BREAD AND WORK

BREAD AND WORK
Social Policy and the Experience of Unemployment, 1918–39

Matt Perry

Pluto  Press

LONDON • STERLING, VIRGINIA

First published 2000 by Pluto Press
345 Archway Road, London N6 5AA
and 22883 Quicksilver Drive, Sterling, VA 20166-2012, USA

British Library Cataloguing in Publication Data
A catalogue record for this book is available from the British Library

ISBN 0 7453 1486 4 hbk

Library of Congress Cataloging in Publication Data
Perry, Matt, 1967–
    Bread and work : the experience of unemployment, 1918–39 /
Matt Perry.
        p.   cm.
    Includes bibliographical references (p.).
    ISBN 0–7453–1486–4
    1. Unemployment—Great Britain—History—20th century.
2. Unemployment—United States—History—20th century.
3. Unemployment—Europe—History—20th century. I. Title.
HD5765.A6P47   2000
331.13'7941'09041—dc21   99–40488
                                                                      CIP

Designed and produced for Pluto Press by
Chase Production Services, Chadlington, OX7 3LN
Typeset from disk by Stanford DTP Services, Northampton
Printed in the EU by TJ International, Padstow

Contents

List of Tables

Preface

Unemployment spread throughout the industrialised world in the years between the two world wars; more virulent in some parts than in others, nowhere escaped. In the USA mass unemployment did not strike until after the Wall Street Crash of autumn 1929. At its height as many as 17 million may have been out of work, hundreds of thousands took to the road in search of work and shantytowns sprang up in the world's wealthiest cities. Without federal relief for the unemployed, local and charitable schemes were incapable of dealing with the sheer scale of misery. Having tried to hold the line against federal relief, the Hoover administration fell, ushering in F.D. Roosevelt's New Deal reforms.

In Europe there were wide variations in the experience of depression: in the intensity and levels of joblessness, in relief systems and in political responses to unemployment. By the mid-1920s most European governments had introduced unemployment relief schemes, though these varied considerably. Not all the unemployed passively accepted their fate. There were riots and hunger marches across Europe, usually led by the Communist Parties. In France, there was no national unemployment insurance system and unemployment was relatively low, but persisted to the outbreak of war. In Germany, a highly developed unemployment insurance system was introduced just two years before the economic crisis broke. As the unemployment insurance scheme's debts mounted in the face of paralysing unemployment, it, and German democracy, fell victim to the slump, which within three years had forced hundreds of thousands out of their homes and left 8 million without work.

The British government had pioneered compulsory unemployment insurance in 1911 and extended it in 1920. This scheme remained controversial: it was unpopular with employers and the Right because they believed it encouraged dole abuse, while the unemployed organisations argued that it failed to provide adequate maintenance for the needy. Britain's unemployment was exceptionally protracted, with at least 1 million out of work from 1920 to 1940. Though concentrated in the staple industries (coal, steel and iron and shipbuilding) and South Wales, Scotland and the North-East, unemployment was a perennial issue of national politics. It was a major concern in all interwar elections and brought down the Labour government in autumn 1931. The 1930s are still remembered as the years of unemployment and the hunger marches.

Every major collapse in international financial markets since the Second World War has raised the spectre of interwar unemployment. Time and again commentators conjure up images of the Wall Street Crash, the dole queues and political instability. This ghost has yet to be exorcised. In the last months of writing this book, the crises of the Far East and Russian economies produced the self-same speculations in the media. These events even prompted the millionaire financier George Soros, to pen a best-selling book entitled *The Crisis of Global Capitalism*.

In the 1930s, the unemployed endured a more or less common and bitter plight. We can piece together with some confidence their archetypal experience. They wiled away their the day tramping from workplace to workplace in search of a job, shuffling in queues at the labour exchange or standing on street corners chatting to friends; their clothes were shabby, their boots in need of repair. They felt hungry and weak and their complexion had greyed through lack of food. Their diet consisted of bread, potatoes and soup; meat was a rarity. A small number committed suicide, more attempted it, more still contemplated it. Their ill-nourished children found it difficult to concentrate at school. The outside world must have seemed irrational, its economic functions devoid of logic. Urban landmarks – the pithead, the factory, the shipyard cranes – stood derelict, idle, rusting. The depression sent the wheels of progress into reverse. Dreams of widening material prosperity were shattered by calamitous, though admittedly temporary, falls in industrial production. The hand of authority tightened its grip as economic circumstances worsened with means testing, police oppression and the threat of the labour camp.

The danger of such a picture though is that the effects of unemployment are too narrowly understood. The images convey a certain reality but miss much. Women and young people were denied the opportunities of work and independence. Strained government finances set one social class against another, and economic instability upset international politics.

This book seeks to elucidate the experience of unemployment in an international context in order to examine why it has had such a profound impact on popular attitudes and policy-makers and why a generation hoped that those days would never again be seen. As such it is a challenge to the current revisionist orthodoxy of the character of British society in the interwar period.

I would like to dedicate this book to Frank Henderson, a friend and revolutionary socialist, who at the age of 16 in 1940 surveyed the ruins of his home town, Coventry, and decided that there was something fundamentally wrong with the world and spent every one of his subsequent years fighting to put it right.

This book would not have been possible without the kind assistance of others. I would like to thank Don MacRaild in particular for his scholarly support and advice. I am also grateful to Chris Bambery, John Charlton, Keith Laybourn and David Martin for reading and commenting on the typescript. Thanks also to Lynne Hunter for encouraging and sagacious comments in its early stages. And thanks to Christine for her patience.

Glossary

American Liberty League – right-wing organisation set up in 1934 to campaign against radicalism and the New Deal. (USA)

Anomalies – various types of claimant who it was believed should not be eligible for benefits, in particular, married women and seasonal workers. (UK)

Arbeitslosenversicherung und Arbeitsvermittlung Gesetz (AVAVG) – the 1927 law which established compulsory unemployment insurance in Germany.

Bonus March – march on Washington by unemployed First World War veterans who demanded their bonus (veteran's pension) early. (USA)

Civilian Conservation Corps (March 1933) – public works programme initially of 250,000 forestry jobs. (USA)

Civil Works Administration (November 1933–March 1934) – forerunner to the Works Progress Administration (q.v.). Work relief scheme engaging 4.2 million by January 1934 in public works such as roads, schools, airports amongst other activities. (USA)

Comintern or Third International or Communist International – the body that brought together and organised the Communist Parties across the world; founded in 1919, disbanded in 1943.

Courts of referees – local bodies that assessed eligibility of unemployed for benefits. (UK)

Covenanted or standard benefit – unemployment benefit for those eligible for National Insurance. (UK)

Deutschnationale Volkspartei (DNVP) – German Nationalist People's Party; Protestant right-wing party.

Deutsche Volkspartei (DVP) – the German People's Party; right-wing pro-business party.

Dole – a slang term originally used for uncovenanted benefits but soon used for all unemployment benefits. (UK)

Emergency Banking Act (1933) – national bank holiday to stop the run on the banks. Federal regulation of the banks to restore confidence. (USA)

Emergency Relief Act (May 1933) – Federal aid to states to provide direct relief for the unemployed. (USA)

Erwerbslosenfürsorge – aid for the unemployed in Germany established in November 1918.

Executive Committee of the Communist International (ECCI) – major decision-making body of the Comintern.

Federal Emergency Relief Administration (FERA) – established to administer direct relief introduced by the Emergency Relief Act. (USA)

Federation of British Industry (FBI) – Employers' organisation established in 1916 with greater emphasis on international and commercial matters than the NCEO.

Freiwilliger Arbeitsdienst (FAD) – Voluntary Labour Service, established in June 1931 by Chancellor Brüning. It was a labour scheme mainly aimed at the young. Later became the Reich Labour Service. (Germany)

Geddes axe – severe public expenditure cuts of 1921 implemented by Sir Eric Geddes, the Chancellor of the Exchequer. (UK)

Genuinely Seeking Work (GSW) Test – a condition of receiving benefit whereby the claimant had to prove that s/he was looking for work. Introduced for uncovenanted in March 1921. Extended to insured unemployed in 1924. (UK)

Ghent system – system of voluntary (usually trade union) unemployment insurance with state or municipal subsidies. (Belgium, Europe)

Gold Standard – exchange rate system that linked currencies to the value of gold. Britain returned to the Gold Standard in 1925 but was forced to leave in September 1931. The United States left in 1933 and the Gold bloc countries (which included France) left in 1936.

KPD – German Communist Party

Langnamverein – Rhineland and Westphalian business association. (Germany)

Local Employment Committees – set up under the 1911 Act, used to assess the GSW for the uncovenanted from 1924 to 1929. (UK)

Means test – enquiry into personal or household income and possessions to determine whether claimant needed support. Introduced for the uncovenanted in March 1921, abolished in 1924. Applied to transitional unemployed in November 1931. (UK)

Musteites – a socialist current, identified with Abraham J. Muste, which engaged in significant unemployed activity – initially, called the Conference for Progressive Labor Action (CPLA). In 1933, they became the American Workers' Party, and in 1934 they merged with the Trotskyist Communist League of America to form the Workers' Party.

National Confederation of Employers' Organisations (NCEO) – Employers' organisation established in 1919 which dealt with matters of domestic and labour policy such as unemployment. (UK)

National Industrial Recovery Act (NIRA) (1933) – prices fixed and production restricted to help business restore profits. Included guarantees for wages, hours and collective bargaining (the last in the infamous section 7a of the Act). (USA)

National Labor Relations Act (1935) – confirmed the right to collective bargaining embodied in section 7a of the NIRA. (USA)

New Deal – President Roosevelt's package of social and economic reforms. (USA)

NSDAP – National Socialist German Workers' (Nazi) Party (Germany)

NUWM – National Unemployed Workers' Movement. (UK)

Poor Law – a system dating from the Elizabethan period whereby funds raised by local rates were used by local authorities to distribute relief to the poor, sometimes on condition of entering the workhouse. (UK)

Poor Law Guardians – locally elected overseers of the Poor Law. Replaced in 1930 by the local council-appointed PACs (q.v.). (UK)

Popular Front – Comintern's perspective from 1935 to 1939 which sought broad alliances with both Socialist and Labour Parties and also Liberals. Formulated by Dimitrov at the 7th Congress of the Comintern in 1935. (USSR)

Public Assistance Committees (PAC) – Local bodies created in 1931 to organise unemployment relief appointed by local councils. (UK)

Public Works Administration (June 1933) (PWA) – part of the National Industrial Recovery Act. (USA)

Reichanstalt – the unemployment insurance fund established in the AVAVG. (Germany)

Reichverband der Deutschen Industrie (RDI) – German Industrial Association. (Germany)

Revolutionäre Gewerkschafts-Opposition (RGO) – German Communist trade union.

Section Française de L'Internationale Ouvrière (SFIO) – French Socialist Party

Share Our Wealth Movement – headed by Huey Long, the Governor of Louisiana, it sought to share the nation's wealth through increases in tax on the rich. Long attracted millions of sympathisers, but was killed in 1935. (USA)

Sinking Fund – the fund used to repay the national debt. (UK)

Social Security Act (1935) – compulsory unemployment insurance based on a payroll tax. Old age insurance based on wages and payroll taxes. Federal aid for state provision for the aged, widows and orphans. (USA)

SPÖ – Austrian Socialist Party.

'Standstill' Act (1935) – An emergency Act to ease the introduction of UAB scales of benefit, the claimant being paid whichever was higher – the UAB scale or former local benefit. (UK)

'Third period' – Comintern's ultra-left and sectarian political perspective from 1928 to 1934. At this time it was argued that the collapse of capitalism was immanent and that the Socialist and Labour Parties were social fascists.

Townsend movement – Dr Francis Townsend organised thousands of clubs to call for pensions of $200 a month for those over the age of 60. (USA)

Umpire – adjudicating officer in cases of appeals in matters of unemployment insurance. (UK)

Uncovenanted (1921–24), extended (1924–27) or transitional benefit (1927–35) – benefit for those ineligible for NI but given discretionary benefit. (UK)

Unemployed Councils – communist-led unemployed organisations. (USA)

Unemployed Leagues – Socialist party-led unemployed organisations.(USA)

Unemployment Assistance Board (UAB) – Set up in the 1934 Act, replacing the PACs, to impose national rates and administration of unemployment relief. (UK)

Unemployment Insurance – system established in 1911 whereby the employers, state and employees contributed to a fund that paid out when an employee was made unemployed. Rules for eligibility changed over time and not all forms of employment were eligible. (UK)

Vereinigung der Deutschen Arbeitergeberverbände (VDA) – Federation of German Employers' Associations.

Wandervögel – literally migrating birds, hundreds of thousands of young, unemployed, homeless Germans who wandered the streets.

Workers' Alliance of America (1935–41) an attempt to organise the local unemployed groups into a national organisation. By the end of 1936 it had an estimated 300,000 members in 1,600 branches. Effectively collapsed in 1938; disbanded in 1941. (USA)

Works Progress Administration (1935–43) – Work relief scheme which by 1943, had 8 million on its books. Public works, but also white-collar, women, young and blacks were engaged. (USA)

XYZ Club – a club that brought together certain Labour Party economic thinkers and sympathisers from the City of London. (UK)

Introduction

> Unemployment makes men seem useless, not wanted, without a country ... unemployment makes men live in fear and ... from fear springs hate.
>
> ... Failure to use our productive powers is the source of an interminable succession of evils.
>
> W.H. Beveridge, Full Employment in a Free Society:
Misery Breeds Hate, 1944[1]

From 1940, as a result of a dramatic intellectual turning point, unemployment was generally seen as an evil force that threatened democratic institutions because, in William Beveridge's words, 'misery breeds hate'. Many believed that in fascism and war Europe was witnessing the bitter consequences of post-1918 economic instability. In 1943, Michael Kalecki, the Polish economist, summed up the popular hopes for a postwar European reconstruction based on full employment:

> Fascism sprang up in Germany against a background of tremendous unemployment and maintained itself in power through securing full employment whilst capitalist democracy failed to do so. The fight of the progressive forces for full employment is at the same time a way of preventing the recurrence of fascism.[2]

At this time, even the Conservative Sub-Committee on Industry stated: 'Unemployment, such as darkened the world between the wars, must not recur'[3] and for nearly 30 years after the Second World War, mass unemployment was banished from much of the world economy.

Its return in the mid-1970s across Western Europe and the United States has brought all too familiar and pernicious results: blighted industries and regions, increasing poverty, hopelessness, demoralisation and despair. In the 1980s and 1990s, European fascists have once again scored electoral successes. In Eastern Europe, unemployment has fuelled uncertainty and instability, adding heat to ethnic, social and nationalist tensions. Despite the fact that unemployment has been disguised by statistical massaging and the diverting discussion of an 'underclass', the corrosive effects of long-term joblessness are obvious for all to see. Its reappearance has shaken the accepted wisdoms of the postwar world: Keynesian full employment, the mixed economy and the universal welfare state. More than anything, this ideological amalgam was defined with reference to the years between the wars.

The 1920s and 1930s inform current political debate. Unemployment is not simply a convention of sociologists, a metaphor of limited use, an ideal-type or an invention that draws together a mixture of heterogeneous experiences. It is a real, irreducible, but historically specific, phenomenon. The experiences, disputes and lessons remain with us still.

Chapter 1 is a survey of the history of unemployment. Over the past 30 years a growing literature has emerged which treats unemployment as a phenomenon with a history of its own. These have emphasised that unemployment is a relatively new phenomenon, a creation of the industrial revolution arising from the specific characteristics of industrial capitalism: generalised wage-labour, the business cycle and technological dynamism.[4] Before industrial capitalism there was undoubtedly hardship, poverty and even a lack of work (though lack of land was the greater problem). Long-term transformations in economic structures were ultimately responsible for the emergence of mass unemployment. Unemployment was not, as Robert Salais would have it, invented; it existed, whether society or the individual was conscious of it or not.[5]

There is another side to unemployment though– how it was perceived and how those without work perceived themselves. This subjective dimension is crucial because unemployment's recognition was late and contested, and sharp ideological disagreements over the phenomenon continue. Today there are still those who deny the existence of involuntary joblessness on any significant scale. Likewise, monetarist historians of the interwar period have reasserted that unemployment was a matter of individual choice rather than the product of forces beyond the control of the unemployed. For example, Matthews and Benjamin have written:

> [I]ndividuals ... make ... choices in the light of self-interest as perceived by them. ...Ultimately, then, young people choose unemployment because it is the rational self-interested choice for them to make.[6]

The very existence of unemployment, in the sense that it is an involuntary condition, is disputed. The historical controversy about unemployment in interwar Britain goes much further than the monetarist case. There is a new historical orthodoxy amongst a wide spectrum of conservative and liberal historians, dubbed revisionism in the 1970s, which doubts the myth of the 'hungry thirties', that lingers in the popular imagination.[7] This book tackles the central assumptions of the revisionist orthodoxy and offers an alternative perspective.

Chapter 2 examines the response to unemployment in Britain from above: from the state and the employers. The poor physical fitness of volunteers for the Boer War had focused government thinking on preventing the physical deterioration, through poverty and unemployment, of the British population. This concern however was balanced by the desire to make 'economies' in unemployment relief in the context of growing numbers of jobless people, government debt and shaky revenues. This basic contradiction unsettled unemployment policy as the Poor Law and social insurance combined, administered by the uneasy partnership of local and central authorities. Further, benefit levels and eligibility varied geographically and over time, so that the organisation of relief was subject to repeated change. Governments seemed to have very few answers to the scale and persistence of unemployment. Ideologically constrained by the economic orthodoxy of the Treasury view, governments aimed for 'safety first'. The belt of public expenditure was buckled tight in the hope that international trade would pick up, thereby resuscitating British export industries. Britain suffered high levels of unemployment in the 1920s due to a sharply deflationary fiscal and monetary policy. This deflation resulted from the attempt to return to the Gold Standard at the pre-war parity, which in turn, once achieved, further damaged the exporting industries as it overvalued sterling by 10 per cent. The consequence for millions of workers was the bitter experience of unemployment, which threatened governments with the possibility of serious political unrest.

For employers, unemployment meant something slightly different. The world economic situation after the First World War devastated some sections of capital: shipbuilding, mining, cotton and engineering had seen markets shrink as war production ended. These distressed staple industries sought government intervention, and the effects of unemployment provided a powerful argument in bargaining for resources. More generally, unemployment allowed business to restructure and discipline its workforce. The context of mass unemployment allowed a shift in the balance of industrial relations: employers could weed out militants through victimisation. This was particularly common in such industries as mining and engineering which suffered the worst of unemployment. Employers sought to put struggling British industry on its feet in world markets through wage-cutting and redundancies; and governments endorsed these measures. Employers' organisations, the Federation of British Industries and the National Confederation of Employers' Organisations, wanted both to rally and disseminate such strategies. Big business lobbied persistently for the reduction of unemployment insurance, on the grounds of its alleged adverse effect on the labour market and widespread abuse. Employers' organisations and the press also propagated the idea of rationalisation, which came in a number of guises and, though patchily implemented, often resulted in deskilling and redundancy.

This chapter challenges the view that unemployment existed in the context of shared interests and consent. Decisions were based on the specific interests of capital and the state. The enactment of these policies necessarily conflicted with working-class interests and resulted in some industrial strife. Despite the claims of liberal historians, unemployment was essentially about coercion. Policies of rationalisation, victimisation, relief and public order all involved government, police or employers in coercive not consensual methods of dealing with the working class.

Chapter 3, then, seeks to give an account of the wider social attitudes that emerged towards unemployment and how the unemployed lived, identifying the tensions between the reality and representations of unemployment. The ideological context of unemployment in the interwar period requires serious investigation. Newspapers, newsreels and novels constructed certain images of those without work. Unemployment was reinvented in a particular way through major recurring themes of pity, benefit abuse and public order. Again, like government and employers' policies, the ideology of unemployment involved conflict, for example, between the right to benefit and the spectre of malingering. A British economist summed up the right-wing view of unemployment insurance (two years before the Wall Street Crash made a nonsense of it):

> The endowment of unemployment isn't made any better by calling it insurance: fire insurance wouldn't do if you let people set their property on fire and keep it burning on condition of signing their names once a week at the insurance office.[8]

Over the past two decades, oral history has provided new insights into the experience of those without work during the 1920s and 1930s. This complements contemporary memoirs, mass observation, official sources (such as the Medical Officers for Health reports and the commissions for the distressed areas), literary accounts (such as *English Journey*, *Love on the Dole* and the *Road to Wigan Pier*) and statistical sources. Through this evidence we can piece together the experience of unemployment. Being out of work was a challenge to personal dignity, a threat to family relationships, a risk to health and brought the temptations of crime, suicide or migration. The unemployed were faced with the Means Test assessors, the stigma of going to the Poor Law Guardians and a dispiriting hunt for a job for which they had to provide evidence under the 'genuinely seeking work' criterion. The state impinged on this experience with work camps, 'less eligibility', unemployed clubs and periodic cuts in benefit.

The current orthodoxy about the interwar years emphasises the growing prosperity, good health and political conservatism of the period. This view greatly underestimates the impact of unemployment, which was not restricted to the distressed fringe. More importantly, it fails to recognise that joblessness did not lead to an easily quantifiable or visible radicalisation, but was a more complex and contradictory experience which was to play a profound role in the construction of attitudes after the war. Revisionist historians have closed the question of unemployed radicalism because social investigators did not find generalised revolutionary feelings amongst the unemployment. As an enquiry for the Carnegie Trust observed:

> It has, perhaps, been assumed too readily by some that, because men are unemployed, their normal state of want and discontent must express itself in some revolutionary attitude. It cannot be reiterated too often that unemployment is not an active state; its keynote is boredom – a continuous sense of boredom.[9]

Yet, it is remarkable that all the serious social studies of unemployment consider its relationship to revolution. This in itself is surely significant. Whilst bitterness and politicisation were usually latent or fragmentary, and overwhelmed by the demoralisation of the dole, they nevertheless existed.

Chapter 4 considers how unemployment posed a problem for Labour, a party that drew electoral support from the working class and was organisationally connected to the trade unions. When out of office, unemployment provided Labour with a tool to criticise the Tories and Liberals. Labour speechified about unemployment as a product of capitalism and its abolition under a Labour government. However, it was during this period that Labour espoused the ideas of economic conservatism (balanced budgets and national competitiveness) and had little to offer economically beyond free trade and tightly budgeted public works. Labour's failure to hold a consistent and independent view on this question proved to be a considerable embarrassment. This chapter investigates the evolution of Labour economic thinking, which was, despite a minority who looked to under-consumptionist or Keynesian ideas, firmly in the camp of orthodoxy. The Keynesian revolution had to storm the defences of the Labour Party as much as anywhere else.

This chapter also examines the record of the two Labour governments on unemployment, looking at economic policy, public works, unemployment insurance and Labour's response to economic crisis. Then, the Labour Party's relationship with the unemployed is probed. We shall see that Labour's attitude to the struggles of the unemployed was, throughout the period, mostly hostile or at best ambiguous.

From the end of the First World War, unemployment again became the subject of working-class agitation. Chapter 5 looks at the major unemployed struggles of 1919–23 and 1931–36. The unemployed themselves built a movement that organised hunger marches, demonstrations, factory protests against overtime and casework for claimants. The National Unemployed Workers' Movement led these protests but did face rivals. This organisation, whose key figures were communists, found itself persistently shunned by the official labour movement and was affected by the shifting line of the Communist International. Recent literature has questioned its impact; Stevenson and Cook argue that these protests were counter-productive. It is fashionable to judge, as Harry Harmer has done, the NUWM by the yardstick of Comintern criticism which castigated the movement for failing to transform itself into a mass revolutionary organisation. The historiography raises a number of issues which this chapter addresses: the relationship between the CPGB and the NUWM, the size and influence of the movement, the relative success of the NUWM and other unemployed protest and whether it brought tangible gains for the unemployed in terms of relief levels and legislation.

The NUWM's history clearly demonstrates strong periodic outbursts of anger and swelling membership combined with (more common) difficulties in maintaining membership and activity. Under these adverse circumstances, the activities of this unemployed movement had a wider significance. It persistently fought the effects of unemployment and put across basic socialist arguments about the nature of unemployment. At the same time, it wrung some important gains for the unemployed and contributed to the process of working-class resurgence so marked by the end of the war.

Chapter 6 considers the character of unemployment in the United States during the interwar period. The contrasts between the US and UK yield abundant insights into the unemployed experience and have been of central importance in framing social policy discussions to the present. There is also a valuable store of American oral history and contemporary social investigation into unemployment waiting for the comparative historian to explore. US political traditions were distinctly hostile to state intervention and emphasised the rugged individualism of the American citizen, so that the emergence of federal provision for the unemployed encountered serious opposition. Economically, the US had become the world's foremost capitalist power with the largest internal market and the most advanced industry. The contrast between the 'Roaring Twenties' and the calamitous collapse of the 1930s was much more stark than in Britain. The sharper character of the economic crisis in the US allows us to see the consequences of unemployment in much stronger relief, not only in terms of the experience of those without work but also in its effect on politics. The New Deal constituted a considerable break with the past. Although Roosevelt eventually introduced unemployment insurance in 1935, US provision for the unemployed differed significantly from the UK with a much greater reliance on work relief schemes. These disparities inform current debates about unemployment policy (even to the extent of the Blair government's use of New Deal rhetoric).

Despite the differences of social policy context and severity, an examination of worklessness shows that the underlying phenomenon was essentially similar on both sides of the Atlantic. The tension between the representation and reality surfaced in both countries. The allegations of abuse and the denial of the scale or effects of unemployment were uttered by the Hoovers and Fords just as they were by their British counterparts. Moreover, the threat of unemployed unrest was keenly felt in the US, and again, it surfaced in short bitter episodes of agitation. The costs of providing for the unemployed also provoked a sharp governmental crises. The British governmental débâcles of 1931 and 1935 had their parallels in the American winter of 1932–33.

Chapter 7 turns to the situation in continental Europe. Interwar Europe provides a rich mosaic of political and economic structure and this diversity allows more general conclusions about the character and effects of unemployment. Again, the material available to the historian is very tempting with studies by social researchers, national governments and international organisations. In social policy terms, two basic state systems of unemployment insurance emerged: the Ghent model of voluntary, state-assisted insurance, and the compulsory unemployment system pioneered in Britain. Both, however, were subject to repeated amendments and revisions because of the destabilising effect of mass unemployment. As in Britain, a deep recession made unemployment insurance the subject of acerbic political argument. The Right campaigned for retrenchment, and the coverage of unemployment insurance narrowed as unemployment increased. In response, several governments intervened in the labour market in a more authoritarian manner, in particular with the development of cheap labour schemes. Others adopted more generous public works. European governments, then, revealed a range of policy opinions and a scale of coercion not experienced in Britain. From the policy perspective, governments were bound by necessity to attempt to find solutions to unemployment, and freedom of action depended on the relative effects of economic crisis, the democratic or dictatorial character of government and the balance of class forces.

The scale, severity and persistence of joblessness varied considerably in interwar Europe. Unemployment was at its worst in Poland, Germany and Austria in the early 1930s. On the other hand, in France, unemployment never reached similar levels but, unlike those European economies that recovered by the mid-1930s, mass unemployment persisted to the end of the decade. As a consequence, the strength of unemployed protest, led mainly by communists, varied from one country to another. This unevenness allows us to judge the relationship between joblessness and radicalisation. The German experience in this regard demonstrates the importance and limitations of unemployed struggles. In this case, the overwhelming majority of the German Communist Party's members were unemployed and through this influx it had become a mass party. Despite this growth and some successful unemployed protests, a mass organisation based on the unemployed provided an inadequate bulwark against Nazism.

The conclusions are both intended to relate to the British, American and European cases of interwar unemployment and to say something about unemployment under industrial capitalism in general. We have not escaped from a world of periodic economic crises and the blight of mass unemployment. The 1930s still have a direct relevance for the present.

Unemployment and economic crisis are interlocking processes. The continuities in the history of unemployment are striking both internationally and over the decades. Revisionist historians assume, sometimes explicitly, that the experience of unemployment was fundamentally different in Britain. Such exceptionalist thinking seems to have precluded serious international comparison or consideration that the depression of the 1930s should be judged as a global process. This book focuses on Britain in the interwar period within an international and long-run context. Unemployment bound the industrially advanced nations in essentially a common though uneven experience. Unemployment was endemic to the interwar world economy and would seem inherent to industrial capitalism itself.

The relative gravity of the basic process shaped national differences. Britain's stability in the interwar period was contingent on economic good fortune and a superficial consensus; and large majorities for the national government in the 1930s masked a deeply divided nation. There are real similarities in the role played by unemployment (escalating costs of relief, financial crisis, mounting business pressure on the government) in the crises of autumn 1931 in Britain, in late 1932 to early 1933 in the USA and the recurrent crises in Germany in the run-up to Hitler's accession to power. Those crises had different outcomes: in Britain the Labour Party was discredited by its inability to deal with unemployment, in Germany the SPD and then the Nationalist Right suffered in similar fashion, as did Hoover in the United States. Current orthodoxy stresses the futility of extra-parliamentary action by the jobless but, by international standards, the British unemployed movement was an impressive achievement in adverse circumstances, it not only scored some notable successes, but also aided the resurgence of working-class confidence in the late 1930s and during the war. It was part of the reshaping of the consciousness of the generation that witnessed the welfare reforms of 1944–48, a change in attitudes that has been an abiding feature of British politics. The structural consequences of war, the fear of social unrest and the actions of pioneers such as Beveridge and Keynes together combined to form the welfare state's foundation just as similar factors had brought welfare concessions at the end of the First World War.

1   Unemployment: History and Perspectives

The right to work. Provisional Government of the French Republic undertakes to guarantee the worker's livelihood through work. It recognises that workers should form associations so that they may enjoy the proper profits arising from their toil.

Government decision taken during the
Revolution of 1848, published in *Le Moniteur*[1]

The poverty reported in the towns, especially in the big ones, is principally the result of the irregular, immoral lives of the workers.

Maréchal Bugeaud, Duc D'Isly, conservative
view during the French Revolution of 1848[2]

Unemployment and Industrial Capitalism

The defining features of the industrial revolution, the factory and the manufacturing town, arrived at different paces across Europe and North America and consequently so too did unemployment. Industrial capitalism connected the growth of manufacturing with the growth of the town. This progress was regional in character and far from uniform across Europe. It was not until the late nineteenth century that the factory dominated European industrial production as putting out, home-working or the workshop remained significant.[3] Urbanisation too varied geographically. Thus, by the beginning of twentieth century, 77 per cent of people in the UK lived in towns, 56.1 per cent in Germany, 41 per cent in France, 40.5 per cent in the Netherlands, but only 22 per cent in Switzerland and 21.5 per cent in Sweden.[4] By this time 39.7 per cent of Americans were town-dwellers. The rise of towns and industry took hold first on the North Atlantic seaboard, then spread to various parts of the North, particularly after 1861, whilst the South remained overwhelmingly agricultural. Thus by 1880, three-quarters of the labour force in the North Atlantic region worked in industry compared to a quarter of the Southern labour force.[5]

Waged work became the predominant form of labour. Even though wage-labour had existed from antiquity, it acquired an increasingly important role in Western Europe from the seventeenth century. Here, wage-labour ultimately outstripped agricultural small-holding and urban self-employment. We now divide the labour market into three categories: inactive, employed and unemployed, categories corresponding to generalised wage labour. These categories are presented as objective universal criteria and, implicitly at least, as timeless phenomena.[6] But unemployment is not a universally applicable and unambiguous category.

The growth of industrial capitalism in the nineteenth century transformed the character of poverty from vagrancy, landlessness and underemployment into unemployment. The industrial revolution and wage-labour separated work from the everyday life of family, home and the natural and liturgical calendar. In the 1950s and 1960s, social historians scrutinised this separation. With the expansion of wage-labour, work evolved from being task-oriented to time-disciplined; time was no longer one's own. The clock sharply divided work- and leisure-time, rather than being blurred by custom, as before.[7] Employers required greater control over the labour process. This took them considerable efforts and time as the early factory owners and their foremen strove to recruit a stable workforce and impose regular attendance, punctuality and an intensive effort over the course of the working day.[8] Though the persistence of putting-out and the workshop should not be ignored, they were undermined in the long run as it became clear that the modern workplace allowed a higher level of productivity.[9]

The growth of the market, commodification and the increasing division of labour also prepared the way for unemployment. This expansion was happening on a global scale from the early modern period. At the core of the capitalist world economy, wage-labour became firmly established, coexisting with serfdom in Eastern Europe and slavery in parts of the New World. With the growth in trade, Europe became a patchwork of interdependent, regional specialisations. On the global scale certain areas such as the southern states of America, India and Africa, were transformed into producers of raw materials, others became the 'workshops of the world'. At the domestic level, work became increasingly specialised as the wide range of activities characteristic of the household subsistence economy withered. This entailed a greater dependence not only on the market for waged work, but also for consumption goods.[10] Unemployment emerged in those regions that had undergone indus-trialisation. In earlier times, households could find several sources of work, consumption or income in agricultural, industrial or commercial activities. However, the increasing division of labour reduced these options. Poire describes the way in which a wider base of economic activities prevented or disguised unemployment:

> In agriculture and in a variety of different family enterprises in industry and commerce, market and household activities were so intermingled that the line between them was difficult to draw and adjustments to the variations in economic conditions were made through changes in the distribution of time between various tasks ... In rural areas and small towns, workers frequently moved back and forth between their own farms and industrial employment in small enterprises with an ease and frequency that also escaped conventional measures of unemployment.[11]

In Europe the persistence of guild production, putting out and the extended family as a unit of production all slowed the emergence of unemployment. Various studies have identified hybrid forms of social production or organisation of labour which delayed or disguised unemployed. One example was the tramping traditions of groups of artisans, who would collectively subsidise the search for work.[12] Another was the petty commercial, service and manufacturing activities undertaken in the black economy or 'penny capitalism' of many working-class families.[13]

In terms of the rhythm of innovation and investment, nineteenth-century capitalism proved to be a much more dynamic economic system than its predecessors. This vitality created obsolescence as new technology, skills and branches of industry opened up and rendered existing ones uncompetitive and outmoded. This restructuring was often traumatic as sections of the labour force and entire regional economies depended on declining industries and skills. The result was a concentration of unemployment in certain trades and geographical areas. Mechanisation or automation, the investment in labour-saving innovations, replaced men and women with machines, creating new sources of unemployment. One early example of this is the immiseration of the handloom weavers of Lancashire.[14] New machinery provoked machine-breaking riots across parts of industrial Europe.[15] In the interwar period, unemployment was similarly concentrated in Scotland, the North and South Wales in the staple industries of coal, shipbuilding, textiles and iron and steel. In the United States, mining areas such as West Virginia or steel towns such as Pittsburgh suffered a similar fate. Europe too had its unemployment blackspots such as the German shipbuilding town of Rostock or the coal and steel areas of Rhineland and the Ruhr. The oscillations of capitalist accumulation have been endemic to the world economy since about the middle of the nineteenth century when different parts of the globe tended to synchronise along the lines of the business cycle.[16] For example, in 1847 and 1873 there were slumps across the world economy. Periodic overproduction, characteristic of the cycle of boom and recession, developed into a major source of unemployment. Previously, the agricultural sector dominated the local economies, a poor harvest increased food prices and thus reduced demand for manufactured goods. Before the industrial revolution as a general rule, it was the harvest and overseas demand that determined the character of business fluctuations.[17] The features of industrial capitalism, its structural change (including the periodic devastation of older sectors), its dynamism, its business cycle, all distinguish unemployment from earlier forms of poverty.

Modern capitalist institutions, the firm and the state, were integral to the development of unemployment. Robert Salais identified the employer–employee contract as an important element in the institutionalisation of unemployment as it formalised the work relationship and its severance.[18] The state passed through three phases of social legislation during the process of industrialisation. Typically, a pattern emerged in which factory legislation was followed by social insurance, which developed into an universalist welfare state. As time progressed this process became compressed with the divisions between the various stages becoming blurred. In Europe, social legislation replaced the Poor Law provisions that had become unsuited to establishing a market of mobile wage labourers or clearly defining the life cycle. The vicissitudes of the business cycle undermined the ability of the Poor Law to regulate poverty. Unemployment became a new source of poverty requiring novel measures. Governments usually attempted to deal with those who were unable to find work through old age or injury before tackling unemployment. This was partly due to the difficulties of isolating unemployment from other causes of poverty, partly due to the fact that, for policy-makers, workers lived in an alien and threatening world. The true level of unemployment was unknown. Eventually, the various elements of social insurance differentiated the elements of the poor from one another.

Unemployment and the Demise of the Poor Law

State regulation of the labour market and the poor influenced the emergence, characteristics and measurement of employment and unemployment. The Poor Law was the generalised form of relief in Western Europe from the early sixteenth century.[19] Municipal or parish authorities administered the Poor Law, which could take the form of the workhouse or outdoor relief. The 1834 Poor Law Amendment Act in England and Wales aimed to abolish outdoor relief in an attempt to create a modern labour market. Outdoor relief had allowed some to rely on casual, seasonal agricultural work which accounted for continued labour shortages in industrial areas. The Speenhamland system of outdoor relief, which had operated in parts of Britain (especially the agricultural South), was heavily criticised as it paid recipients according to family size so that for many families the margin between wages and relief was small. The answer for the government lay in the harsh regime of the workhouse, which segmented inmates, including members of the same family, by sex and age.

The reformed Poor Law was ultimately incompatible with the new dynamics of poverty created by unemployment. 'Less eligibility', the workhouse and the labour test deterred dependency on relief. The workhouse remained as a stick to coerce workers into the factories, but it had to be complemented by outdoor relief as a last resort. In rural areas, the Poor Law authorities, dominated by well-off tenant farmers, sought to maintain adequate supplies of labour in order to match high seasonal fluctuations of demand.[20] Derek Fraser, a historian of British social policy, has shown the strong continuities between the old and new Poor Laws and the manner in which educational and medical improvements under its aegis laid the foundations for extended welfare reforms.[21] However, M.E. Rose described unemployment as 'the Achilles' heel of the Poor Law system'. When attempts were made to impose the amended Poor Law on the northern towns during the winter of 1837–38, there was a huge surge in working-class opposition, which fuelled Chartism. Even northern employers questioned the application of a system designed for the South. In the towns where work was organised in large productive units the problem was not chronic underemployment but acute unemployment. Given that this was the case, many northern Poor Law unions simply refused to implement the new system. The amended Poor Law could cause severe problems in rural areas too. In 1838 the English Poor Law template was imposed on Ireland's impoverished peasant population; during the famine, from 1845 to 1851, the system completely collapsed.

The inadequacy of the Poor Law in dealing with unemployment cannot be passed off as the teething problems of the 1834 reform. Indoor relief and the labour test were effectively waived for the large numbers of urban workers who flocked to the Board of Guardians in times of slump. The winter recessions of 1860–61, 1867–68 and 1868–69 threw the Poor Law in London into crisis because of the surge in unemployed applicants for outdoor relief. The Lancashire cotton famine of 1863–65, a consequence of the American Civil War, brought similar problems. These sharp increases in applicants undermined the principle of the new Poor Law as the numbers on relief raised the spectre of mass pauperism. At the same time, the costs to the ratepayer escalated and charities worried that their efforts would encourage the formation of a dependent class of paupers. In response, the Charity Organisation Society and the Local Government Board attempted to distinguish between deserving and undeserving cases through home visits and investigation.[22] In the longer term the principle of less eligibility could not overcome the problems that unemployment posed to the Poor Law and these difficulties resurfaced in sharpened form in the mid-1880s.

After Poor Law reform, governments attempted to regulate the modern labour market through factory legislation. This was true not simply of Britain, the first industrial nation; factory legislation pre-dated other forms of social policy in most industrialising countries. One element of the life cycle of the modern labour force, childhood exclusion, was formalised through the prohibition of child labour, and the extension of compulsory education altered the nature and definition of the working population. Modern definitions of economic activity exclude children: activity rates are measured amongst the population between 15 and 65 years. This was the first way in which state regulation began to define the labour force. Child labour, which was widespread in previous generations, was gradually eclipsed despite difficulties and reluctance in enforcing legislation in its early days. Factory legislation, particularly in its latter stages, also came to define the limits of activity of all employees through the regulation of the working day. Factory legislation codified not only the working population but also the characteristics of the workers' activity. Consequently, economic activity in the form of a standard working day and week takes the form of comparable units of quantification. Factory legislation therefore laid the foundation for measurable unemployment.

The era of state social insurance began in Imperial Germany with Chancellor Bismarck's reforms of the 1880s. He introduced sickness insurance, industrial compensation, old age and sickness pensions through three major pieces of legislation. As a result, by 1890, 12 million workers were covered by the first two schemes.[23] Other capitalist states introduced similar legislation. Social insurance initially redefined the poor along the lines of age and ill health, and later unemployment. Britain pioneered the first unemployment insurance scheme in 1911. Although this covered only a small proportion of the workforce, it was extended in 1920 to all workers except those in domestic or agricultural work. By 1925 there were 15 national unemployment insurance schemes. Often labour exchanges developed alongside social insurance. Germany was the most advanced in this respect. By the 1890s, every major city had a labour exchange. By the early years of the twentieth century, governments had established labour exchanges in Switzerland,

Austria, Belgium and Norway. In France by 1904 an estimated million jobs a year were filled by exchanges that were run by government, the unions and private sector.[24] In 1909, the National Labour Exchanges Act established a national network of employment exchanges across Britain.

The impact of this intervention on the labour force was to clarify the boundaries of the active population. An out-of-work 70-year-old suffering from an industrial injury could now be formally excluded from the labour market. Previously, it would have been very difficult to distinguish him from an unemployed, 20-year-old bricklayer. The emergence of pension insurance set the upper limits on the labour force in the same way that compulsory education and the factory laws set the lower limits. Sickness insurance maintained workers at times when ill health prevented them from working. Both measures negatively defined employment and allowed for the withdrawal of less productive individuals from the labour market. Unemployment insurance, which was the most radical break with orthodox economic and poverty relief thinking, was the final element that distilled the previously undifferentiated mass of urban poor. Obviously, this had important implications for the definition and measurement of the labour force. It allowed for those who became unemployed during the productive years of their life cycle to be sustained in periods of recession ready to return to work when the economy picked up.

The era of the welfare state denotes the period in which most industrialised countries moved towards universal welfare systems. Typically, social policy spending had evolved from around 2 per cent of national income in the early 1880s to around 30 per cent a century later. The universality has been resisted in some countries, including the US, but even there welfare expenditure has risen massively. During this period the process of differentiation of the poor which began with the era of social insurance was completed. The post-1945 Keynesian welfare consensus promoted state regulation of the labour market and economy to an extent it had never done before.

Though the pattern of social and economic development across Europe and North America was not regular or uniform, the objective criterion for the emergence of unemployment was the transformation of wage-labour by capital accumulation, the factory and the town. However, it is also necessary to consider unemployment at the subjective level. Unless it has achieved a certain ideological or insti-tutional maturity unemployment cannot be measured or be part of public debate and consciousness. It would be a mistake to ignore or gloss over the subjective or ideological aspect of unemployment as this is fundamental to its historical development, particularly when we consider that the definition and ideology of unemployment have been so hotly contested. We are therefore drawn to the conclusion that whilst unemployment was born out the objective conditions of modern capitalist development, it was understood, contested and defined subjectively. It had to be fixed in the consciousness of men and women; in other words, it needed to come to ideological maturity. But the conceptualisation of unemployment poses a paradox. Generalised industrial wage-labour, the division of labour and the cycle of accumulation preceded the regulation of unemployment. The manner in which the ideology lagged behind material reality needs explanation.

The Late and Contested Recognition of Unemployment

For many years economists were blind to the existence of unemployment. In 1776, Adam Smith's *The Wealth of Nations* expounded the virtues of a laissez-faire capitalist system in which markets naturally matched supply and demand through the price mechanism. This applied equally to the labour market, therefore unemployment could not be an inherent feature of market economies. This was also expressed by Say's Law, which stated that output creates its own demand. According to this logic, unemployment should not, theoretically speaking, exist.[25] Therefore, Smith, and with him the other classical economists – David Ricardo and James Mill – found no room for unemployment, recession or the business cycle in their explanation of the economy. Nor did the next major advance in modern economics, the Marginal School of Marshall and Jevons, fundamentally alter this. Mark Casson has noted that it was not until the beginning of the twentieth century that economists began to consider unemployment seriously, and whilst Beveridge published *Unemployment: a Problem of Industry* in 1909, Casson described Pigou's *Unemployment* (1914) as the first major pre-Keynesian theory of unemployment.[26]

Not only economics but also social orthodoxies proved an obstacle to the recognition of unemployment. Thomas Malthus, Jeremy Bentham and Samuel Smiles more than any others epitomised the social thought of nineteenth-century Britain. Each in his own way erected intellectual barriers to the recognition of unemployment. Bentham took a minimalist view to state intervention and the welfare of the poor. Both these policies were prerequisites for a general awareness of unemployment. His utilitarianism preached that the greatest good for the greatest number – which translated, in practice as the misery of the poorest – should not interfere with the contentment of those better off. Malthus, on the other hand, conceived of social problems primarily in terms of population and the food supply. Poverty, therefore, resulted not from the characteristics of capitalism, but from the promiscuity and fecundity of the poor; in a word, overpopulation. From a different perspective, Smiles, in *Self-Help* (1859) and *Thrift* (1876), believed that all the woes that befell an individual could be overcome by personal effort:

> It is shown that failure is the best discipline of the true worker, by stimulating him to renewed efforts, evoking his best powers, and carrying him onward in self-culture, self-control, and growth in knowledge and wisdom. Viewed in this light, failure, conquered by perseverance, is always full of interest and instruction.[27]

Social problems resulted from the moral torpor of the poor who, through sacrifice and hard work, could reverse their situation. The thought of Bentham, Smiles and Malthus, despite having quite different starting-points, complemented one another as conceptualisations of poverty that obscured unemployment.

The very vocabulary of the nineteenth century concealed unemployment. It was misdiagnosed as idleness, pauperism, indigence, poverty or distress. Garraty pointed out that people could only conceive of a society in which everyone needed to work: 'it followed that an idle person was not so much morally inadequate but anti-social'.[28] In similar fashion, 'pauperism' had a strong grip on the nineteenth-century imagination. Social policy was aimed at preventing the undeserving poor, who were capable of work, from depending on relief. At times of widespread unemployment, ratepayers, Poor Law authorities and charity workers agonised that they were encouraging pauperism. The term 'pauper' also obscured unemployment as he or she could be ill, old, insane, destitute or without work. 'Distress' also linguistically clouded a clear view of unemployment. Whilst the term did denote economic hard times rather than malingering, it was too vague to distinguish between the situation of the artisan, agricultural labourer, industrial worker or small proprietor. Poverty, too, was a general concept that would include unemployment as an unspoken component. As Rowntree's two studies of York in 1899 and in 1935–36 observed, unemployment was not the major source of poverty in Victorian Britain that it was to become in the interwar period.[29]

The spokesmen of their age, the champions of capitalist progress, unconsciously resisted the very idea of unemployment. Raymond Williams described how this resistance took place by conflating the social position (unemployment) with the personal trait (idleness):

> There has been a steady resistance to this necessary distinction ... The resistance is still active, and in relation to the words is

especially evident in the use of idle, in news reporting, to describe workers laid off, locked out or on strike.[30]

The Discovery of Unemployment

The late conceptualisation of unemployment is remarkable. First entering the *New English Dictionary* in 1888, it was not until the 1890s that unemployment came into general use in the English language. The *Oxford English Dictionary* states that unemployment came into common use *circa* 1895. The French word *chômeur* (an unemployed man) was a creation of the 1870s and the German *Arbeitslosigkeit* (unemployment) became common in the 1890s.[31] In the US, there were only rare references to the unemployed before 1850 and the term only became common in the 1870s.[32] Thus, unemployment preceded its official recognition, the delay perhaps being explained by the continued existence of old ideas about work and idleness.

In Germany, the first two national official enumerations of unemployment were in the population census and the census of production in 1895. The French census did not record unemployment until 1896. Salais explained the failure to establish a specific unemployment category:

neither in those without occupation of which they were a component, called the 'acrobats, bohemians, vagabonds and prostitutes' nor in the 'unclassified population', an undifferentiated mass for which the statistician could only give a general figure.[33]

The British censuses followed the same pattern. In the 1881 Census of England and Wales, the 'unoccupied class' was not an equivalent to unemployment or a even partial recognition of the phenomenon, but

were managing their estates and property; directing charitable institutions; prosecuting literary or scientific researches, or engaged in other of the multifarious channels by which unpaid energy finds vent. If these were deducted from the 182,282 unoccupied males, and a further deduction were also made for those who were incapacitated for work by physical defects, the remainder, constituting the really idle portion of the community, would be very small.[34]

In the US, it wasn't until the 1910 census that the guidelines for enumerators dealt with unemployment, but even then the census officials were instructed to record the unemployed individual by their occupation when in employment.[35]

Clearly, if unemployment was to be recognised, this 'common sense' had to be challenged. Most discussions of the role of the working class, and its relationship to social policy, centre on the 'social control' debate whereby welfare was introduced as a form of containment of popular demands. The term itself is an abstract catch-all which has been fashioned at times into a straw man. As such, it has obscured the precise ways in which the working class affected the origins of the welfare state. Research has demonstrated the complex interaction of forces that played a part in this process. These include 'enlightened' employers, the growth of the state bureaucracy involved in social policy, individual reformers, the strains of modernisation and the example of foreign pioneers. On one level we are not concerned as much with the origins of the welfare state as its narrower connection with the recognition of unemployment. The modern word 'unemployment', E.P. Thompson noted, emerged in the 1820s and 1830s in the trade union, radical and Owenite literature, even though it had not, as yet, entered the discourse of the early Victorian reformers.[36] The acceptance of unemployment as a social problem coincided with the emergence of mass socialist parties in a number European countries and the political threat they represented. The political demand for the 'right to work' was crucial to the development of unemployment as an idea. The banners of the Lyons silk-workers' revolt in 1831 read 'Live working or die fighting'.[37] The right to work was first given literary currency by the writings of the French utopian socialist Charles Fourier.[38] The slogan penetrated the emerging utopian socialist groups and literature across Europe.

The right to work was one of the popular demands made during the French revolution of February 1848 which led to the establishment of the National Workshops and the Provisional Government's declaration of the right to work.[39] The closure of the National Workshops in June led to an insurrection in Paris. At their trials, impoverished insurgents would explain that they had joined the secret revolutionary clubs because they had been promised the right to work.[40] The demand had a powerful hold over the urban poor, many of whom were destitute and without work because of financial and harvest failures. The significance of the slogan was that it stressed the involuntary character of worklessness. The indignant militancy and activism of the Lyonnais silk-weaver or the Lancashire millworker hardly fitted the notion of passivity and sloth associated with pauperism or idleness.

The importance of working-class and socialist organisations in the recognition of unemployment went beyond ideology and slogans.

Alexander Keyssar, in his study of unemployment in Massachusetts, observed a time-lag between working-class and middle-class awareness of unemployment, which spanned the last quarter of the nineteenth century. He pointed to the connection between the under-standing of unemployment as a social problem and unemployed demonstrations, protests and riots. In Boston, the socialist Morrison Swift and the radical Christian Urbain Ledoux led these unemployed protests and they had a subtle but profound effect. Whilst they failed in their declared goals, they succeeded in mounting a moral and symbolic challenge to the authorities. These movements elicited greater charitable and relief efforts, provoked the serious investiga-tions of unemployment and their most enduring achievement was placing unemployment as a problem 'on the doorstep of government'.[41]

Britain presents a similar story of labour's role in the emergence of unemployment. The trade unions that organised unemployment insurance funds collected the first statistics of unemployment. Protest also played a fundamental part. In response to the bitter recession of the winter of 1885–86, the Social Democratic Federation (SDF) and radical trade unionists organised unemployed demonstrations, culminating in riots on 8 and 9 February 1887 in Trafalgar Square. Langan argued that working-class militancy over the issue of unem-ployment, and the 'Right to Work' campaign in particular, prompted the Board of Trade to recognise and act on the issue in the 1890s.[42] Harris believed it to be one of the influences on the Liberal government's introduction of unemployment insurance in 1911. As the Home Secretary Winston Churchill told a *Daily Mail* reporter in 1909: 'With a "stake in the country" in the form of insurance against evil days these workers will pay no attention to the vague promises of revolutionary socialism.'[43]

The European socialist parties, championing the rights of the emerging industrial working class, attempted an alternative explanation of the workings of capitalism. Ideologically, Marx's economic analysis of capitalism played perhaps the most important role here. Marx argued in the first volume of *Capital* that a relative surplus population is a necessary condition of modern industry. It is essential to accumulation as, without this, the rapid cyclical boom with its increased demand for labour could not take place. The relative surplus population also acts as a threat to the worker:

> The industrial reserve army, during periods of stagnation and average prosperity, weighs down the active army of workers; during periods of over-production and feverish activity, it puts a curb on their pretensions. The relative surplus population is therefore the background against which the law of supply and demand does its

work. It confines the field of action of this law to the limits absolutely convenient to capital's drive to exploit and dominate workers.[44]

According to Marx, the source of this 'industrial reserve army' was threefold. First, employers are able, through new technology, to replace labourers by machines. Second, employers can extract more work from their existing labour force, either by extending the working day or by intensifying work. Third, this 'reserve', made possible by the first two factors, is given a cyclical character by the fluctuations in industrial activity. Garraty argued that Marx put unemployment in 'a new context' as it was not an aberrant but 'an entirely normal and necessary aspect of capitalism'.[45] From this point, unemployment could be treated as a subject of social investigation and reform. Whilst this perhaps overstated the importance and influence of Marx on contemporary debates, it does point to the way in which he profoundly challenged existing attitudes to unemployment.

Charles Booth, the influential social reformer, took up the notion of a labour reserve in his *Life and Labour of the People in London* (1889–1902). Booth's work was significant because it viewed unemployment as a social problem – one that was morally degenerating but not simply reducible to personal character. He divided the working class into categories according to levels of skill, regularity of work and moral standards. At one end of the scale, the respectable working class engaged in regular skilled work and, at the other, the unskilled, casual labourer was infected with criminality and alcoholism. Irregular work, casual labour and bouts of unemployment, classically associated with the East End of London, threatened to blur the divisions within the working class. If unemployment spread to the respectable working class it would have a degrading effect on the morals and quality of labour. Booth proposed labour colonies, which had already been established in Belgium and Switzerland, to resolve the problem.[46]

William Beveridge, who was seen as a pioneer in the economic treatment of unemployment, adopted Booth's definition of the working class and unemployment. However in these pre-1914 debates unemployment was conceptualised in a much narrower fashion than it would be after 1918. A consensus emerged that unemployment was a problem principally concerned with casual labour. Beveridge's solution of decasualisation through a national network of labour exchanges therefore, flowed from this understanding. In the interwar period even though casual labour certainly did not disappear, the spotlight shifted to the staple industries and depressed areas that were suffering unemployment.

Unemployment acquired its present meaning through a process of ideological and institutional contingency and contestation. Viewed in the long run, unemployment was brought into the realm of public recognition and policy through two obviously connected factors: a critique of industrial capitalism and the protest of those threatened by unemployment. Across the industrialising parts of the globe, in Lyons, London or Boston, unemployment emerged by this same combination of factors. However, the ideological conflict that gave unemployment its name continued. Though unemployment could no longer be denied, the attitudes that had prevented its recognition remained. Notions that the unemployed were undeserving or work-shy persisted (and, indeed, persist to this day). After its birth, unemployment continued to be the subject of a continuing gap between reality and representation, and a matter of contrasting political agendas, images, policies and struggles. Historians of the interwar period have neglected this continuing contestation and our study of interwar unemployment in Britain, the USA and Europe will attempt to correct this oversight.

Unemployment in Britain between the Wars: Revisionism and its Critics

A strong liberal and conservative consensus about the interwar Britain has emerged. Its project has been explicitly to replace the postwar image of the 1930s. These historians have a set of common assumptions, themes and language. 'Revision', 'reappraisal', 'myth', 'the failure of extremes' are the watchwords of this consensus. They share, to a considerable degree, a number of central propositions about the 1930s. First, they urge that improvements in health, prosperity and leisure have been ignored. Second, Britain was governed by consent, and violence and extremism were alien to British political culture. Third, the 'guilty men' (Neville Chamberlain, Stanley Baldwin, Ramsay MacDonald, etc.), those blamed in the 1940s for the previous decade's appeasement and unemployment, should be seen in a more favourable light. This inter-pretation sounds a counterpoint to the popular myths about the 1930s. These myths underpinned the 1945 settlement and were summed up by the slogan 'Never Again' – that is, there would be no return to the 1930s. These myths were based on a collective memory and experience, albeit a selective one, of the years between the wars. Was there really an orthodoxy amongst academic historians that the 1930s were a 'low, dishonest decade'? Or has there been an over-reaction to a largely imaginary foe? If this is true, the self-styled revisionists are not entirely deserving of the name. The overstatement of their case can be seen in their attempt to marginalise the political activity of the unemployed. This forms part of a wider approach that ignores the experience of the working class in the 1930s. The revisionist literature deals, in the main, in consumers, voters, cinema audiences, 'the British people', the unemployed and so on, not in class, ethnic or gender terms.

Though in many ways anticipated by Mowat's study (1955), John Stevenson and Chris Cook's *The Slump* played a seminal role in forming the new Liberal-Conservative consensus.[47] Chris Cook was also joint editor of a collection of essays that challenged

> the accent ... either on the basic continuity of British institutions or on the failure to grapple with certain problems seen in the light of the new triumphant Keynesian collectivism to which major elements of all parties gave their adherence.[48]

Another collection of essays, *The Failure of Political Extremism*, edited by Andrew Thorpe, further elaborated the political aspects of the new historiography. The like-mindedness of many British historians was born out of the changing political, intellectual and academic climate of the mid-1970s. The works that have been mentioned thus far are mainly of political history; they have been complemented by works of monetarist economic historians (notably Aldcroft, and Benjamin and Kochin).[49] Ross McKibbin also weighed in against the orthodox Keynesian view established by Skidelsky (and others), arguing that the international experience demonstrated that a British New Deal was not really an option.[50] Furthermore, non-monetarists economic historians, such as Tomlinson, Peden and Middleton, have taken the view that Keynesianism was an impossibility in the early 1930s for institutional reasons. (The peacetime state was neither large enough nor had the mechanisms to bring about full employment.)[51]

Obviously there are a good number of historians that stand out against this consensus, either in general or over particular aspects. Consequently, several important historical debates have emerged. Keith Laybourn's *Britain on the Breadline* stands in contrast to the revisionists, surveying a broad range of social issues of the 1930s. On a more specific level, Webster and Mitchell have taken issue with the optimistic view of health espoused by historians such as Winter and a number of studies of unemployed struggles have challenged the 'Jarrow School' view of consensus and unemployed passivity.[52] Others writing tangential to these issues, for example, on the Labour Party, also provide an important counterweight to the revisionist view.[53]

The first major attempt to tackle the revisionist history of the 1930s was John Saville and Alun Howkins' review of *The Slump* in the *Socialist Register*. They pointed out that improvements in the standard of living based on real wages ignore that, for many, wages were interrupted by unemployment. Even in supposedly booming sectors such as construction or the motor industry, work was strongly affected by the seasons. They argue that *The Slump* neglected the experiences of the working class and women. This experience has been opened up, for all its weaknesses, by oral history. Saville and Howkins offered the following example of how the real experience of economic change is crucial. Thousands left the distressed areas to find employment in new industries in the prosperous South which meant being uprooted from familiar surrounding, friends, associations, home and family. Nor do the revisionist historians have an appreciation of the effect of the depression on class relations, as 'there is no good statistical measure, by which to address, in an imaginative as well as a rigorous fashion, a bullying foreman with the seigneurial right of hiring and firing'.[54] The review then takes *The Slump* to task over the way in which the radicalisation of sections of the British population in the late 1930s is skirted around. For example, Stevenson and Cook incorrectly suggested that the surge in Communist Party membership resulted from a fad of middle-class intellectuals.

There are some very substantial problems with the assumptions and categories that underpin the revisionist analysis. These include the use of the term 'extremism', the reliance on electoral statistics as an indicator of social attitudes, the uniqueness of Britain in the 1930s, and the relationship between social struggles and reform.

'Extremism' is a highly problematic term with its self-evidently value-laden associations, an extremist, as any dictionary or thesaurus will reveal, is excessive, unreasonable, wild. For the revisionists, the NUWM, militant anti-fascism and the CPGB occupied the extremist margins of politics, they were effectively alien to British politics. In response, it should be stressed that unemployed radicalism was not an irrational, extraneous factor, but was bred by the very conditions of the interwar period. Similar conditions had fostered the growth of unemployed protest elsewhere in Europe and in Britain in the decades before the First World War. The distinction between unemployed activists and their neighbours was not a question of kind but of degree. Far from being unlettered extremists, those involved in the unemployed movement were often amongst the most well-read, articulate and thinking members of their class; examples, perhaps, of Gramsci's notion of the organic intellectual. Those who believe that liberal democracy generates a harmonious civil society use the term to equate conflict with aberrant or deviant behaviour.

They ignore class and gender as part of an explanatory framework and relegate them to the passing details of narrative. This is a fundamental mistake. Consider, for example, A.J.P. Taylor's question (quoted by many, including Stevenson and Cook): 'Which was more important for the future – over a million unemployed or over a million private cars?' The answer depended surely on whether you were a middle-class car owner or a jobless worker. This mystifies how the interwar consensus was produced and the social interests that lay behind it. The consensus of the day was forged in high politics between government and big business. This consensus was not all-conquering but subject to a near permanent ideological friction with the demand of 'work and maintenance', to which policy concessions were begrudgingly made. This notion of ideological contestation is indispensable to an explanation of the developing politics of unemployment.

Several historians have placed great emphasis on the analysis of electoral statistics to undermine accepted nostrums about the 1930s. A great deal can be learnt from such statistics, but we should also sound a note of caution as voting patterns are relatively limited indicators of social attitudes. For example, votes cannot simply be equated with wholesale endorsement of a party's policy or even its manifesto (which invariably differ). In particular, elections are incapable of measuring the nuances of mood, attitudinal development, hesitations, confusions and contradictory ideas held by individuals or at large. Time and again in history we find electoral results at odds with the developments of social protest, movements and even revolutions. Consciousness is uneven and undergoes rapid shifts in periods of social unrest. For example, consider the student insurgency and militant general strike of France in May 1968, which was rapidly succeeded by an overwhelming Gaullist electoral victory.

The revisionists take a strongly historicist line and assume the 1930s in Britain to be (internationally and historically) unique and incomparable. Thus, they contradict Beveridge's central proposition that unemployment was a general threat to democratic institutions. British constitutionalism, according to the liberal historians, was more resilient than elsewhere in Europe because of the gradual and peaceful character of British history. The problems with such a view are that it offers a highly selective version of British history; it is not in any way quantifiable (in fact, there is no still British constitution and the vote had only recently arrived for women and unskilled manual workers); and it is dependent on the very use of hindsight that revisionists condemn in others. Surely we are on firmer empirical ground if we take as our starting-point the relative scale of economic crisis (levels of unemployment, falls in output, bankruptcies, etc.). Such a line of inquiry suggests that the British economy was in a favourable position when compared to its European counterparts. Zimmerman found that, of six European countries, Britain was least severely affected by economic depression.[55] Those other countries suffered much greater political instability than Britain. As the origins and course of the depression were beyond the understanding or control of British policy-makers, the relative fortuitousness of the British situation is hardly cause for national self-congratulation. Nor should the 1930s be treated in isolation from what preceded or followed. At its beginning, the catastrophic defeat of organised labour in 1926 shaped the political pattern of the 1930s and this has to be seen as the context for the 'revolution that never was'. Revisionists also over-react to the temptations of teleology and hindsight, and in asserting the 'openness' of the late 1930s they ignore the structural constraint and contingency of an increasingly probable war. Baldwinite consensus depended on appeasement and recovery. The collapse of appeasement sounded the death knell for that consensus.

Perhaps the most difficult question for the historian of the 1930s is the relationship between protest and social reform. Revisionists eschew any connection between reform and class relations or struggle. Two issues are involved: first, the short-term and immediate response to protest, and second, the longer-term development of the welfare state. Harmer states that the impact of the NUWM on the government was 'minimal'. Even in the short term this is highly disputable. Reforms often occur over the longer term when the immediate battles have been waged or the immediate threat has passed and the lessons gradually assimilated. This raises the general question of causality in history and it is perhaps no coincidence that Saville and Howkins should describe *The Slump* as standing in the 'A.J.P. Taylor school', which views causality as the product of the immediate, sequential and often accidental actions of individuals. The literature of historians and historical sociologists on the origins and development of the welfare state suggests an interaction between social conflict and reform that is not direct, intentional, immediate, but, none the less, significant.[56] Of course, there are those who lay greater emphasis on party political factors or modernisation, but a strong case has been made that neither the 'great liberal' nor the blind forces of modernisation are adequate explanations of the development of welfare states.[57] Goran Therborn emphasised state traditions and class relations in the origins of the welfare state and, in particular, though not exclusively, the threat from below posed by labour movements. From this perspective, the contribution of the unemployed struggle to a more general recovery in working-class organisation and consciousness in the mid- to late 1930s was highly significant with regard to welfarist developments during the war.

Sources of Controversy: Revisionism and Historical Methods

Most historical disagreements are reflected in the protagonists'
attitudes to the sources. This holds true for unemployment between
the wars. Mrs Keen, a cotton operative who had been without work
for four years, warned: 'Unless you live here, amongst these things,
you couldn't understand and I can't put them into words.'[58] Her
sentiments, which are echoed in many unemployed testimonies,
identify one of the central problems faced by the historian of unemployment: How can we understand what unemployment was really
like? We have so many cultural and political references to unemployment and depression that it is difficult to distinguish between reality
and representation. As the experience of unemployment existed in
the realm of everyday life, the traditional avenues of investigation,
politicians' papers or memoirs and official documents, are ill-suited
to answering this satisfactorily.

Most historians researching the question of unemployment in
interwar Britain have started with official documents; and with good
reason. Annual reports of the Education, Health and Labour
Ministries provide a wealth of information about the jobless. In
addition, the government commissioned many specific reports into
questions such as unemployment relief, the conditions of distressed
areas, and the effects of the depression on health. The two reports of
the Royal Commission on Unemployment Insurance provide an
extensive discussion of the nature of unemployment and its relief.
These efforts continued in the annual reports of the Unemployment
Assistance Boards. However, the volume and exhaustiveness of this
material should not blind us to its omissions and bias. Government
reports were written from a particular standpoint with specific aims;
sometimes the official agenda was obvious and intruded on their
conclusions. For instance, the report on health in Sunderland set out
to rebut a local doctor's claim that the North-East's high unemployment was causing ill-health.[59] Bias also affected government
documents in more subtle ways. The first annual Unemployment
Assistance Board was very carefully prepared to gain that controversial body the most favourable press coverage. Detailed instructions
were sent to district officers on how to compile reports using case
histories rather than statistics and giving particular emphasis to
countering 'allegations' made about the means test.[60] Rivalry within
and between ministries sometimes affected official evidence. Most
importantly, the voices of the unemployed themselves were absent.
The investigators were politicians, civil servants, businessmen and
trade union leaders, and the latter were always outnumbered by
figures from the Establishment.[61] Elsewhere, Home Office and
Cabinet Papers were concerned about the threat of unrest and even,

in the immediate postwar months, revolution posed by the unemployed. Police surveillance of the unemployed movement offered distorted evidence of the experience of unemployment. The Metropolitan Police files are a vital source of information on the hunger marches. There are obvious problems with such adversarial and covert information as these agencies clearly sought to contain unemployed radicals. The files had a number of purposes: reporting to political masters; the dissemination of an official version to the press; and internal police use.

Take the example of the size of demonstrations which the police consistently under-reported. The official estimate for the Hyde Park reception of the 1936 Hunger March was 12,000, but the number given by organisers and participants was 100,000; the *Daily Herald* claimed 250,000; however, other newspapers quoted police figures. Historians applying the rules of their trade accepted the police estimate rather than the latter as better evidence, but this is a mistake because the police were not neutral.

Bias in official documents, then, resulted from the fact that the unemployed were the object of observation, containment and administration rather than subjects given freedom to voice their experiences, concerns and demands. Official reports reveal nothing that was conducted in guarded and personal conversations of ministers and civil servants. The difference between the diary entries of Thomas Jones, deputy secretary to the Cabinet, and Cabinet conclusions is striking. Official documents are generally withheld for 50 or 70 years, some even longer, but some are destroyed or lost. Dave Colledge and John Field noted that the files on labour camp disturbances had been 'weeded' out, and thought this to be no accident.[62] Then there is the odd story of the 'missing' files of the Metropolitan Police on the hunger marches pertaining to the use of special branch informers in the NUWM.[63]

The paradox of government sources extends to statistics. The government alone is capable of producing the data needed to understand certain aspects of unemployment. Most obviously, the Ministry of Labour produced fortnightly unemployment figures and hence our knowledge of the scale of unemployment was much more accurate than before the First World War. The coverage of the labour exchanges and the insurance schemes was an improvement on the trade union statistics which pre-dated the National Insurance Act of 1911. The 1920 Unemployment Insurance Act initially covered 11 million workers, rising to 15.4 million by 1938. However, agricultural and domestic workers were ineligible and therefore these figures slightly exaggerate the rate of unemployment (as unemployment was more likely in the insured trades) but underestimates the absolute number unemployed. These statistics do, nevertheless, allow a

detailed assessment of the national, regional and industrial pattern of
unemployment and, as foreign governments were producing unemployment statistics, the interwar period was the first in which
international unemployment rates could be meaningfully compared.
This comparison reveals British unemployment to be of a more
chronic character than elsewhere, but the acute depression of the
early 1930s brought considerably greater unemployment in the US
and Germany. Unemployment statistics may be misleading because
of the geographical units used. Thus many local pockets of acute
unemployment may be missed in the aggregate figures. For example,
the appalling unemployment figures for Jarrow were merged with the
less shocking figure for Hebburn in 1935. The major problem with
the statistics from our perspective, however, is that they are purely
quantitative and therefore of little help in assessing the subjective
experience of unemployment for its millions of victims. George
Orwell, in *The Road to Wigan Pier*, made the point that the figures
comforted middle-class opinion as 'facts' could be discussed dispas-
sionately.[64] Official publications may be essential to the study of
unemployment but over-reliance on them offers a 'top-down' view
and marginalises the experiences of the workless.

If government sources are problematic, to what extent do the
efforts of private individuals, philanthropists and social investigators
provide a solution? The methods of the social investigators of the
interwar period were profoundly influenced by Charles Booth, who
tried to quantify poverty and make the distinction between the
deserving and undeserving poor. Contemporary local studies of social
conditions took place in Bristol, Brynmawr (South Wales), Liverpool,
London, Southampton, York, Tyneside and Sheffield.[65] These
provide detailed local empirical investigations of poverty providing
results from questionnaires, interviewing and official statistics. The
faith that scientific observation would reveal both the objective
character of the problem and its remedy underpinned these
endeavours. Despite much useful detail and analysis, objectivity was
not achieved as the studies were imbued with the contemporary
middle-class man's political agenda of charity and social reform, his
social assumptions of a woman's place, the need for cleanliness,
sobriety and the production of healthy racial stock.

Cleanliness provides a good example of the influence of the investigators' prejudices on their work. Middle-class standards of
cleanliness were not appropriate for the poor, often overcrowded and
overworked, households that they investigated. Their standards were
based on having time, energy, a good standard of housing and, above
all, domestic servants. Investigators were also affected by a sense of
superiority (even biological superiority given the prevalence of
eugenics). A Pilgrim Trust investigator talked of 'the usual crop of

residual cases ... low grade families of the virtually unemployable';
one man was put in this category because he was 'continually
grinning or scratching his head'.[66] A Mass Observation survey, which
graded the population by class, had a category of

> People who are crude, dirty and irresponsible. Have no community
> feeling outside their own grade ... Quite content to live and
> produce children on the dole. Of their circumstances they would
> say 'It's good enough for the likes of us'. It seems they know their
> own value.[67]

Certain left-wingers – George Orwell, J.B. Priestley and Fenner
Brockway – produced an alternative model to this empirical approach
which was more literary and attempted, in varying degrees, to portray
the experience of the unemployed.[68] Despite these efforts, neither
approach breaks down the problem of the middle-class outsider
attempting to understand the unemployed. Orwell admitted to
having a childhood repulsion of the working class and he continued
to think that all workers' houses smelt bad. This highlighted a
problem surely common to all middle-class investigators who found
working-class life alien, squalid and even threatening.[69] Their
solutions were formulated from an outsider's perspective: what can
be done for 'them' and what values should be instilled in 'them'?
Typical of both these responses are efforts 'from above': charity or
social reform. Even left-wingers such as Orwell and Priestley were
ambivalent about the self-activity of the unemployed and the efforts
of the communists to agitate amongst them.

Several types of document record the subjective experience of the
workless. The 1930s novels – Walter Greenwood's *Love on the Dole*,
Walter Brierley's *Means Test Man* and Hans Fallada's *Little Man –
What Now?* – all deal with unemployment as a central theme, and
were based on the authors' experience of unemployment.[70] They
have a dual relevance: for their wide contemporary readership and as
an authentic expression of the unemployed life. Testimony of the
unemployed themselves, oral history, also provides an insider's
account of the depression years. Here we find a rich source of
information, vivid memories, opinion, feelings and macabre
anecdotes. Since the mid-1970s, many local projects have sought to
uncover the experience of the depression from prosperous Leicester
to distressed Newcastle. These accounts provide insights, but again
this type of source has its own drawbacks: sample size and memory.
The small numbers often involved in oral history projects raise
questions of the representativeness of the chroniclers. In *The Worst of
Times*, Nigel Gray freely admitted that his purpose in collecting
accounts of the depression was to refute the revisionist trend amongst

historians. Also, the prism of memory tends unwittingly to reshape testimony. Memory tries to make sense of events in the light of subsequent personal development, suppressing some episodes, distorting others. Having said that, oral history does allow us to penetrate the world of the everyday life in a way that other sources plainly do not. Indeed, a number of particularly valuable volumes, such as published BBC interviews with the unemployed, brought together testimonies at the time and therefore avoid the distortions of memory.[71] These collections, edited by Beales and Lambert, and Greene, cover several important aspects of unemployed life: budgets, personal and political feelings and ways of making ends meet. Ironically, the credentials of the *Time to Spare* series were strengthened because ministerial criticism forced the BBC to check the series' factual details and representativeness.[72]

The literature of the National Unemployed Workers' Movement provides another source of information 'from the inside'. Wal Hannington, its leader, wrote several major accounts of the condition of the workless, the unemployed movement and government policy. The movement also produced countless pamphlets, newspapers and leaflets and has left a store of photographs, biographies and memories. Their great advantage is that, despite the distortions produced by its communist leadership, this was a political movement run for and by the unemployed and as such records their experience and struggles. In so many of the other sources, the unemployed are treated as victims of fate: passive recipients of relief or charity, a mob to be feared or individuals broken by poverty. In contrast, the NUWM stressed that if the unemployed themselves acted, they could improve their lot. The language of the NUWM was simultaneously marked by a communist rhetoric and expressed the bitterness of many unemployed that is silent in many other sources. The juvenile instruction centres were 'slave camps', the Unemployment Assistance Act the 'slave bill', Neville Chamberlain a 'baby-starver', the means test 'mass murder', relief scales 'the starvation of mother and child'. A word of caution must be sounded about Hannington's writings, in particular the claims made of government concessions and of communist–NUWM relations. Naturally enough, Hannington too easily equates improvements with the activities in which he invested so much enthusiasm, energy and self-sacrifice. At times he allowed himself a degree of heroic licence in his narrative of the titanic clashes between government and the unemployed. He consequently presents a one-sided case to the exclusion of other factors, and offers an extremely optimistic view of the NUWM's relationship with the CPGB, which was often fraught. At times the CP were extolling revolutionary action from the unemployed, at others the NUWM's liquidation to joint bodies with the official labour movement. Here

McShane, the Scottish NUWM leader, provides a useful corrective as he had broken with the CPGB by the time he wrote his memoirs. Liberal and conservative historians have generally underplayed the importance of this literature and the impact of the movement. Whilst it is necessary to understand the NUWM's literature in the light of the twists and turns of communist policy, this does not mean that there was no substance to Hannington's claims to have won concessions from government. Harry Harmer goes to considerable lengths and tortuous reasoning to disprove the NUWM leader's claims because he believes the evidence of a communist is of little worth.[73] That there is no explicit evidence in government sources does not necessarily invalidate such claims. The government was unlikely to admit even in secret Cabinet minutes that militant struggles on the part of the unemployed brought results. There is plenty of evidence that the government did everything it could to prevent and discourage the hunger marches and also that they were concerned by the political effects of distress.

Although evidence from the inside is often subjective and difficult to evaluate, its very subjectivity is its strength. After all, unemployment was a personal, subjective experience as well as a mass phenomenon dictated by economic circumstance. Insiders' evidence is neither better nor worse than official documents: it is different, better suited to some tasks, less so to others. Historians' attitudes to these sources have shaped the way in which the history of the interwar period has been written and rewritten. Ignoring or underplaying insiders' evidence as too problematic has resulted in an over-reliance on those viewing unemployment from without and a dependency on sources with middle-class or government agendas. This has been a serious flaw in the revisionist view of the 1930s.

THE BRITISH EXPERIENCE

2 Government, Employers and Unemployment

> The temper of the men is becoming increasingly bitter ... There is
> much muttering about the ostentation and luxury of the 'idle rich'
> and agitators have seized upon the real discontent and distress to
> carry on a ceaseless propaganda of class war. Peace with Russia as
> a panacea for unemployment is their constant theme.
>
> Thomas MacNamara, Minister of Labour
> to the Cabinet, 9 December 1920[1]

The years between the wars marked an awkward transition between
the old and the new, between British world leadership and middle-
power status, between laissez-faire and 'organised' capitalism,
between nightwatchman state and welfare state. That transition was
already taking place before 1914; it was accelerated by war. In the
case of unemployment, the state had created unemployment
insurance, employment exchanges and unemployment statistics
before the First World War. All were in a state of immaturity.
Unemployment insurance established in 1911 catered for only a
small minority of the working class and was not intended to provide
enough to live on (or 'maintenance' in the parlance of the day).

The employers' attitudes and relationship between business and
government are of critical importance to assessing the politics of
unemployment 'from above'. The interwar period opened with a
series of concessions given to appease a discontented working class,
unemployment relief being perhaps the most notable of these. Both
employers' representatives and government spoke in the conciliatory
tones of corporatism, combining high-level negotiations and new
institutional structures for conflict-resolution. After this initial phase,
policy followed a less compromising course of attempted reorganisation of the benefits system and retrenchment, but it was not until the
late 1930s that unemployment relief was restructured so as to not
cause government further embarrassments. In addition to relief, the
government adopted a range of policies to deal with unemployment,
such as regional policy and public works. The attitudes of business
underpinned the formulation of government policy; unemployment

was, after all, an economic phenomenon and therefore part of their traditional domain. The employers, by lobbying government and public campaigning, clearly sought to minimise the costs of welfare on business. Through ownership of the press and their representative organisations, they exerted considerable influence on the government. Their presence on Royal Commissions and on government reports is an obvious example of this. Governments generally listened sympathetically to the business agenda and often articulated similar themes, notably the need for economies and the spectre of dole abuse, but there were important limits to the extent to which the government could implement this programme set by electoral considerations and unemployed protests. As a result of these counteracting forces the government needed to display its seriousness about tackling the problem of unemployment, but all too often these conflicting agendas led to half-measures (labour camps, assisted migration and public works) and palliatives (the encouragement of philanthropy).

Concessions Born of Unrest, 1918–22

In 1917 the government commissioned an investigation into industrial unrest. Its report warned that the working class, whilst still in large part patriotic, was showing pre-revolutionary stirrings. It detailed the unofficial shop stewards' movement's growing influence. Independent of the trade union bureaucracy, the shop stewards were responsible for the contagion of wartime strikes. High prices, the conscription of skilled workers, the erosion of custom and practice, the dilution of skilled labour and poor housing all fuelled the widespread grumbling about an 'inequality of sacrifice' and government's 'broken promises'. Investigators were worried: the industrial future was one of 'woeful uncertainty'.[2] The mood hardened for the first two years after the war as the years 1917–20 marked the high tide of working-class unrest; a 'moment of insurgency' as Cronin called it.[3] 1919 was the year of the Clydeside 40-hour strike which brought tanks onto the streets of Glasgow, two police strikes, the rail strike and the dual threat of a miners' strike and the enactment of the 'triple alliance' (an understanding whereby miners, transport and rail workers would strike together). In that year 2.4 million had been on strike and in 1920 trade unions reached the unprecedented peak of 8.3 million members.[4] In this context Lloyd George, heading an anxious Coalition government, promised a 'land of milk and honey', a 'land fit for heroes', 'a really new world'. To smooth over industrial troubles, he dabbled with corporatism, the creation of institutions allowing co-operation between government, unions and employers.

In early 1919 the National Industrial Conference, which the press heralded as the 'Peace Conference for Industry', brought together employer, trade union and government representatives and established the Provisional Joint Committee.[5] These efforts served the government's and employers' purposes at the time, and the trade union leaders were seduced by their inclusion at the top table. The Sankey Commission into the Mines which discussed nationalisation of the coal industry mirrored this delaying strategy of reconciliation. It effectively stalled miners' militancy and its recommendations, published in August 1919, were ultimately officially ignored. Lloyd George's corporatism spoke the language of reconstruction and seemed more positive than the rank-and-file militancy of the shop stewards. But these manoeuvrings on their own were not enough to diffuse discontent.

As Lloyd George and the employers played for time the trauma of industrial defeats and mass unemployment checked working-class confidence. Full employment and relatively successful industrial skirmishing had encouraged working-class defiance. On Armistice Day, Wal Hannington, later the unemployed leader, ran up the red flag at his factory; he was not sacked because it would have 'caused a strike' and toolmakers were 'not easy to replace'.[6] But those conditions were soon to collapse. In September 1920 unemployment among trade unionists was only 2.2 per cent; seven months later it had soared to 27.6 per cent.[7] The world recession of 1921–23 and an employers' wage-cutting offensive undermined the trade unions' bargaining position. Unemployment, virtually absent from the British economy for ten years, instilled fear amongst workers once more. The 1921–22 employers' offensive shattered workers' confidence. In spring 1921 the national miners' strike was defeated and the following year the engineers and textile workers suffered reverses. Employers were able to identify and blacklist militants, such as Hannington, who were now easy to replace.[8] The relations between the union leadership and the shop stewards' movement was another crucial element in this equation. The all-important miners' strike was defeated. On 'Black Friday' the triple alliance crumbled when Jimmy Thomas, the railworkers' leader, refused to call his members out on strike. The dispute's failure also resulted from the activities of miners' leaders who 'usurped powers of negotiation and decision', ignoring a two-thirds ballot in favour of continuing the strike.[9] J.T. Murphy, speaking at the 1922 Congress of Communist International, explained that the 'objective conditions' of 'empty and depleted workshops' had broken the shop stewards' movement.[10] Sidney Webb too recognised this correlation. 'In all industries, indeed,' he wrote, the employers' insistence on reductions of wages has had to be accepted, not necessarily because their economic inevitableness [sic] has been demonstrated, but because of the presence on the labour market of large masses of unemployed who could not have been prevented from accepting the employers' terms.[11]

As the unemployed were considered both a threat to public order and a drain on expenditure, governments had to appease the trinity of unemployment insurance fund solvency, adequate relief and retrenchment. Policy constituted a series of confused, *ad hoc* measures, which attempted to balance these three contradictory concerns. Miscalculation aggravated the problem. Governments, from Lloyd George's coalition onwards, repeatedly underestimated the scale and permanence of unemployment, and projections were far too low in the planning of relief. The 1920 Unemployment Act assumed 5 per cent unemployment; in the Blanesburgh Committee report of 1927 the projected rate was still only 6 per cent, and it was not until 1936 that a more realistic average level of 16.75 per cent was assumed.[12]

Up to early 1922 governments conceded more and more (although relief was miserly to begin with as unemployment benefits were intended to supplement working-class savings). In 1918 the Out of Work Donation provided emergency benefit for the unemployed without insurance contributions.[13] The National Insurance Acts of 1916 and 1920 extended unemployment insurance so that, after 1920, most workers (11.75 million in all) were covered. Benefit was also raised on Christmas Day 1919 from 7 to 11 shillings a week, and in October 1920 to 15 shillings. Other concessions were made to the unemployed in the form of public works. In December 1920, the Unemployment Grants Committee was set up to finance local authority work-creation schemes. As a temporary measure, during spring 1921, roughly coinciding with the miners' strike, weekly benefits were raised from 15 shillings to 20 shillings. In a move that made concessions to the notion of maintenance, claimants who had exhausted their right to insurance benefit, from August 1921, were allowed 'uncovenanted' benefits, and two months later the unemployed received allowances for their dependants. The sum for an unemployed man with a wife and two children was raised from 15 shillings a week to 22 shillings.[14] Employers criticised these measures for encouraging abuse and idleness, but tolerated them because they believed that unemployment insurance made union co-operation more likely.[15]

The Coalition government's fear that unemployment would cause widespread unrest had prompted this generosity. The Cabinet received regular secret, often alarming, reports on revolutionary organisations from Sir Basil Home Thomson, the Assistant Commissioner of Scotland Yard and Director of Intelligence. In September 1921, Thomas MacNamara warned the Cabinet of the consequences of inadequate relief for the unemployed, and even the King wrote to Lloyd George about unemployment: 'The people grow discontented and agitators seize their opportunities: marches are organised; the police interfere; resistance ensues; troops are called out and riot begets revolt and possibly revolution.'[16]

To a large extent the government's commitment (established by the Cunliffe Report of 1918) to restoring sterling to the Gold Standard determined the course of unemployment during the 1920s. As the Gold Standard had facilitated a dramatic pre-war growth in world trade with the City of London at its heart, all parties agreed that a return to the Gold Standard, at sterling's pre-war value ($4.86), was a priority. In order to achieve this, prices were kept down through high interest rates and deflation. Painfully high unemployment in Britain's major exporting industries (coal, iron and steel, shipbuilding and textiles) followed. Even so, when Britain re-joined the Gold Standard in April 1925 the pound was still overvalued by 10 per cent. With exports dear and imports cheap, those economic sectors sensitive to international competition were severely disadvantaged and suffered high unemployment throughout the 1920s. Joblessness on this scale had not been experienced before. In the years 1905–14, unemployment had averaged 4.4 per cent whilst for 1920–29 average unemployment had almost trebled to 12.3 per cent. With mass unemployment prolonged as never before, its relief became an intractable problem.

Reform and Retrenchment, 1922–39

For both labour and capital, the British system of unemployment insurance was an awkward hybrid: an insurance scheme and a state hand-out, welfarism and Poor Law, and concession and retrenchment. Because of over-optimistic forecasting of both the numbers and duration of unemployment, the insurance principle was repeatedly breached. Consequently, increasing joblessness periodically plunged the Unemployment Insurance Fund deep into debt precipitating government cuts. The government faced the dilemma that, because of long-term unemployment, large numbers would exhaust their right to benefit but would bitterly resent and probably resist the imposition of the Poor Law.

From 1921–22, once the threat from below had subsided, the government sought to recover these concessions. But their attempt to end uncovenanted unemployment insurance benefits and turn their recipients on to the Poor Law in August and September 1921 fell apart. Many unemployed workers were skilled and saw themselves as 'respectable'. These people hated the Poor Law and felt that to be treated as paupers was abject degradation. Local Poor Law Guardians would also be unable to cope with the scale of unemployment in the depressed areas. Using the Poor Law to replace uncovenanted benefit or reduce the scales of relief was therefore not an option. The direct path thwarted, the government selected a more disguised retrenchment: expenditure on unemployment was reduced through administrative measures to disqualify or cut benefits to individuals.

The two main methods of clawing back concessions were the means test and the 'genuinely seeking work' test. This began as early as March 1921 with the application of a genuinely seeking work clause to uncovenanted benefit. The unemployed had to appear before Local Employment Committees and demonstrate that they were looking for work – onus of proof being on the claimant. In February 1922, in the context of expenditure cuts (known as the Geddes axe) uncovenanted benefit also became subject to a means test and the unemployed were now deemed to be not genuinely seeking work if they would not accept a job regardless of their prior wages and craft.[17] Despite increases in unemployment benefit and eligibility, the 1924 Labour government introduced the genuinely seeking work clause for all claimants. The advantage for the government was that these administrative measures were implemented gradually and without the fanfare of a sudden change in the eligibility of the mass of the jobless.

The problem of uncovenanted unemployment continued to perplex government and vex business. Various voices, notably those of employers, called for this group to be turned over to the Poor Law but the Cabinet feared such a move. Employers, prominent Conservatives and the press also pressed the issue of malingering and abuse. As a contemporary expert on unemployment, R.C. Davison, remarked, despite the lack of substantiating evidence, 'One party still hankered after a task of work in return for maintenance and was always suspicious that benefit was being abused by undeserving and even fraudulent claims of both sexes.'[18] In order to address these concerns, Stanley Baldwin, the Conservative Prime Minister, appointed a committee under the chairmanship of Lord Blanesburgh in 1925.[19] By January 1927, when it published its report, the Unemployment Insurance Fund was £21 million in debt. The Blanesburgh Committee suggested cuts in unemployment benefits, the abolition of extended benefit, stricter contributory eligibility and tight application of the genuinely seeking work clause. These proposals were rapidly embodied in the Unemployment Insurance

Act, with the exception of the abolition of extended benefits and suggested contributory regulations, which were delayed. The Act's immediate effects were a 1 shilling reduction of male weekly unemployment benefit and greater scope for the genuinely seeking work clause.[20]

Between 1921 and 1930 3 million lost their benefit through genuinely seeking work disallowances. Its operation was intrusive and arbitrary. Local Employment Committee officials and Courts of Referees sat in ritualistic judgement over claimants who had to prove that they were searching for (often non-existent) work. Information was gleaned from neighbours and tradesmen about the interviewees. Even their 'attitude' was scrutinised for genuineness; sometimes the interviewee's nervousness was enough for disqualification. Unsurprisingly, given these impressionistic criteria, disallowance rates varied considerably by region. In London its implementation was particularly vicious: in Stepney as many as one in four were disallowed through the clause (and 37 per cent disallowed by all means). In 1927, one in ten were being disqualified by the genuinely seeking work interviews and 18 per cent by all methods.[21]

The means test, introduced for transitional claimants in autumn 1931, became the hated symbol of the treatment of the unemployed in the 1930s. Under the means test people living in the same household were examined jointly to assess whether the unemployed needed assistance. Savings had to be exhausted, furniture sold and adult children had to support elderly parents (or vice versa) or leave home in the pursuit of 'national economy'. Although government reports denied this, the means test broke up families and caused considerable anguish. Many of those assessed also despised the fact that middle-class clerks would come to the house once a month to inspect the family resources, savings or insurance books and household furniture, and would 'size you up and down to see how much food you needed and then allow you not quite enough money to buy it'.[22] The effects of the means test – family stress and break-up and its degrading associations with the Poor Law – were widely recognised.[23]

The Labour government fell over pressure to impose unemployment benefit cuts (which will be dealt with in Chapter 4). The 'National' government succeeded it. Although Ramsay MacDonald was the Prime Minister, the National government was dominated by the Tories. In late 1932 the government faced a crisis brought about by the means test and the cuts. Some Public Assistance Committees (PACs) were facing fierce local opposition and many did not savour implementing the means test. The unemployed had mounted the most militant and violent campaign witnessed to that point, with clashes with police on the 1932 hunger march and rioting in Birkenhead, Liverpool and Belfast. Opposition voices were also heard from some Tory MPs, Church leaders and local authorities themselves. Some PACs made it clear they would not co-operate with the means test and there was considerable variation in its implementation. At one extreme Durham County PAC was suspended in December.

The Transitional Payments (Determination of Need) Act of November 1932, which softened certain aspects of the means test such as its household savings regulations, resolved the immediate crisis. Perhaps more importantly, the government and the PACs struck a tacit agreement wherein the latter were given considerable latitude in implementing the means test in return for dropping public opposition to it.[24] The structural flaw of unemployed provision, caught between insurance and relief, remained as it had since March 1921 when uncovenanted benefits first buttressed the crumbling Unemployment Insurance Act.

The National government now turned its attention to reorganising public assistance but, from the start, internal divisions and indecision plagued these attempts. The Royal Commission on Unemployment Insurance, which published its final report in November 1932, suggested a tripartite system of clearly distinct unemployment insurance; unemployment relief under Ministry of Labour control, but local authority administration; and the Poor Law which would not deal with the unemployed unless they had been disqualified. Neville Chamberlain, the Chancellor of the Exchequer, and Henry Betterton, the Minister of Labour, clashed over reform of unemployment relief.[25] Chamberlain wanted an independent national assistance scheme which would replace the Poor Law and cater for all who needed relief and were not in receipt of unemployment insurance benefits (including the old, mentally ill, etc.). Betterton proposed that unemployment assistance should be under Ministry of Labour control, but administered by local authorities. The slowness of its passage reveals the difficulty in seeking agreement: thus, the Unemployment Assistance Bill was not presented to the House of Commons until November 1933, passing into law in May 1934, and only becoming fully operative in January 1935. Both Chamberlain and Betterton sought to distinguish 'assistance' from unemployment insurance, to take unemployment relief out of politics and avoid any perceived association with the Poor Law which, they realised, would not be acceptable to 'respectable' workers. The outcome, the Unemployment Assistance Board, failed on both latter counts. In fact, resistance to the UAB was the highpoint of unemployed protest for the whole interwar period. The government seriously miscalculated, partly because of ignorance of working-class budgets. As a result, 48 per cent in receipt of the new scales lost money. Panicked by the speed and breadth of opposition, the government hastily introduced the 'Standstill' Act in February 1935, which allowed everyone on the new regulations to receive whichever scale, UAB or PAC, was the greater for them.

This débâcle did not prevent the 1935 re-election of the National government, which announced in July 1936 the decision to implement the new UAB scales in November. Even these were postponed and it was not until May 1938 that UAB standard, nation-wide scales were brought in.

Half-measures: Public Works, Labour Camps and Special Areas

Public works had long been in existence as part of the machinery of the Poor Law. Before the First World War A.L. Bowley and later the Webbs saw their potential for regulating the level of employment over the course of the business cycle. The Labour Party adopted this notion of counter-cyclical government contracts and public works during the war.[26] By the end of the postwar boom the Coalition government was using public works to dissipate unrest and government unpopularity. In December 1920 the St David's Committee (or Unemployment Grants Committee – UGC) was established to promote local authority public works with local councils applying to the UGC for wage subsidies (up to 30 per cent initially) on their public works proposals. The UGC scrutinised applications according to certain criteria: grants were only given to areas of acute unemployment, schemes were to prefer ex-servicemen and work was to be of public utility (for example, sewerage, roads, electricity and water supply). As unemployment continued into the 1920s, the UGC, initially a winter stop-gap, widened its scope. In September 1921, the government matched local authority borrowing pound for pound in order to speed up the expansion of public works, and in March 1924 the criterion of acute distress was relaxed. By the summer of 1923, 10,000 projects had been approved entailing £40 million of government subsidy. In part because of the local authority control there were a number of problems with the scheme. Local public works projects became exhausted because councils found that there was a limit to their infrastructural needs, so applications fell off. Relief works tended to plunge councils in industrial areas into ever greater indebtedness. Central government could not conjure with the level of employment on the counter-cyclical principle (unemployment itself proved more intractable than before). In part the problem lay with central government because general retrenchment in public expenditure from early 1922 onwards counteracted the effect of public works on employment.

From December 1925 to November 1928 the Conservative government sharply restricted UGC grants as part of a general retrenchment policy. Grants were approved only if a local authority had suffered 15 per cent unemployment in the previous year. As a result the cost of grants fell from £17.6 million (July 1925–June 1926) to £0.8 million (July 1926–June 1927). In 1927 Sir Arthur Steel-Maitland, the Minister of Labour, even declared public works 'a wasteful use of capital and a mistake'. The public outcry at the persistent unemployment in the pits and shipyards caused a reversal in this policy. Conditions in the mines in particular had worsened after the ending of the government subsidy and the defeat of the strike. In November 1928 the government sought to coordinate UGC grants with industrial transference to encourage migration from the depressed areas. Now UGC applications were granted to prosperous areas on condition that they employed a proportion of migrants. The expansion of public works continued under Labour, with 1,850 schemes approved between July 1929 and June 1930 at a cost of £37 million. In August 1929, the UGC, which had been under Treasury control, was now given statutory status through the Development (Loans Guarantees and Grants) Act. In June 1930, all authorities were allowed maximum grants. The government also attempted to ease the implementation of public works through the Public Works Facilities Act in August 1930 by speeding up compulsory land purchases. Despite the depression initially encouraging the use of public works, it was to cause their eventual demise. The 'substantially accelerated' public works expenditure was insufficient and too slow to turn back the advancing tide of unemployment. At its height in March 1931, the UGC directly created only 59,177 jobs whilst unemployment stood at 2,655,000. The UGC was ultimately a victim of the August 1931 crisis.[27] Officially, the UGC sanctioned its last schemes in January 1932, and after then only already approved schemes were honoured. In its life-span the UGC granted £191 million for public works, of which only £67 million was expended and for every million spent 2,500 were directly employed so that the average employed on the scheme over its ten-year existence was roughly 12,500.[28]

Believing in the philosophy of the free market, interwar governments rejected intervention to tackle regions blighted by persistent unemployment. Their answer to the particularly high unemployment in South Wales, Scotland and the North-East was mainly in the form of assisted migration, land settlement and voluntary social services. That unemployment was acute in certain trades (mining, shipbuilding, iron and steel) and regions was obvious from the early 1920s, but governments maintained the fiction that a restoration of trade would cure this malady. In January 1928, the

Baldwin government set up the Industrial Transference Board to encourage migration from the depressed to the prosperous areas. Initially concentrating on mining areas, the government's logic was that migration would create labour reserves for those parts of the country where demand could grow quickest. In government thinking, migration was a better option than either public works or doles in depressed areas. In autumn 1928, the UGC channelled transfer grants to local authorities in prosperous areas if they employed a proportion of depressed areas men on public works schemes. Both the Baldwin and Labour governments widened the scope of the scheme. As recession bit in 1930, migration withered and local authorities and trade unions began to complain about migrant labour as unemployment grew throughout the country. Migration had become even less attractive. Not only were there the unfamiliar surroundings far from home, family and community, there was also no guarantees of even a short-term job. Many returned home.

The government also attempted to regenerate the labour market through labour camps. Originating in 1929, there were various categories, such as the Juvenile Instructional Centres and the Transfer Instructional Centres and in all 187,214 were admitted to the camps. Their official purpose was to 'recondition human material', to maintain the working potential of the long-term unemployed. Governments worried about the unemployed's physical or moral degeneration which might render them unfit for work or war.[29]

With the recovery of 1933–34, the question of the distressed areas resurfaced as sharp regional disparities in the scale and length of unemployment developed. In November 1934, unemployment stood at 16.9 per cent for Great Britain as a whole, but 35.3 per cent for the Special Areas. Long-term unemployment became distressingly widespread in these areas. Whilst the long-term unemployment rate was 29.7 per cent in Great Britain as a whole, it was 51.4 per cent in the Special Areas.[30] Public sympathy for the unemployed in the depressed areas grew once again. In March 1934, the government commissioned a report which resulted in the Depressed Areas Bill in November. Two commissioners assumed responsibility for promoting schemes of land settlement, allotments, occupational centres, public works and infrastructural improvements. As the initial budget for this temporary scheme was only £2 million, these measures provoked wide criticism. Aneurin Bevan called the measure 'an idle and empty farce', and it was 'a mere flea-bite and a sop' for the Lord Mayor of Newcastle.[31] Chamberlain, at the time Chancellor of the Exchequer, stated in private that the legislation was not 'a question of spending a great deal of money, but showing the matter had not been pigeon-holed'.[32] The *Manchester Guardian's* political editor discovered several Tory MPs who believed it 'a good inexpensive way of evading the question'.[33] These criticisms prefigured the frustrations of Malcolm Stewart, the Commissioner for the English and Welsh Special Areas, who resigned in 1936. In his final report, he pointed out that the Act had not and could not make any impact on the numbers unemployed and questioned the continued usefulness of the Commissioners unless they were 'endowed with authority to take independent action'.[34]

Not immune to such criticisms, the National government made considerable pledges in relation to unemployment and the Special Areas in the general election of 1935. This public concern did not abate in 1936 when the National Hunger March, the Jarrow Crusade and the King's visit to South Wales concentrated minds on the issue. In response, the government created development boards which set up trading estates at Team Valley (Gateshead), Treforest (South Wales) and Hillington (near Glasgow). The Special Areas legislation was amended in 1937 to allow factories tax, rent and rate rebates for up to five years. As elsewhere, unemployment in the distressed areas fell between 1933 and 1934. All in all, the effects of Special Areas policy on unemployment were proportionately small. By May 1939, 273 factories had opened on the trading estates employing 8,500, a figure that seems small in comparison to unemployment of 226,193 in the Special Areas two months later.[35] The numbers of jobs created neither reversed regional disparities nor matched those created by rearmament. As regards industrial transfer, those assisted by government schemes, averaging 32,000 a year in 1929–38, were far outnumbered by those who migrated voluntarily. Cynicism prevailed: ministers and government officials generally did not believe that anything could be done for these areas. Projects were typically underfunded, but paraded as evidence of action.

In addition to the relief of unemployment, governments explored various avenues to tackle unemployment: public works, regional policy, migration and labour camps. These methods, at least on the scale attempted, proved inadequate in confronting the persistent unemployment especially of the depressed areas.

Employers' Organisations, Bosses and Unemployment

The First World War brought the closest co-operation between the state, employers and trade unions that had ever been experienced up to that point. Across Europe there were attempts to head off working-class militancy with corporatist arrangements, whereby government, employers and unions came together in new institutions and resolved their differences. Britain was no exception, either in terms of corporatist experiment or in working-class militancy. The government required trade union collaboration in order to secure industrial peace, boost production and change working practices. Agreements were made that new practices would exist only for the duration of the war and employers would not permanently dilute skilled labour or extend the working day. Whitley Councils were established to bring together unions and employers to forge a new consensus on an industry-by-industry basis.[36] The role of the state had grown to unprecedented heights, taking a major role in reorganising production for industrialised warfare. Employers, worried by threats to their prerogative posed by both the state and the unions, created new national representative organisations: the Federation of British Industries formed in 1916 and both the National Confederation of Employers' Organisations and the Economic League three years later. These organisations gained considerable influence in the Houses of Commons, the FBI admitting that 70–80 MPs were connected with firms that were FBI members. Nevertheless, they did not represent the whole of British capital, but were particularly strong in engineering, shipbuilding, cotton and coal. The NCEO also had important links through the Parliamentary Industrial Group of MPs and was able to influence the political process by lobbying and delegations or reports to ministries. At the local level, these organisations were mirrored by the activities of the Chambers of Commerce and Ratepayers' Associations.[37]

The NCEO essentially wanted quiescent unions and government to leave the running of industry entirely to them. Corporatism was short-lived and was quickly dropped when the employers felt confident enough during their 1921–2 offensive. Initially, employers' representatives had consented to a 48-hour working week, counter-cyclical public works, a housing programme and state support for new industries. The Provisional Joint Council of employers and trade unions proposed on 4 April 1919 'some steps which might be taken to alleviate unemployment'. These included a ban on overtime, government stabilisation of employment and raising of the school leaving age. The Council were 'unanimous in their view that the normal provision of maintenance during unemployment should be more adequate and of wider application than is provided by the National Insurance (Unemployment) Acts'.[38] These conciliatory attitudes were soon to change. In July 1921, the NCEO withdrew from the NJC and at the Gairloch conference in October, in conjunction with the government it sharply re-drew the agenda.[39]

The Economic League provided employers with blacklists of known trade union activists and communists, and preached the virtues of the capitalist system in public and workplace meetings. The Economic League enjoyed support from major industrialists and an overlapping membership with the NCEO and FBI. It also colluded with the police by supplying (and being supplied with) information. The *Daily Worker* published evidence of the Manchester Police passing information to the local Economic League and it is likely that such activities were widespread.[40]

Where unemployment was concerned, the agenda of employers' organisations remained fairly consistent after the Gairloch conference. Of course, these attitudes had already been hinted at as employers questioned the Out of Work Donation on the grounds that it led to widespread fraud (claims that the government felt compelled to investigate and discovered were largely unfounded).[41] Despite initially welcoming the 1920 Act as a means of securing trade union co-operation, employers viewed the insurance system to be too great a burden on industry. They railed against malingerers who were encouraged by over-generous and uncovenanted benefit. They also complained loudly about those who were better off on the dole. By 1923, once the threat of widespread disorder had been dispelled, the NCEO urged the government to end uncovenanted benefit or at least for it to be separated from the insurance system. They believed that an unemployment insurance system should be based on low cost and low benefit and that those who did not qualify through contributions and rules set down should be dealt with by a reformed Poor Law. The NCEO fostered the interwar conservative hegemony on the unemployment question. The NCEO's influence on this matter, which was its major preoccupation, was exercised through various channels. Its regular delegations and consultations constituted a special relationship with the Ministry of Labour. As an example of this relationship, in November 1922 the Ministry requested a special report on employers' attitudes to unemployment insurance.[42] The NCEO also had close links with the Conservative Party and from February 1919 they organised up to 40 MPs in their Parliamentary Industrial Group. In July 1929, this became subsumed within the Trade and Industry Committee of the Conservative Party, but three months later Henry Mond formed the Parliamentary Committee of the NCEO. On a more diffuse level, NCEO members, MPs, ministers and government committee members mingled in the rich associational culture of big business and parliamentary leaders and of course sometimes the distinctions between these groups blurred at the edges.

The government committees also demonstrate the attitudes of employers to unemployment. Government enquiries into unemployment, even those commissioned by Labour, had a strong business representation, both through committee membership and through submission and consideration of evidence. In the Blanesburgh Committee, J. Forbes Watson and John A. Gregorson (NCEO) pressed for cuts in benefits to 1920 levels and the abolition of extended benefits. As they saw it:

The evils of the present system have become more and more apparent as time has gone on. Unemployment Benefit and Poor Law relief have to a large measure become merged, and it has been possible for a workman through possessing an insurance card – though he has no contribution to his credit – to draw as much as 65s. a week from these two sources. The problem, as the Confederation sees it, is reflected in the enormous cost, but also in the resultant sapping of thrift and independence.[43]

Their reasoning was that extended benefits constituted an 'insupportable burden upon industry'. They believed that unemployment benefit should not provide maintenance, but supplement working-class thrift and self-help; benefits should be lower than the lowest wages and bear no relation to subsistence. As it stood, unemployment insurance threatened 'permanent injury to the spirit of independence and thrift of the people' and corroded 'the claimant's incentive to seek work'. They did agree with the principle of unemployment insurance, but only if contributions and benefits were kept to the 'lowest possible limits'. In the Morris Committee (set up to look into the not genuinely seeking work clause), Gregorson sought to keep rigorous controls on the bogey of abuse through retaining the need for unemployed workers to satisfy committees that they had the right attitude and sought work even where it was non-existent.

During the growing crisis of 1931, the NCEO told the government that spending on social services, in particular unemployment, was 'far greater than the country could afford' and was in part 'responsible for industrial depression'.[44] Their document of February 1931, *The Industrial Situation*, called for the cutting of unemployment benefits by a third and for stricter conditions for eligibility to be enforced. The 'colossal expenditure' on social provision in their distorted logic was not a consequence of unemployment but its cause, as it was 'in no small measure accountable for our industrial depression and ... has in large measure deprived them of employment'.[45] The 'blue book', as it became known, sold 50,000 copies and contributed to the mounting crisis of the Labour government. Business opinion had turned sharply against the levels of unemployment benefits being paid: *The Economist,* for example, talked of the 'impossibility of continuing unemployment insurance as an undisguised dole, on the basis of a supposedly inexhaustible cash-box, wide open to every claimant'.[46] The NCEO in a published memorandum to the Royal Commission on Unemployment Insurance criticised unemployment insurance for having

fostered a belief in this country that this country has unlimited resources which can enable it to act as a universal provider against

all ills by paying weekly benefits which are demandable as a legal
right, without conditions attached and without reference to their
contribution or needs.

Moreover, such a system was 'insidiously sapping the whole social,
financial and industrial stability of the country'.[47] Numerically and
intellectually dominated by financiers and industrialists, the May
Committee's report into government finances provided the most
powerful vehicle for business views during the crisis. Its howls of
anguish created the ideological climate for cuts in unemployment
benefit. The government proposed severe retrenchment in late
August and because this was not enough for business leaders, the
Labour government fell.

By the time of the wartime Beveridge Report, their attitudes had
changed little. They questioned whether the issues of social insurance
should be discussed during the war, blaming slow rearmament on
levels of unemployment benefit 'having concentrated on social
security to the detriment of national security'. In their opinion, the
government should not commit itself on this issue and spending
'must be directly related to ... industrial performance' and should not
'weaken the incentive of the population to play their full part in
maintaining the productivity and exporting ability of the country at
its highest level'.[48] By then, the NCEO was clinging to the old
hegemonic formula that Beveridge and others were superseding.
During the interwar period, the NCEO had been crucial to the
political consensus by articulating the interests of big business and by
providing an organisational connection between it and government.
Its influence was both public, through its literature and press
reception, and discrete, through the influence of the *bona fide* insider
to the corridors of power.

The relationship between big business and government was far
stronger than an ideological one. Notwithstanding the suspicion of,
even hostility to, state involvement in industrial affairs, unemployment did act as a catalyst for a number of initiatives that connected
business and government. Both the Exports Credits Scheme and the
Trade Facilities Act allowed industrial subsidies in return for
increased (or accelerated) employment. During its operation between
November 1921 and March 1927, £75 million was expended in
subsidies under the Trade Facilities Act. In another handout to
business, the De-Rating Act of 1928 relieved industry of 75 per cent
of its rates bill. A small number of specific industries, notably sugar
beet, also received direct state subsidies.

Perhaps most significantly, industry, finance and government
converged to varying degrees over the question of industrial rationalisation. During the 1920s the idea of rationalisation became

fashionable in employers', government and official trade union circles. Rationalisation was as elusive as much as it was a misnomer. Sometimes rationalisation signified the use of Taylorist and other methods of 'scientific management'. These systems conceived of human labour as an adjunct of the machine. Frederick Taylor declared that he wanted to turn the factory worker into a 'trained gorilla' to perform tasks mechanically and repetitively for the most intensive use of his labour power. Others, such as Charles Bédaux, fashioned complex systems for measuring and integrating human and machine movements. Henry Ford's adoption of the assembly line was a great propaganda coup for scientific management and allowed the more systematic dissemination of other techniques. These associations gave rationalisation a scientific, technological, modern mystique. However, more often than not rationalisation signified either amalgamation and monopolistic practices (output quotas and price-fixing) or the scrapping or 'sterilisation' of excess or obsolete industrial capacity.

A considerable chasm existed between the much vaunted potential of rationalisation and its meagre achievements. Enthusiasts prescribed rationalisation as an answer to British relative decline, especially in the export industries. Attitudes had changed by the late 1920s. It became clear that trade revival would not restore prosperity to the staple industries. The Baldwin government (in its last months) and the MacDonald government became vocal advocates of voluntary industrial reorganisation. Fearing state intervention, the Bank of England made tentative steps in the direction of industrial intervention to pre-empt government 'interference'. The Bank had on two previous occasions taken over and reorganised industrial concerns: Vickers-Armstrong in 1925 and the Lancashire Cotton Corporation in 1929. In both these cases bad debts threatened the banking system and this prompted the Bank's actions rather than any enthusiasm for rationalisation. In November 1929, however, on the Bank's initiative, the Securities Management Trust was established to provide funds and City expertise for rationalisation. In March of the following year, the Bank headed a financial consortium, the Bankers' Industrial Development Company (BIDC), to finance mergers and new fixed capital.

Because the government rejected compulsion or state planning to reorganise and upgrade industry, intervention was a series of inconsistent *ad hoc* measures rather than what could be termed an industrial policy. Rationalisation's progress was a piecemeal, ambiguous combination of state encouragement, City lending and neglect.

Rationalisation policy, where it existed, varied from one industry to another as three depressed industries, shipbuilding, coal and iron and steel, demonstrated. The development of rationalisation was perhaps most marked in the shipbuilding industry which witnessed the closure of 36 shipbuilders between 1920 and 1930. Funded by a levy on members and BIDC money, in March 1929 the Shipbuilders Employers' Federation adopted a 'self-pruning' scheme, the National Shipbuilders Security Ltd (NSS). This scrapped 38 yards and over a quarter of all berths, at a net cost of £1.33 million.[49] This gave employers respite from the damaging uncertainty of cut-throat price competition. That was cold comfort to shipbuilding workers in towns where the yards had been closed. One such yard, Palmer's in Jarrow, was closed and was not to be re-opened for 40 years under the NSS terms. Ellen Wilkinson, Jarrow's MP, could not see the rationality in 'murdering' the town. In the coal industry, the MacDonald government tried to resolve the problems of fragmented ownership, shrinking markets and declining profits through the Coal Act of 1930. Part I of the Act created compulsory regional marketing boards for the mining companies to set production quotas and prices, but inter-regional competition undermined cartelisation's supposed benefits (stable prices and elimination of cheaper but less efficient competitors). Part II of the Act, which set up a Reorganisation Commission to encourage and organise voluntary amalgamation, was equally unsuccessful for similar reasons. In the iron and steel industry the government introduced a tariff in 1932 on the condition that the industry would rationalise, but this failed to materialise on any significant scale and monopolistic practices were further extended by joining the European Steel Cartel in 1935.

At its core rationalisation raised the slogans, ideology and programme to overcome intensified capitalist competition and economic crisis. Paradoxically, the gains that individual firms made through rationalisation were often neutralised by their general adoption. For example, increases in productivity could lead to competitive advantages (and less labour) in the short term, but that advantage would be lost over the longer term if adopted elsewhere. Rationalisation drew together a number of contradictory, often self-defeating, phenomena and in general proved inadequate in reversing the problems of the staple industries. Whereas competition and bankruptcy could lead to mergers and acquisitions, rationalisation schemes often restricted competition. Perversely, the greatest ratio-nalisation (the adoption of scientific management and industrial concentration) took place in the new industries.

Employers differed in their approach to unemployment and industrial relations in part reflecting the divisions between heavy and light industry, export and domestic orientations, size of firm and market position. In the aftermath of the General Strike, between 1927 and 1933, Sir Alfred Mond, of ICI, spearheaded an effort to secure trade union co-operation for a programme of modernising

British industry and industrial relations. Mond represented a section of export-oriented big business with large market shares. The Mond–Turner talks (Ben Turner was the President of the TUC) had the advantage for employers of gaining trade union sanction for industrial reorganisation. It also furnished industry with contacts and a *modus vivendi* in the event of a Labour government. As regards unemployment, participants agreed that rationalisation and the regularisation of work by employers was the key to the fight against joblessness. Even the modest accords, which for example opposed the practice of blacklisting, were too much for the Engineering Employers' Federation, which remained hostile, and the NCEO, which was distinctly unenthusiastic about Mond's conciliatory approach.[50] Despite these differences amongst sections of industry, what engineering and coal employers sought to achieve by lock-out and victimisation, Mond sought through finesse. In essence, he wanted support from a rightward-moving TUC leadership for a programme of rationalisation; in other words, trade union sanctioning of job losses and the replacement of labour with machines.[51]

One strand of employer opinion was open to a more interventionist state and for a break with the apparent consensus of the 1930s. The most significant of these was the Political and Economic Planning group. Formed in 1931, it produced a journal of that name and included Israel Sieff, the Managing Director of Marks and Spencer, and Sir Basil Blackett, a director of the Bank of England. At the same time a number of Conservative 'Young Turks', including Harold Macmillan and Robert Boothby, formed the Next Five Years group espousing a similar approach, in conjunction with Keynesianism.[52] In addition, notable individuals, such as Sir John Jarvis, an industrialist and Conservative MP, became publicly involved in charitable efforts to alleviate hardship in depressed areas, establishing the Surrey Fund for the Relief of Jarrow.[53] In the 1930s, the government encouraged private charitable initiatives particularly in the shape of the National Council of Social Services; between 1932 and 1939, the government, through the Ministry of Labour and the Special Areas legislation, provided £1.5 million for the NCSS; before that, the Lord Mayor's Fund for the Relief of Women and Children in the Mining Areas (1928–30) had raised £1.7 million with a spell of the government granting a pound-for-pound subsidy.[54] The interwar period was the era of 'new philanthropy' in which the voluntary sector channelled largely public funds into innovative areas of social service.[55] The prosperous were to come to the aid of depression-hit areas and the more that these activities were reported in the newspapers the more it seemed that government alone was not responsible for the relief of the unemployed.[56] There were several

charitable initiatives along the lines of the Surrey Fund: the city of
Bath adopted the Cornish town of Redruth, BBC staff adopted an
unemployed club in Gateshead, and Ministry of Health staff adopted
a club in Crook, Co. Durham.[57] Although mainly a middle-class
affair, some employers were involved in the National Council of
Social Services which provided clubs for the unemployed. However,
despite the more 'progressive' stance of some, the NCEO expressed
the general attitudes of the employing class in Britain for most of the
interwar period.

Conclusion

Revisionist historians have commented that British governments were
more successful than other interwar governments in constructing a
broad, stable, political centre-ground.[58] Contemporaries also
attributed this to the alien character of extremism to the British
mentality and the resilience of the traditions of British constitutionalism and democracy. When viewed through the lense of
unemployment this case is highly questionable.

At times this stability was seriously threatened, especially in the
immediate postwar years when both the Coalition government and
employers were desperate to diffuse working-class discontent and
were acutely anxious that unemployment might aggravate the
situation. For these reasons, concessions followed in rapid
succession. As circumstances unfolded, defeated strikes and unemployment disappointed the hopes of working-class militants. The
clamour for retrenchment resulted from these changed circumstances. Governments acted more cautiously as they had to consider
the possibility of reigniting discontent if retrenchment went too far.

This centre-ground was not as broad in its origins as it might at
first appear. The range of palliatives notwithstanding, governments
stuck firmly to a conservative agenda, which they largely shared with
the press, business and, so it would seem, the electorate. This agenda
sought to reduce the costs of unemployment relief, it opposed
significant government intervention, let alone planning, to fight
unemployment, and it held to economic orthodoxies of balanced
budgets, the market, retrenchment and sound finance. This was
essentially a capitalist hegemony generalised through ruling-class
penetration into the workings of British democracy, its associations,
such as the NCEO, and its ownership of the press. After the
uncertainty of the first postwar years, although Britain was governed
largely by consent, this was manufactured from on high rather than
developing from the bottom up. This consent was crucially
contingent on major concessions of the immediate postwar period

and attempted revisions in that settlement demonstrated the fragility of consensus.

British governments did prove to be more stable than their European counterparts. Although unemployment was severe and persistent it was not as acute as in Germany and recovery in the 1930s, when it did arrive, was much stronger than in France. From 1933 the British economy underwent a recovery based on construction, new industries and rearmament. These favourable economic circumstances were fundamental to the degree of stability and consensus that British governments achieved. The fortunes of the British economy turned favourably in 1931 when it left the Gold Standard, but ironically, the government, City and Bank of England fought desperately to prevent this happening. The conditions of relative immunity to European instability thus owed more to luck than to judgement.

3 The Experience of Unemployment

I remember vividly the half-starved men hanging around on the street corners, passing a Woodbine round for each of them to enjoy a drag, until a policeman arrived on the scene and dispersed them. They weren't allowed to gather on street corners for an innocent chat. Maybe they were plotting revolution! I remember them playing pitch and toss – that is if they had a few ha'pennies in their ragged pockets.

Frank Unwin, *Reflections on the Mersey*, 1982[1]

I remember just after the Armistice, I had been sent out to look after some German POWs. They had a certain look ... It was a strained, greyish, faintly decomposed look. I did not expect to see that kind of face for a long time but I was wrong. I had seen a lot of those faces on this journey. They belonged to unemployed men.

J.B. Priestley, *English Journey*, 1934[2]

Various claims have been made about the unemployed in the two decades between the wars. The monetarist historians Benjamin and Kochin described them as a 'volunteer army' that chose unemployment. Some have stated that they were essentially immune to 'political extremism'. Others are sceptical about the usefulness of the term 'unemployment' because it has become a portmanteau for a variety of different situations and because of the persistence of casual, part-time and seasonal work.[3] Given the political significance of the 1930s as a defining moment of British political history, the unemployed experience is of critical importance. However, the representation and reality of unemployment are not easily distinguished: representation of the unemployed was drawn from and in turn affected their treatment. Although it would be foolish to talk of a static or single message, media and ideological representations of the unemployed did return time and again to certain key themes such as abuse, disorder and the charitable efforts of the rich.

The Representation of Unemployment

The ideological and media representation of unemployment, more so than its reality, shaped social attitudes towards those without work, especially amongst the middle class. As today, British national newspapers were owned by a handful of enormously wealthy individuals; in 1930, nine national newspapers were Tory whilst Labour and the Liberals controlled only one each. During this period, newspaper circulation swelled on a diet of advertising, cheaper prices, free gifts, competitions and sport, rather than their political affiliation alone.[4] The mainstream press usually discussed unemployment within the confines the consensus of the interwar high politics. According to this, unemployment was an evil about which little could be done. Newspapers habitually viewed unemployed demonstrations and organisations as the work of the 'reds', marchers as 'Moscow dupes' and their actions as a threat to property and public order.[5] The *Daily Mail* published the political and criminal records of the 1922 national hunger marchers in an attempt to discredit them.[6] *The Times* correspondent vitriolically denounced the 3,000-strong American 'hunger' march to Washington (the journalist added inverted commas to show irony), 'The majority were negroes and some were women, and the remainder were racially indistinguishable, for the most part as of Central or Eastern European origin.'[7] In other words, they did not look sufficiently hungry, male, white and American. Government and press co-operated on a number of occasions to reinforce the message. In 1932, Sir John Gilmour, the Home Secretary, fed red scare-stories to obliging editors, who printed instructions to shop owners on the hunger march route to board up their premises. This tactic was repeated. The Home Secretary, Sir John Simon, wrote a Cabinet memorandum with regard to the 1936 hunger march: 'the best course would be to arrange, probably through the National Publicity Bureau, for selected journalists to be interviewed and given material for exposing the origin, motive and uselessness of the march'.[8] The *Manchester Guardian* and *The Times* were silent during last week of the 1934 Hunger March in accordance with government wishes.

Other newspaper themes stigmatised those without work. Editors would run stories about the abuse of unemployment benefit, of youth crime and unemployment and of the 'insupportable burden' of unemployment insurance on national finances. Although abuse articles were common throughout the two decades, they peaked at times of 'economy' campaigns. For instance, the papers were running stories of a dole claimant with capital investments of £3,000 on the same day that Ramsay MacDonald proposed the 10 per cent cut in the dole.[9] Only the month before, the *Daily Mail* ran a story 'A Cab Driver's

Views on Dole Thieves', in which a London cabby fed his journalist fare tales of dole abuse implausibly beginning, 'Down our way there's a bloke ...' and 'Next door to where me and the missus live in Camberwell, there's a girl of 22 ... .'[10] A few months later, an article in *The Times*, reporting on the hated means test cuts, talked of 'recognised types' who perpetrated 'dole abuses', claiming 'fraudulent benefit over considerable periods' from 'false addresses'. It cited the case of a man who paid 7 shillings rent, received 34 shillings trade union insurance, 15s 3d in transitional benefit and owned £1,200 in securities. This juxtaposition of government savings on unemployment, repetitious and sensationalist phraseology and lurid stories of fraud rationalised MacDonald's cuts which the Tory newspapers had so eagerly pressed for. In 1938, *The Times* ran a campaign of virulent anti-'shirker' articles describing young unemployed men as 'parasites', 'malingerers', 'shiftless' and 'work-shy'. These were 'lazy young men who do not show any disposition to bestir themselves' and were slack in 'moral fibre and will as well as muscle'. The editor even asked, 'Why, for example, should it be necessary to recoil from the system of Labour Service in Germany merely because in that country it is immediately precedent in time and openly preparatory in character to compulsory service in the army?'[11]

These stories presented the exaggerated and atypical as the norm, and consequently they planted in the popular imagination the idea that the unemployed were undeserving. All the talk of 'shirkers' and abuse had its effect on popular attitudes making the unemployed ashamed of their plight. In *Time to Spare*, a mother on the dole talked of the shame of bringing children into the world to live in such conditions. Many feared the stigma of the Poor Law and in particular the prospect of a 'pauper's funeral' or the workhouse.[12] The unemployed Derbyshire miner in Walter Brierley's novel, *Means Test Man*,

> held back from free intercourse with his fellows feeling himself not whole. He had heard it said of others, 'He's been out of work that long he doesn't want work. While they'll keep finding him some dole he'll not bother.'[13]

In a series of letters to the *Sunderland Echo* in autumn 1931, 'a Miner's Wife' berated the unemployed for idleness and wasting money on pictures and gambling.[14]

Newspapers balanced these negative images of the unemployed with stories from the perspective of the sympathetic spectator of unemployment. A number of themes dealt with unemployment in positive, optimistic terms. The charitable efforts of middle-class volunteers in the National Council of Social Services were carefully charted. Royal consolation for the unemployed reappeared in local and national press. Both George V and Edward, Prince of Wales featured prominently in articles on unemployment. The royals obliged the press's hunger for connecting the unemployment issue with the monarchy in Christmas messages, state openings of Parliament, the Silver Jubilee of May 1935 and the occasional visit to the depressed areas or an unemployed club. In the King's Silver Jubilee message, George lamented,

> In the midst of this day's rejoicing I grieve to think of the numbers of my people who are still without work ... I hope that during this Jubilee year all who can will do their utmost to find them work and bring them hope.[15]

Several days later the Prince of Wales' speech on unemployment in South Wales was widely reported:

> There is growing feeling that a special effort should be made to end the protracted misery of unemployment, particularly in South Wales. For this reason I sincerely hope that the Jubilee year may be crowned with great national endeavour to remove the burden of wretchedness and demoralisation of unemployment ... I know how deeply the King is concerned.[16]

Stories reporting the conditions in the depressed areas often found a cause for optimism on which to end. These included the charitably funded clubs where the unemployed could mend their boots or read a newspaper, football matches organised for the unemployed of two different towns, university students painting the houses of the unemployed, or unemployed holiday camps.[17] The distance between this superficial optimism and the often bitter reality is demonstrated by a *Daily Express* article entitled '16 girls have found a new heaven'. These young women had been found work in a London woollen factory through Sir John Jarvis's Surrey Fund for the Relief of Jarrow. However, the paper failed to report that eight were sent home, two because of ill health (one with rheumatism, anaemia and heart trouble), a married woman who was homesick and the rest because their new employer deemed them to be 'troublemakers'.[18]

These themes sought to raise national spirits during the depression; and all carried the message of social harmony, deferential suffering and a sympathetic nation. These were images of the unemployed that suited the interests of government, big business and millionaire newspaper tycoons alike.

Mass circulation daily newspapers were not the only way in which such ideas could be communicated. The cinemas projected conformist values, ideas and attitudes to expanding audiences. By 1938 weekly audiences had reached 19 million.[19] The newsreels popularised the stereotype of the British pulling together in hard times with their brisk and cheery narration. The issue of unemployment was often treated to the familiar optimistic gloss. Typical of these images were royal visits to depressed areas in the Silver Jubilee year, thousands of South Wales unemployed miners loyally cheering the King in South Wales, who in return uttered a few words of sympathy. In addition to the bias of the newsreel cutting room, Scotland Yard requested the newsreels companies not to film the 1934 and 1936 hunger marches.[20]

Films, on the other hand, largely avoided the unemployment question. This resulted, despite occasional disagreements, from a consensus of film studios and censors. The British Board of Film Censors (a film industry, rather than a government, body) often banned films or scripts dealing with industrial conflict, politics, 'sex' and horror. In 1936 a *Love on the Dole* script was rejected on the grounds that it was 'a very sordid story in very sordid surroundings', it was 'coarse and full of swear words' and there were 'scenes of mob fighting with the police'. All in all, *Love on the Dole*, a realistic and immensely popular portrait of unemployment, conveyed 'too much of the tragic and sordid side of poverty'.[21] The field was clear for unemployment to be addressed through the musical and comic genres by Gracie Fields, Charlie Chaplin, George Formby, Flanagan and Allen and Al Jolson. Al Jolson (*Hallelujah, I'm a Bum*, 1933) and Flanagan and Allen (*Underneath the Arches*, 1939) starred in musicals as unemployed vagrants. Gracie Fields faced unemployment twice, first on screen in *Sing As We Go* in 1935 and then in *Shipyard Sally* in 1939. In the first she implausibly led hundreds of sacked textile workers down the street to rousing strains of the film's title song. In *Shipyard Sally*, she had a similar effect on unemployed shipyard workers on the Clyde. As one historian pointed out, in the fantasy world of Gracie Fields, 'Unemployment ... was not met by industrial unrest ... but by appeals to reason, cheerful discussions with government and industrialists and the re-opening of the shipyards and cotton mills amid displays of patriotic fervour.'[22] Ironically, the world that the film-makers and censors created was attractive to working-class and unemployed cinema-goers who sought escape. As one put it, 'The pictures help you live in a different world for a little while. I almost feel I'm in the picture.'[23]

Much of the information available to journalists came from government sources through regular statistics or official reports. The British ruling class, by virtue of its immense patronage and its ownership of the newspapers and film industry, was able to exert its considerable power on the recurrent themes of national solidarity, selective sympathy, paternalistic charity, dole abuse and excessive unemployment expenditure. Of course, there were tensions between and within government and business, but on balance the coherence and uniformity of their ideas are striking. This ideology also found a popular echo in the prejudices, gossiping intrigue and even denunciation that were the other side of the coin of neighbourly support in working-class communities. The danger for the historian, then, is to linger over the representation of unemployment rather than probe beyond the surface to the realities of unemployed life.

The Reality of Unemployment

As unemployment is related specifically to wage-labour and all that accompanies it – the working day, the separation of work and leisure and labour discipline – it was (and is) integral to working-class life. The importance of work to the fabric of working-class experience cannot be underestimated. Unemployment broke the mainstay of the worker's daily routine, of gender and family relations and of the life-cycle. The jobless youngster was denied initiation into the world of work, a key rite of passage to adulthood. Unemployment was a threat to identity for people who often defined their manhood (less often womanhood) in terms of their trade. Unemployed husbands had been raised to believe that they were a 'Mary-Ann' if they shared household duties. Social investigators noted that these pressures and lack of money meant that family life was more likely to become strained.

Employment also gave a worker's day its meaning: clocking in, timed breaks, imposed work-rates, the factory hooter, gave time a routine, pace and punctuation. As Marie Jahoda, a pioneering social psychologist of the 1930s, put it some years after her original researches into unemployment:

everyone living in industrialised society is used to firm time structures and to complaining about them. But when this structure is removed as it is in its absence it presents a major psychological burden. Days stretch long when there is nothing that has to be done; boredom and waste of time become the rule, particularly when the first shock has been overcome and the search for employment has been given up as futile.[24]

Wage-labour is a particularly disciplined form of work, one that was only achieved after a generation's conflict over work intensity at the beginning of factory production.[25] This work discipline engendered a strong work ethic amongst large sections of the working class. As J.B.

Priestley observed on his travels through England, 'the ironist in charge' created the greatest unemployment where there was 'a tradition of hard work and very little else'.[26] John Evans, an unemployed miner, stated, 'I've been brought up to work. Some people have been born to leisure. Others have leisure forced upon them, but there's a world of difference between them.'[27] The sociologist Henry Mess described the unemployed as having to endure 'anxiety gnawing at their minds' in a state of 'tormented leisure'.[28] Whereas unemployment threw the individual back into the home, the workplace provided friendship networks, a trade or company identity and often membership of trade union. One Lancashire textile worker voiced her acute sense of loss and the isolation of unemployment: 'I loved the mills: I loved the company and the people and everything about them. The mill was home to me.'[29]

The search for work often involved walking long, disheartening distances; for some it even meant migration as tens of thousands left the depressed areas for the prospering South and Midlands. At certain times, unemployment regulations meant that the worker was quizzed about his search for work on pain of disallowance. The unemployed were forced into an often hopeless routine of tramping from one pit, shipyard or factory to another knowing that there were no jobs. E. Wright Bakke, studying the unemployed in Greenwich, found that they were spending on average 23 hours a week looking for work.[30] Contemporary sociologists noticed this gruelling quest resulted in successive stages of fading hope and demoralisation.[31] In some industries especially where casual labour was the norm the search for work took the form of turning up outside work in the hope of being picked out by the foreman. The docker's 'pen' or the shipbuilder's 'market', as they were known, allowed employers to pick and choose on the grounds of family, religion, skill, age or politics.[32] Mass unemployment also blurred the divide between the vagrant and the unemployed worker as many took to the road and slept in the Poor House in the search for work.[33]

Unemployment assumed many guises according to town, industry, age, sex and duration. With the collapse of the postwar boom in 1920, unemployment in the UK remained above the 'intractable million', as it was known, until May 1940.[34] In the peak year of 1932, 3.4 million were unemployed, some 17 per cent of all employees and 22 per cent of insured workers.[35] Although unemployment was a problem throughout the interwar period, it was much worse in the 1930s. Throughout the period the majority of the unemployed were out of work for less than three months, but a minority were less fortunate. Long-term joblessness reached a peak in 1937 when 27.1 per cent of the unemployed had been out of work for a year or more (at that time the average spell of unemployment was 41.6 weeks).[36]

The lack of work most adversely affected Scotland, South Wales, the North-East and Lancashire, in shipbuilding, coal, textile, iron and in some sectors of engineering industries. Long-term joblessness was also more concentrated in these areas. The regional concentration of unemployment led to the notion of the distressed (or depressed or special) areas. High unemployment was not restricted to these areas and many unemployment blackspots were excluded from special area status. Of those administrative units with more than 20 per cent male unemployment in the 1931 census, 9 out of 26 – Cardiff, Middlesbrough, Wigan, Ashton-under-Lyne, Blackburn, Bootle, Liverpool, Oldham and Birkenhead – were not to be designated 'Special Areas'.[37] These figures failed to record the plight of the isolated rural mining communities in Shropshire, Staffordshire or Cornwall which were nominally in prosperous parts. Angus McInnes asked how many towns like Stoke were badly affected by the depression, but have been subsequently ignored because they lay outside the special areas.[38] Eric Hopkins, in his study of thriving Birmingham, noted that the Black Country towns to its north were in much tighter straits.[39] The 1931 census figures show that even in the affluent South there were enclaves of very high unemployment. In London, which had lower than average unemployment, Shoreditch and Poplar had male unemployment of 17.2 per cent and 18.9 per cent respectively. Unemployment also existed in prosperous areas and brought with it its own problems as the long-term unemployed suffered greater isolation and shame than counterparts in areas where unemployment was the norm.[40]

Unemployment disproportionately affected both younger and the older workers. Harry Hardcastle's fictional experience in *Love on the Dole* articulated the real indignity, helplessness and confusion of the young worker facing unemployment. He had been accepted for an engineering apprenticeship at the age of 14, but was sacked once the apprenticeship was over only to be replaced by younger, cheaper new apprentices, a practice that was quite widespread. On the other hand, 47-year-old John Evans was told he was too old to work and many who were 40 or over in certain areas or industries believed they would never work again.[41]

The pressures of unemployment on working-class families forced women into unpleasant and onerous work trying to balance work and household commitments. Many young women were reluctantly driven into domestic service, often having to leave home to do so.[42] For the period between the wars unemployment rates were lower for women than men. Social surveys largely ignored the problem of women's unemployment as titles such as *The Unemployed Man* and *Men without Work* suggest. Even in Hilda Jennings' *Brynmawr* – the exceptional case when social investigation was headed by a woman –

this issue was overlooked. It would be quite wrong to assume that unemployment was less of a problem for women. Women's employment, although often creating a double burden of home and workplace, did break the restricted, often stifling, insularity of family and immediate neighbours. Oral histories show that friendships, self-esteem and a degree of independence lost by the unemployed were as important for women as men. The statistics also under-recorded the scale of women's unemployment as married women in particular dropped out of the statistics due to benefit regulations that treated them as anomalies. As a result of the anomaly regulations of June 1931, the female unemployment rate was 90 per cent that of the male rate in 1930 but only 54 per cent in 1932.[43] The regulations assumed that women would retire from the factory on marriage, but this was often not the case, particularly in certain industries such as textiles. Women were also less likely to be in trades covered by unemployment insurance, for example as domestic workers, and therefore were less likely to figure in unemployment statistics tied to the insurance scheme.[44] The statistics also ignored the 'informal' economic activities that many women engaged in to make ends meet: clothes-mending, taking in lodgers, washing, outwork. Women's occupations and trades (except textiles) did suffer less than the heavy staple industries which were predominantly male. Several expanding and new economic sectors like food-processing and retail provided opportunities for women, but at low rates of pay and invariably under male supervision.

When husbands were out of work the pressures of stretching the family budget fell on the wife. As John Rankin put it,

> That's a problem for my wife, and God knows how she solves it. The brunt of it falls on the wife; a man hands in his money and knows in his heart it is a hopeless proposition to keep a house on it for a week.[45]

Unemployment, in the words of a survey of working-class wives, was 'the worst misfortune' that could befall a woman. It compounded all the other problems. One wife described her state of mind and health:

> But I often get in a low state. I get irritable and the poor bairns suffer. I've had my teeth attended to through the welfare centre, I've been paying two pence a week for over two years for my new teeth. I don't know how long I'll have to pay for. I've never asked the amount, I don't want the shock. Now I feel as though my eyes need attention, but I've got no means. My head aches, and if I start

to read everything goes black. I often find myself in perspiration through weakness. I only put it down to worry.[46]

Only a small proportion of women were entitled to free medical care as it was only in pregnancy and when nursing a newborn that assistance could be claimed. If a woman worked in an insurable trade she could, like her husband, see a 'panel doctor' under the National Insurance Act, but many women were not in these occupations. Margaret Spring Rice found only 13 of 1,250 in her survey were covered. Repeated childbirth and lack of medical facilities (for example, contraceptive advice and abortions), meant that working-class women experienced very poor health. In Rice's 1939 survey 45 per cent were found to have anaemia and 15 per cent were diagnosed with gynaecological ailments; only 31.3 per cent described themselves in consistently good health. The report found evidence that women's health was adversely affected by childbirth and an inadequate diet. It discovered numerous cases of women going without food to feed their unemployed family; the Pilgrim Trust investigators also noted this. The unemployed households' poor diet particularly affected women's health.[47]

Although at any one time the majority were always in a job, most workers at one time or another experienced unemployment. In 1930 whilst unemployment averaged 1.9 million, a total of over 5 million were unemployed in the course of the year and three-fifths of insured workers had experienced unemployment since 1920.[48] Even for those in work, the threat of unemployment hung over many. John Rankin, a shipyard worker on the Clyde, described the weekly cycle of fear:

When Tuesday is passed you know you are safe till next Friday – and if Friday passed you know you're all right till Tuesday, and so it goes on. But sooner or later the foreman will come up to you and tell you to get out.[49]

The two periods of rising unemployment, the early 1920s and the three years after the Wall Street Crash, reduced trade union membership and sapped workers' confidence inside the workplace. Militants feared victimisation; a foreman could point out that those queuing for the dole who would be happy to have your job. Such discrimination was particularly widespread in certain industries that had high unemployment and traditions of militancy, such as mining and engineering, or where the unions had a weak foothold, such as commercial transport. The Pilgrim Trust found claims of victimisation were very common among South Wales miners. Hywel Francis found that of 170 South Wales volunteers for the Spanish Civil War, 26 were victimised trade unionists.[50] Despite the silence of

government documents on the matter, oral history reveals this
widespread experience of militants. For example, Joseph Farrington's
father was sacked after leading a strike. When he asked the Labour
Exchange for the reason given for his dismissal the reply was that that
was 'strictly confidential'. He was blacklisted by the 'masters'
federation' so that when he eventually found work he was laid off at
the end of the week by a foreman who apologetically could offer no
explanation, 'I don't know why, but I've been told to give you your
cards.'[51] A Newcastle Transport and General Workers' Union
Secretary's report described the effect of unemployment in
commercial transport:

> This section is in a very difficult position from the organising point
> of view owing to the innumberable employers engaged in the
> industry, together with the low ebb of Trade Union spirit amongst
> the workers employed. The fear of victimisation by the employees
> precludes many men from joining the union in these times of
> exceptional unemployment. Owing to the latter factor employers
> hold the whip hand for the present, and many men are working
> long hours rather than be unemployed.[52]

Pressures that unemployment exerted on the individual could be
considerable. The unemployed were more likely to commit suicide
than those in work despite revisionist historians' dismissing this as
based on 'circumstantial evidence'.[53] According to the Registrar
General's figures, suicide peaked at the time of greatest unemployment in 1932 when two unemployed men committed suicide every
day.[54] As a consequence, questions were raised in the House of
Commons about the young men committing and attempting suicide.
For men 25 years and under between 1921 and 1932, the numbers of
suicides rose by 60 per cent and the number of attempted suicides
doubled. Accused that the harshness of the means test was
responsible for the increase, the government remained silent.[55] Some
evidence links suicide and unemployment more directly: of the 24
failed suicides in Birkenhead in 1932, 13 gave unemployment as the
chief reason for their attempt on their own life.[56] In a study of five
London boroughs for 1936–38, Sainsbury found that the
unemployed were nearly five times more likely to commit suicide
than those in work and in about a third of unemployed suicides,
unemployment was given as the principal reason.[57] These statistics
can be supplemented by a host of newspaper, cultural and oral
evidence. In an oral history of the North-East, Charles Graham
remembered a character nicknamed 'Dead Bodies' who regularly
earned 7s 6d from the police every time he fished a suicide victim out
of the Tyne.[58] Suicide certainly didn't attract much media coverage,

particularly when we consider that, in 1930 for example, there were around 25 times more suicides in Britain than murders. Newspaper reports on coroners' verdicts sometimes revealed the link between unemployment and suicide as with the case of a 65-year-old man from Blackburn who was found by his wife with his head in the gas oven in January 1938. The victim had been out of work for some time and suffered from high blood pressure, depression and insomnia. The coroner's verdict was that suicide resulted 'while not of sound mind through ill-health'.[59]

Though unemployed life was an arduous daily battle, working-class communities developed ways of coping: the weekly visit to the pawnshop, delaying the rent at the risk of eviction or the moonlight flit, poaching, allotments or coal picked from slag heaps and outcrops in mining areas. The opportunities for such activities varied from place to place. In mining areas or small towns, allotments, pilfering from the fields or poaching were much more significant than in large towns or cities. A 1937–38 survey of working-class budgets found that weekly produce from gardens or allotments averaged 1.25 lb of potatoes and 0.25 lb of cabbage and half an egg in industrial households and averaged 7.5 lb of potatoes, three eggs and a pound of cabbage in agricultural households.[60] In the mining villages of Co. Durham in 1920 there were 20,000 allotments. In general, neighbours and family might help out. In larger urban areas, the street allowed some opportunities for small-scale money-making. Mary Chamberlain, in her oral history of Lambeth, commented, 'There was the casual selling – of beetroots, perhaps or tarry blocks, or firewood that could be scrounged for no capital outlay ... In many cases it was difficult to discern where begging stopped and entertainment began.'[61] Of course, the danger with these informal activities was that you could fall foul of the authorities. The labour exchange might discover or neighbours might inform on undeclared income. Picking coal, poaching or being a bookie's runner might lead to a brush with the police. An NUWM pamphlet recorded the case of Robert Burn, a 50-year-old unemployed miner, who was picking coal from a slag heap, was chased by police and drowned whilst trying to escape.[62]

Housing and Health

The unemployed often suffered the very worst housing conditions. Hilda Jennings described the 'very bad state of repairs' of the older cottages in a South Wales pit village:

> The roofs are leaking badly, the external walls are damp, windows are too small, and in many cases the woodwork so decayed that the

windows would not open. In a few houses the sculleries do not contain windows, and one block of 7 or 8 houses contain only two dilapidated WCs, the drains from which are defective.[63]

As economic conditions worsened, people were forced to sub-let or wait before leaving their parental home. In his diary, Orwell noted a two-up-two-down house in which three families with five adults and six children lived.[64] Overcrowding was at its worst in the depressed regions. The 1931 census for England and Wales revealed shocking overcrowding in Sunderland, Gateshead, South Shields and Newcastle, where 23 per cent of the population lived in conditions of more than two people per room. In stark contrast, six county boroughs had an overcrowding rate of less than 2.5 per cent.[65] In 1936, a report on overcrowding in England and Wales found 3.8 per cent overcrowding, indicating a very considerable improvement, but some areas continued to experience very severe housing problems; 20.6 per cent of households in Sunderland were overcrowded, as were 12 per cent in Durham.[66] One consequence of overcrowding was poorer health as some diseases, such as TB, measles and pneumonia, are closely correlated to housing conditions. Hilda Jennings studied the link between overcrowding and TB in Brynmawr. Between 1919 and 1929, over half the local TB deaths were connected to overcrowded conditions, with recurring fatalities in the very worst houses. New housing estates did not necessarily solve the problems as tenants were to discover on the Mount Pleasant estate in Stockton-on-Tees which had an exceptional death rate because higher rents cut significantly into household expenditure on food.[67]

The relationship between unemployment and health was one of the most important political questions of the 1930s. The government maintained that the trade depression, despite causing hardship, did not adversely affect the nation's health. Sir George Newman, the Chief Medical Officer for Health, wrote, 'There has been no general excess of sickness, ill-health or physical incapacity attributable to unemployment.'[68] The government case rested on the general long-term improvement in mortality rates. These fell from 22.5 per 1,000 for 1861–70 to 12.1 per 1,000 for 1921–30.[69] During the 1930s, a formidable but disparate group of critics challenged this official complacency, claiming that malnutrition was widespread, particularly in the depressed areas. A vocal minority of health professionals, local medical officers, doctors and medical researchers, took a dissenting line. The debate within the profession was complicated by the advances of nutritional science and in the diagnosis of certain illnesses (such as anaemia, rickets and TB).[70] Beginning with Fenner Brockway's *Hungry England* in 1932, criticism was popularised in literary form by politicians, pressure groups and intellectuals.[71] A number of organisations (the Rowett Insititute, Save the Children Fund, the Child's Minimum Council, Committee against Malnutrition, Political and Economic Planning, the National Unemployed Workers' Movement) campaigned specifically over the issue of unemployment and its effects on health. The debate ranged over various health indicators: infant and maternal mortality, the incidence of rickets and TB, heights and weights of adults and children.

Even Newman's most basic assertation that unemployment had no adverse affect on general mortality was challenged. Dr G. M'Gonigle, the Medical Officer of Health for Stockton-on-Tees, studied the relationship between unemployment and the death rate of 777 families in Stockton for 1931–4. He found that death rates (standardised for age and sex) were 39 per cent higher among the unemployed.[72] Unfortunately, the government never conducted such a direct comparison between the health of unemployed and employed.

As maternal mortality had declined least of the mortality rates and had even demonstrated a slight increase in the five-year average from 1924 to 1933, government critics seized on maternal mortality as demonstrating the relationship between the depression and ill-health.[73] Lady Williams set up an experiment in supplementary feeding of mothers in the Rhondda Urban District. For those given the additional food the maternal death rate more than halved (from 11.29 to 4.77 per 1000 live births), and deaths due to maternal sepsis fell from 7.11 to 0.87 per 1,000 births.[74] After this study, Ministry of Health commissioned two enquiries into maternal mortality.[75] The *Report on Maternal Mortality in England* found no link between regional patterns of maternal mortality and unemployment or overcrowding, but some correlation with rainfall and the economic activity rate of women. These conclusions were obviously of comfort to government circles. The report on Wales, however, revealed 21 per cent higher rates of mothers dying in childbirth in depressed Wales than in the remainder of the principality.[76]

Arthur S. MacNalty, Sir George Newman's successor, compiled both these reports, which revealed the assumptions of the Ministry of Health. They confirmed the established official view that no link between unemployment and a deterioration in health existed. The question of nutrition was side-stepped as 'beyond the scope of this investigation'. This did not however prevent pronouncements on 'unbalanced diets' because of wrong feeding through ignorance rather than an 'insufficient quantity of food'.[77] Again, the Welsh report attempted to shift responsibility for poor health onto its victims.

While the infant mortality rate showed general improvement, there were wide discrepancies between regions and social classes.

According to the 1931 census the average for the ten boroughs with the highest infant mortality rates was 103.9 per 1,000 live births; for the lowest ten boroughs was 37.4 per 1,000 live births. The ten worst boroughs (South Shields, Barnsley, Oldham, Merthyr Tydfil, Wigan, Gateshead, Middlesbrough, Stoke-on-Trent, Warrington, Sunderland) were noted for unemployment and overcrowding; while the most fortunate (Rutland, Isle of Wight, Oxfordshire, Eastbourne, Bath, Southampton, Berkshire, Buckinghamshire, Surrey, East Sussex) suffered from neither. The 1930s saw by far the slowest fall in infant mortality of any decade in the period 1900–50 (4 per cent fall whilst the decennial average fall was 30 per cent).[78] Class background determined the chances of survival of infants. In 1930–32, infants of unskilled workers were nearly five more likely to die from a range of diseases (measles, whooping cough, diarrhoea, enteritis, TB and parasitic diseases) than those at the top of society.[79]

The debate broadened from mortality to morbidity. Here the statistics were far from systematic or consistent. Certain diseases, such as TB or rickets, were perceived to be indicators of malnutrition and poor housing. A 1932 Ministry of Health circular declared that 'severe rickets is fast disappearing in this country generally, but in some areas the milder form of the disease is still prevalent among infants and young children'.[80] Sir George Newman boasted that school inspections demonstrated that only 1.2 per cent of children in elementary schools in England and Wales were treated for rickets and a further 2.6 per cent noted for observation. Dr M'Gonigle claimed that rickets was much more widespread because it was difficult to diagnose without X-ray technology. A study of 1,638 children in 33 London County Council schools found only 12.5 per cent of children free from all signs of rickets, in the 'best' schools the figure was 22.3 per cent and in the 'worst' 8.7 per cent. Another study in Co. Durham found similar proportions of rickets as the worst schools of the London study.[81]

Research discovered malnutrition in the children of the unemployed. A Save the Children Fund report identified poor school performance because of hunger in several areas, though these results were not uniform. In Pontypridd, standards were low, 'owing to lack of nourishment', in Co. Durham vitality was lower and lack of boots affected attendance, but in Jarrow 'no definite change' was detected. The report concluded: 'There is a residuum of children whose health is already impaired and whose future as citizens and as parents is being imperilled by the conditions under which they are now being compelled to live.'[82] A Newcastle study of pre-school children found that 5 per cent of children from the professional backgrounds were below the 'normal height range', compared with 47 per cent of children of the 'labouring and artisanal' classes. The percentages below the normal weight range were 13 per cent for the children of professional classes and 48 per cent for the 'labouring and artisanal' classes. As for anaemia, the study found that no children from the professional classes had less than a 70 per cent haemoglobin level whereas 23 per cent of the poorer category had. The report discovered that the average weekly expenditure on food per male unemployed adult was 4s 5.8d whilst the minimum adequate standards of the time required 5s 7.5d (BMA) or 5s 1.5d (Ministry of Health).[83] School Medical Officer of Health reports recorded the heights and weights of school-children according to their parents' social class and employment status. Bernard Harris in a recent study of these reports came to the conclusion that in some areas, though certainly not all, there was a correlation between unemployment and children's heights, but he cautioned that any simplistic link between unemployment and health would flounder on the host of other variables involved.[84]

The government came across its most formidable medical opponent in Sir John Boyd Orr of the Rowett Research Institute. Ritchie Calder (the reporter and academic) described Sir John's influential work, *Food, Income and Health*, as 'political dynamite'. The book came to the devastating conclusion that:

The average diet of the poorest comprising 4.5 million, is by the standard adopted, deficient in every constituent considered. The second group comprising of 9 million is adequate in protein, fat and carbohydrates, but deficient in all the vitamins and minerals.[85]

The government went to great lengths to silence their critics. Boyd Orr and M'Gonigle were threatened with being struck off the Medical Register. Boyd Orr recalled pressure from civil servants and ministers to suppress his report.[86] With hindsight, even former ministers retreated from their former positions. Eustace Percy, one-time Minister of Education, to whom Newman was responsible, later admitted that the Chief Medical Officer 'was beginning to retire a little into the false serenities of old age .... [H]e doubted the existence of any serious malnutrition in south Wales', which led the minister to give 'rather stilted assurances to this effect'.[87]

This debate did exert political pressure on the government to improve scales of relief. The leaders of the Jarrow March repeatedly pointed out that their town had the highest infant mortality rate in the country. The government's and medical establishment's last line of defence was that wrong feeding was responsible for malnutrition where, and if, it existed. Not poverty but working-class women's ignorance was the reason for ill-health. The unemployed spent too much on bread and other cheap staples which 'filled you up', but did not provide the necessary proteins and vitamins for a healthy diet. Dr M'Gonigle pointed out that those who had for long denied the existence of malnutrition were now blaming it on wrong feeding.[88] As one Sunderland housewife, whose husband was now 'skin and bones' and had been out of work for over 12 years, put it: 'Our medical officer wrote an article the other day and said white bread, marge and tea was no good for anyone. Well, that's our main diet and there's thousands like me.'[89]

The debate largely ignored the psychological effects of unemployment upon health. A study of the insured population showed higher rates of mental illness amongst the male unemployed than those in work. According to Dr James Halliday's study of 1,000 male patients in Glasgow, there were 9 per cent more unemployed than employed with debilitating stress or 'psychoneurosis'.[90]

Historians do not agree about the relationship between unemployment and health. Partly because of the inadequacy of aggregate statistics which do not allow us to isolate the unemployed for statistical analysis, partly because of the range of contradictory variables at work (the improvement in medical science, the falling cost of living, economic recovery from 1933 and the effects of unemployment). These disagreements will continue. We can say with confidence that the official optimism exaggerated the prevalence of health improvements and minimised disparities between classes and regions, which were considerable. Also, whilst there was improvement in the standard of health, this was slow compared to what went before or after. The diets of the unemployed were often below nutritional requirements and therefore probably accounted for the persistence of ill-health and acted as a drag on general improvement.

An Authoritarian Social Policy: The Administration of the Unemployed

Unemployment benefits were conditional on the discouragement of those deemed to be 'undeserving'. Unlike the Poor Law, a modern bureaucratic apparatus of expert civil servants increasing distinguished the deserving from the undeserving. Ranged against the unemployed was a towering authority structure: at the bottom, the labour exchange clerk, the means test official and the policeman who would 'move you on'; at its middle layers, the investigation officer, the Courts of Referees, Public Assistance Committees, Unemployed Assistance Boards, and at the summit the Ministry of Labour, the Umpire and the government.

One consequence of this bureaucratisation was that administrative procedure, the use of statistics and euphemism obscured the human suffering of the workless. The state bureaucracy (and big business) clouded unemployment's reality with rhetoric. According to this language, men were 'displaced'; industries were 'rationalised' or 'self-pruned'; there were 'special' areas; plants were 'sterilised'; there was the need for 'economy' and 'sound finance'. To the unemployed this language was alien and disarming. The impersonal nature of the bureaucracy meant that there was no one to blame, making the unemployed feel the victims of forces beyond their control.

The 'genuinely seeking work' clause, the Anomalies Act of 1931 and, above all, the means test were all designed to reduce the numbers receiving benefit and to cut benefit levels. Consequently, the administration of unemployment was experienced as a punitive, demeaning and intrusive process aiming, as one government adviser said to the Wolverhampton Board of Guardians, 'to weed the scallywags from the genuine fellows'.[91] This process reinforced the authority of the employer and foreman who were already in a buyer's market for labour. Anyone who had been sacked was ineligible for unemployment benefit and Courts of Referees would not entertain appeals on the grounds of unfair dismissal. Though both employers and trade unions had a place on the Courts of Referees, Ministry of Labour appointment procedures ensured that trade union representation was always in a minority.

Even the weekly routine of interaction with officialdom brought anxiety, frustration and bitterness. The unemployed were expected to sign on one, three or even five times a week. Max Cohen, in his memoir, *I Was One of the Unemployed*, remembered being herded into the employment exchange:

> Everybody loathes the Exchange. Crowds struggle to get up the narrow stairs into the building and out again as soon as possible. The stairs are blocked. Men become wedged in inextricable positions. There is no shouting or horse-play. It is merely a mad, passionate determination to avoid waiting in the hated queue a moment longer than is essential.[92]

A Carnegie Trust report found that the labour exchange clerks treated the claimant 'not as a person, but as a number with a card, to be dealt with as quickly as possible'.[93] Many experienced the anxiety of being summonsed to the investigation officer at the labour exchange. A change in circumstances or a petty infringement could threaten eligibility for benefit, and anyone found to be defrauding the system could face imprisonment. An unemployed mass observer Joe

Willcock recorded the reactions of the unemployed in the labour exchange,

> Can anyone wonder at, or see how the claimants can be anything else but nervous ... When these men are spoken to by a supervisor, you can see the claimants go red and flustered, I saw two out of three with shaking hands these men have been sent for by letter or told by the clerks at the various signing boxes. You can hear the Super say 'Can't you read what it says there', pointing to a footnote on the form presented by the claimants. Another is sent to the Super because he has lost his card, 'Have you anything to prove your identity?' This man in a flustered manner, looked all over his pockets and said, 'Eh I've got a gas bill, but it's not for my present address'. Super. 'Let's see it alright go to your box'.[94]

No wonder claimants feared the letter from the labour exchange or the summons from the investigation officer. In 1932 alone, 669,261 were brought before the Courts of Referees of whom 460,593 were disallowed.[95] The benefit regulations, with their legalistic wording and repeated revisions, were unfathomable to individual claimants, so reinforcing their sense of powerlessness. Claimants often had to rely on word of mouth and rumours that would circulate at the regular haunts of the unemployed: the public library, the street corner or the unemployed club. The NUWM produced several pamphlets explaining the workings of new regulations, claimants' rights or what to say at the Courts of Referees. Many activists became expert at representing their unemployed comrades.

Of all the indignities which the unemployed shouldered in the interwar period, the means test 'inquisition' was the most despised. Although official accounts denied that the means test split families and Pilgrim Trust quoted one individual who came to see his means test investigator as a friend, a wealth of evidence uncovered by oral history clearly exposes extreme bitterness towards the 'tin gods' or the 'English Gestapo'.[96] The regular official home visits were seen as a particular slight on the independence and respectability of those out of work. These officials would 'get to know everything about us', any household savings or income from relatives and they would decide if there were a piano, spare bed or sideboard that could be sold.[97] A repentant means test investigator remembered a typical reaction to an inspection:

> She is trying hard not to show it, but I know nevertheless, that she mistrusts us – Means Test – men walking into your house demanding to know all your business ... This is the greatest blow to pride that you've had in years. You've always kept yourself to

yourself, held your head up even in this house of mixed society, and now you're asking yourself, 'Has it really come to this?' And you're worried, too, about that polished oak sideboard; you're wondering whether you'll be ordered to sell it. No, you don't like us mother; but no one can blame you for that.[98]

The entire plot of Walter Brierley's novel *Means Test Man* is structured around the rising tension and anxiety between an unemployed man and his wife as they wait for the next visit from the means test officer. After inspections, the PAC or UAB often interviewed claimants. These 'all-powerful' committees were 'the select body of ladies and gentlemen whose duty it is to assess the needs of that other larger body of hungry-looking ordinary men and women waiting outside in the Public Hall'.[99] An unemployed man described the fear before the interview, 'The thing is a nightmare, and chokes me as I trudge around, the suspense of waiting for the blow to come is numbing my brain, and fills my thoughts at every turn.' Edward Warburton, a former means test investigator, recounted an interview with an irate disabled veteran whose transitional benefit was disallowed because of his war pension. A committee member moralised at the unfortunate old soldier,

Now, come, come, my man. Don't give way to hysteria. Face facts, as you did in 1914. Say to yourself: 'My country is in danger again, only in a different way. She needs help, now, even as she did in 1914.' Just look at the thing from a patriotic angle.[100]

Max Cohen, who left relatives because of the means test, bitterly described its consequences as 'dole-drawers starved in strange lodgings'.[101] Two historians of social policy poignantly noted the means test's 'enduring image' as a 'young couple who were told that their savings would have to go towards the maintenance of one of their parents, the family that was told to live off the pension paid to a veteran'.[102]

While the experience of unemployed men was abject, in many respects the treatment of women was even worse. The administrators of unemployment relief viewed women as second-class citizens. The criteria for relief were often more harshly interpreted and rates of benefit were, from November 1920 onwards, lower for women than men. The 1923 TUC Congress in Plymouth debated equal treatment for unemployed women, one speaker quoting the case of a women with 15 years' shop experience who had her benefit disallowed because she refused to go into domestic service for 10 shillings a week.[103] One woman pottery worker remembered being disallowed because she had been accompanied by her child when signing on.[104]

Married women who claimed benefit were singled out as 'anomalies' and faced a massive wave of disallowances after the June 1931 Act. The minority report of the Royal Commission in Unemployment Insurance outlined how the anomaly regulation had affected women. From 21 September to 23 November 1931, 72,401 married women had been disqualified from benefit, by publication of the report in 1932, 179,888 had been disqualified. The minority report described how the courts of Referees tried to snare women by the often mutually exclusive criteria for benefit of proof that they were in an insurable trade and that they had reasonable expectations of a job given local circumstances.[105] To add insult to injury, some employers would not employ married women and would lay off female employees if they married. Questions were asked in the House of Commons about such women, who were discriminated against by the employer and the anomaly regulation which meant that once sacked they would not receive benefit.[106]

The Unemployed Condition: Dole and Revolution?

The election victories of the Conservatives in 1931 and 1935 seem to confirm the view that the 1930s were a period of right-wing consensus. The experience of mass unemployment did not, so it would seem, lead to a political radicalisation. Some contemporaries were puzzled by this: 'Unemployed! We conjure up a picture of a sullen figure in a cap and choker brooding sedition and capable of effort only in the avoidance of work.'[107] Psychologists and social investigators looked to science to understand the unemployed condition and provided important insights into the attitudes of the unemployed.[108] However, their work assumed that there was a behaviourial reflex response to unemployment which existed in all cases. The problem with this approach is that it deals with the relationship between unemployment and radicalisation in terms of rigid abstract alternatives rather than an open manner in which historical circumstances and events are considered. For the behaviourialists, either unemployment fosters revolution in general or not at all; they came to the latter conclusion.

But this question is not that straightforward, for some contemporary collections of unemployed testimony did reveal an intense bitterness:

Some of you think that an unemployed man gets apathetic. He doesn't. The chief mental effect to most, I am sure, is bitterness. It's just a general bitterness. You feel you must do something. You feel you could break something.[109]

The hopeless routine of unemployment tempered this radical impulse. In *Time to Spare*, one talked of having 'no hope for change'; another, though against violence, wanted 'revolutionary change'; a third had 'no hopes' but thought that 'something ought to be done pretty soon'; still another asked: 'can you blame us for being so bitter?' For an unemployed engineer interviewed in 1934, unemployment had 'definitely lessened' political interest and was amazed the 'great mob permitted it'; an engineer had thrown himself into 'revolutionary movements from time to time, but it all seems so futile'.[110] A miner from the Durham coalfield, quoted in *Out of the Pit*, stated,

> At first I used to feel bitter and want[ed] to do something violent, I got books from the county library, socialist books and books on economics. I read a lot about revolution and communism and joined some demonstrations. But it leads to violence and you can't take risks [with] the authorities when you've got a wife and kids. That's what makes a lot of us armchair revolutionists ... As long as you've got dole regular, well you think twice about doing anything militant.[111]

C.A. Oakley, of the National Institute of Industrial Psychology, observed that many unemployed men were isolated, demoralised and lost interest in politics; E.W. Bakke, the American sociologist, agreed.[112] The consensus amongst psychologists was that the unemployed could be categorised by various states or stages (unbroken, resigned, apathetic, distressed). Personality and the length of unemployment determined these stages, which were the product of an unemployed condition. When describing the distressed stage, psychologists had to admit very real bitterness and rage:

> The distressed. The anxious, bitter, hopeless individuals who do not know which way to turn and who alternate between fits of gloominess and violent outburst. These are too disorganised to become revolutionaries; they more frequently go into flights from reality.[113]

The major problem with the attempts of psychologists and social investigators to grapple with the unemployed condition is that they see it as independent of events, changing political consciousness and the development of working class or unemployed organisation. The view that the unemployed condition could be summed up by a succession of clear stages is unsatisfactory both because it ignores the impact of changes in the political and economic circumstances and because it forces individuals into a single 'stage', whereas it was more likely that they took on characteristics from different stages or passed from one to another and back again depending on circumstance. To understand the role of the unemployed in the politics of the interwar period these insights have to be understood in conjunction with the ebbs and flows of unemployed struggles, which were not automatically determined by the levels of unemployment or poverty.

Wal Hannington explained the limits of unemployed radicalism by a combination of this demoralisation and government concessions.[114] At times, as we shall see by a close examination of unemployed struggles, the bitterness of those without work expressed itself, sometimes violently, on the streets. On a number of occasions, the government was forced into retreat and perhaps H.N. Brailsford was right in stating that 'An abandonment of insurance against unemployment would destroy any British government that attempted it.'[115] Brailsford was not alone, Bakke believed unemployment insurance 'has kept unrest to a minimum' and Philip Snowden, Chancellor of the Exchequer, expressed similar views in the House of Commons.[116]

Conclusion

Whilst the media represented the unemployed as troublemakers, shirkers, comedic simpletons or charity cases, the real lives of the unemployed revealed a more mundane struggle to make ends meet, the foot-slogging search for work, the pangs of hunger, the victimisation of militants and even suicide in the most desperate cases. Their means of support – the system of unemployed provision – had developed into an alien bureaucratic machine with its form-filling, home visits, queuing, austere offices, language of bureaucratic euphemism and basic authoritarianism. With the genuinely seeking work clause, the anomaly regulations and the introduction of the means test, this regime became more miserly and punitive in response to the spectre of abuse and desire to make government economies. Though social investigators and psychologists searched for a simple behavioural response to unemployment, they unwittingly uncovered the paradox of bitterness and despair. This helps to explain the dynamic of unemployed agitation wherein outbursts of short-lived protest and revolt punctuated the general gloom of the unemployed.

No simple formula equates increasing unemployment with radicalisation. In so far as it is correct to talk of an unemployed condition, that condition is by its nature contradictory, combining both bitterness and despair. To explain the reactions of the unemployed we must move on to a consideration of the Labour Party, which treated the unemployed 'as a reservoir of votes' and unemployed protest.[117]

4 The Labour Party and Unemployment

> The pressing question of our time ... it must be faced with a determination to spend whatever sums, however large, may be necessary to remove the scandal from our society of a class of human beings industrially and individually superfluous.
>
> Philip Snowden, *Labour and the New World*, 1921

The Labour Party was founded in 1906 and made its decisive breakthrough on the home front of the First World War. The wartime coalition government co-opted Labour and trade union officials as junior partners in the war effort. Labour was swept along by the tide of working-class confidence which lasted until the early 1920s. It equipped itself with a socialist programme, *Labour and the New Social Order*, and a constitution that was sufficiently vague to placate the different shades of opinion in the Party. During the interwar period, Labour gradually ousted the Liberals as the main opposition party to the Tories. In the long run the rise of the Labour Party resulted from both the enfranchisement of the working class in 1884 and 1918 and the continued commitment of trade union officials and the socialist movement to have parliamentary representation. Historians have characterised the interwar period as the age of Baldwin, a period of conservative consensus in high politics; but there were two brief intermissions in 1924 and 1929–31 when Labour for the first time formed minority governments.[1]

Unemployment offered Labour a unique opportunity to demonstrate its ability to manage and reform capitalism and thereby ameliorate the lives of Labour's working-class supporters. The improvements for the unemployed under Labour governments were modest: the first government slightly increased benefits and the second abolished the genuinely seeking work clause. This chapter will argue that Labour failed both at the level of government and in its relationship with the unemployed. Whilst it shunned the extra-parliamentary actions of the workless, its parliamentary efforts led it to accept cuts in benefits for Britain's most needy. It is this failure of the reformist Left, rather than British exceptionalism, that explains (alongside other factors, such as the strength of economic recovery and the doldrums of British trade unionism after the General Strike) the poor fortunes of left radicalism in the 1930s.

Labour Party Thought and Unemployment

The Labour Party, then as throughout its history, was far from ideologically uniform. Containing many political currents, the Party's two major schools of thought were the 'guild socialists' who believed in workers' control of industry and the Fabians, who favoured state control. What united both these currents with trade union leaders was the belief in incremental parliamentary change, the 'inevitability of gradualness'. The Labour Party combined an explanation of unemployment as the product of capitalism to be solved by socialist planning with policies in the here and now which differed little from the Tories' and Liberals'. Even the figures associated with the right of the Labour Party, such as Jimmy Thomas and Philip Snowden, enthusiastically predicted unemployment's demise under socialism. As Thomas noted: 'There will be no profiteers, no unemployment, no slums, no hungry children. No man will be expected to work an excessive number of hours, and no man who is fit to work will be able to shirk it.'[2] Labour Party and trade union leaders reasoned that mass unemployment revealed capitalism's irrationality which only socialism could bring to its end.

When in opposition, Labour repeatedly criticised the government's unemployment policies. In theory, the labour movement demanded 'work or full maintenance' in unison; this was the Party's unemployment watchword. But in practice this slogan conveyed a variety of meanings: for trade union leaders, it was a defence against the unemployed being used to undermine union rates of pay; for the Labour Party, it meant a commitment to improving the lot of the unemployed if parliamentary conditions allowed; for the NUWM, it meant the rallying cry in the fight for work, for better relief and against the Poor Law.

Labour believed that unemployment resulted from 'failed prevention'. During the war, Labour had warned that at the end of hostilities, only careful preparation could prevent unemployment. The state, it was argued, should concentrate work contracts in lean years, embark on public works and reduce the supply of labour by raising the school-leaving age and limiting the working week. It was Labour's policy 'to maintain at a fairly uniform level year by year ... the aggregate demand for labour'.[3] Unemployment, according to Labour thinking, was preventable and therefore resulted from government neglect. To underline this, the Parliamentary Labour

Party (PLP) introduced Prevention of Unemployment Bills in 1919, 1920, 1921, 1922, 1923, 1925, 1926 and 1927, although these had no chance of a parliamentary majority. This pantomine was outdone when, in March 1923, Labour introduced a debate on whether the House should support the transition to socialism.

Foreign policy played a key part in Labour's challenge to unemployment. The Labour Party blamed Lloyd George's peace settlement for aggravating postwar unemployment. The Versailles peace treaty, they contended, was punitive to the defeated and injurious to British exports, 'Their aim appears to be to prevent the revival in these countries; their result is to create unemployment elsewhere.'[4] The trade embargo on the Soviet Union exacerbated the weakness of international trade. Labour called for an international economic conference to reduce German reparations, to provide loans for devastated areas and persuade governments to balance budgets. The Labour leadership reckoned that these measures, by reducing inflation and stabilising exchange rates, would allow a return to the Gold Standard, which would in turn result in a revival in international trade.

At home, Labour criticised Coalition and Conservative governments for the 'miserably inadequate' unemployed maintenance and the failure to implement sufficient public works through the St David's Committee (otherwise known as the Unemployment Grants Committee). In terms of economics, Labour's rhetoric prescribed socialist planning, nationalisation and the elimination of unemployment, but its short-term policy was one of capitalist orthodoxy. Until late 1931, the economic policy and thinking of the Labour Party was dominated by Philip Snowden and Ramsay MacDonald. Chancellor and Prime Minister respectively of both Labour governments, they shared orthodox liberal economic ideas. Snowden in particular kneeled before the icons of nineteenth-century British liberalism: free trade, the Gold Standard and balanced budgets. As such there was little to distinguish Labour from the economic thought of mainstream parties and economists of the time.

There were two major breaches in the economic consensus of the interwar period. First, Stanley Baldwin's Conservative Party became increasingly protectionist and, second, David Lloyd George's faction of 'new' Liberals by 1928 had embraced Keynesian employment policies. Baldwin, three times Conservative Prime Minister (1923–24, 1924–29 and 1935–37), argued that protection could solve unemployment and he was prepared to go to the country over the matter. In 1923, he addressed a public meeting with these words: 'The unemployment problem is the most crucial problem of our country. I can fight it. I cannot fight it without weapons. The only way is fighting this subject by protecting the home market.'[5] In the election of December 1923, the Labour Party stood for free trade against Baldwin's protectionist platform. MacDonald countered with a pamphlet, *Labour's Policy versus Protectionism*, which condemned protection as 'bribery, corruption and log-rolling' and proposed free trade and a conciliatory foreign policy as the main weapons in the battle against unemployment.[6] Labour were keen to fight the election on these terms and even ousted the Liberals as the main electoral representatives of free trade. Their manifesto dropped nationalisation while proposing income tax cuts which would benefit the middle class. In the course of the next few years, protectionism gained ground in Parliament, press and country, until it finally triumphed in 1931. The issue divided business opinion and major campaigns were mounted by press barons to shape opinion in this direction. A revenue tariff even attracted sections of the Labour and TUC leadership as an expedient in the years of economic crisis. Snowden, however, remained steadfastly opposed and was able to mobilise enough free trade opinion to scuttle protectionism in Labour's ranks.

Snowden's economic conservatism was all too apparent when he castigated the Coalition government (1918–22) for profligacy at a time when the major reason for rising expenditure was unemployment relief.[7] Snowden and the Labour Party were again to clash with Lloyd George over their plans to use budget deficits to finance work-creation in the 1929 election. Lloyd George's 1929 election manifesto, *We Can Conquer Unemployment*, was a radical plan to combat unemployment. Although some have seen it as an electoral manoeuvre, Keynes and Henderson leapt to its defence in *Can Lloyd George Do It?* The Liberal programme projected 600,000 new jobs a year by spending £250 million on public works. All this would be complemented by 'international appeasement' aimed at stabilising the price of gold. Domestically, they sought to stimulate new industries and relocate workers from distressed areas. They did not foresee the need for a significant budget deficit as the employment generated would increase tax receipts, reduce the costs of unemployment and could be financed through loans. The Labour Party's response, *How to Conquer Unemployment*, attacked the Liberals: 'Mr. Lloyd George ... is ready to mortgage the future as ever; ... wise men throw such things in the waste bin without much ado.' This confused document condemned the Liberal programme as ineffective and superficial and 'a thing of shreds and patches, of sound projects flitched from Labour sources'.[8]

Despite considerable propaganda about unemployment, the Labour Party had left a number of issues unresolved. Given the three-way split of the electorate, how would Labour gain office and win the necessary majority to implement its programme? Would it accept minority government? It was unclear precisely how Labour would implement its programme given the prevailing economic and international circumstances. Labour espoused job-creation through public works, but on the understanding that the budget must balance. But as long as Labour accepted the agenda of a balanced budget and a return to the Gold Standard, public works on the scale required to tackle the intractable million were out of the question.

Dissenting Economic Views

During the 1920s two groups dissented from Labour's economic orthodoxy: Sir Oswald Mosley and John Strachey came under the sway of Keynes; and a number of Independent Labour Party (ILP, a party affiliated to the Labour Party) members, who were receptive to J.A. Hobson's under-consumptionist theories. Mosley, a former Conservative MP, joined Labour and the ILP in 1924. Influenced by Keynes' journalism, he sought a radical solution to unemployment, challenging the economic orthodoxy of a return to the Gold Standard at the pre-war parity. In these efforts, he teamed up with John Strachey, who like Mosley was an aristocratic outsider in the Labour ranks. In 1925 both authored pamphlets of the same title, *Revolution by Reason*, espousing essentially the same case. Unlike other radical Labour economists, they maintained that an increase in demand was more important than the redistribution of wealth. An Economic Planning Council, a 'general staff of union and business experts', was necessary to plan credit expansion and state purchasing and bypass government red tape. They countered orthodox criticisms in Keynesian fashion: increasing the level of demand would only create inflation once full employment had been achieved. They also declared that the pound should float if necessary, decrying the prevalent 'export fetishism' whereby trade improvement was simplistically equated with British economic revival. Again in line with Keynes, the major economic antagonism was between industry and finance so that their programme supposedly articulated the common interests of industrial capital and labour. Once Mosley had regained his place in Parliament through a by-election in Smethwick in December 1926, the leaders of the PLP saw him as a rising talent to nurture.

The other dissenters, J.A. Hobson, E.F. Wise and H.N. Brailsford, were ILP intellectuals. They asserted that capitalism had been thrown into economic crisis because it suppressed the consumption of the masses: 'the power of the masses to consume fails to keep pace with the power of the machines to produce'.[9] Hobson pointed to the war economy to illustrate his case. Were consumption at three quarters of its wartime level, he reasoned, it 'would not merely avert unemployment ... but would furnish economic conditions for a continually increasing productivity'.[10] Brailsford, writing twelve years later, restated the view that the errors of 'our traditional exaggeration of the external market' had been to the detriment of 'internal purchasing power'. In other words, the solution to the economic crisis was to put more on the worker's plate.[11] These ILP members formed the Living Wage Commission which produced a report spelling out the under-consumptionist case. Perversely, such ideas were both marginal and pervasive within the Labour Party. MacDonald and Snowden stressed the need for economic responsibility and the goal of demonstrating Labour's suitability for office; this line held sway in the Party. When *The Living Wage* was debated at the 1927 Labour Party Conference it was rejected by 20 to 1.[12] But, in diluted form, under-consumptionist thinking could be often detected in Labour Party rhetoric, programmes and manifestos. Despite similarities, this under-consumptionism differed from the ideas of Keynes and Mosley. For the latter two, the answer lay with raising the general level of demand through government stimulation of productive investment. For the under-consumptionist, wealth redistribution to the poor (through wage increases and family allowances) would result in a greater proportion of wealth being immediately spent rather than saved or speculated.

The challenge to the ideas of Snowden and MacDonald was a rather marginal affair and the Party's lack of economic expertise and debate proved to be debilitating in the crisis of 1931. As Francis Williams, *Daily Herald*'s City editor, later noted in his memoirs, key Cabinet ministers had a poor grasp of economics: Snowden 'had nothing to offer but the most orthodox and deflationary of remedies', Sidney Webb was 'too much of a Fabian gradualist to recognise a world depression when he saw it'; and Henderson's 'intellectual understanding of economic principles [was] negligible'.[13] In terms of economic thought, the Labour Party accepted throughout the 1920s its leadership's mixture of practical orthodoxy and socialist rhetoric. The years of opposition did not put their thought to the test. In government, rhetoric's veil would be removed to lay bare their policy's realities. Seemingly uninfluential at the time, economic alternatives within the Party would prove significant later as they created the potential for internal dissent, controversy and, ultimately, policy reformulation.

1924 – Labour's First Term

The December 1923 election resulted in a minority Labour government. Ramsay MacDonald had formerly ruled out minority government as the Party would be unable to carry out its programme and manifesto pledges, but on 21 January 1924 he accepted office. His about-face was to demonstrate, as his letter to the King put it, the Labour Party's 'capacity to govern'.[14] The first Labour government was rather disappointing: small reforms were made in relation to housing, taxes and unemployment, but it certainly did not live up to its own advance publicity in which Labour had scalded Coalition and Tory governments for failing to implement adequate public works programmes and for relying on relief rather than work-creation. Labour also repeatedly declared that only they could end unemployment.

On 12 February 1924, the new Prime Minister's opening address spelled out the priorities of his government to the Commons 'not first of all on the relief of unemployment, but on the restoration of trade. We are not going to diminish industrial capital in order to provide relief.'[15] In order to achieve this he unimaginatively proposed an expansion of the Trade Facilities Act and Export Credit schemes. The Trades Facilities Act set up state-guaranteed loans to British firms in the hope that this would encourage a restoration of trade and therefore employment. He also embarked on certain public works proposals and specific measures to deal with women's unemployment. On the latter question, Margaret Bondfield, the Parliamentary Secretary to the Minister of Labour, reeled off platitudes about the domestic responsibilities of women, 'the great work of all housewives in the country in making the home, and in developing that home life which has been the backbone and the main stay of this country'.[16]

The Labour government's attempt to reform unemployment insurance ended in an awkward compromise. In its first weeks, it abolished the three-week gap during which uncovenanted benefit was withheld after twelve weeks. John Wheatley, the Minister of Health, also annulled the 1921 order restricting the granting of relief by Poplar Council, although this order had never been enforced. The Labour government's major initiative was the Unemployment Insurance (no. 2) Act. In some respects this heralded genuine gains for the unemployed. The Act widened eligibility to the unemployment scheme, increased the levels of benefit (from 15 shillings to 18 shillings for men, from 12 shillings to 15 shillings for women) and abolished the means test. However, the latter's abolition, announced by Thomas Shaw in the early days of Labour's term, incensed Snowden, who intoned against 'undesirable characters trading on the country's generosity'.[17] Such improvements caused less Tory and Liberal criticism than might have been expected because the economy was improving, the Unemployment Insurance Fund deficit was steadily falling and to receive benefit uncovenanted unemployed were to be 'genuinely seeking work' (the GSW clause), rather than 'capable of and available for work but unable to find suitable employment'. This clause was intended to clamp down on abuse, about which opposition politicians, employers and the press, without any substantial evidence, voiced anger and anguish. Racist arguments about 'aliens' who 'come over here' and were 'kept in idleness' sum up the naked prejudice of much of the abuse propaganda.[18] Placing the onus of proof on the claimant did not worry Labour as they thought that disallowances would fall principally on women. This concession ultimately disqualified millions of unemployed from their benefits. The Labour Party defended this regulation despite the fact that Shaw received several delegations of trade unionists and was asked a series of parliamentary questions about the sometimes punitive and arbitrary character of the GSW and the Local Employment Committees (LECs) that applied it.[19] For example, he was told that some LECs were demanding unobtainable certificates from employers or foremen as proof of job search.

Philip Snowden's and Labour's first budget, the so-called 'housewife's budget', did little to tackle unemployment. The Capital Levy (a tax on the rich), which would provide money for war debt repayments, had been abandoned. Snowden described the Capital Levy, Labour's one major progressive tax proposal, as an 'electoral millstone'. Instead, Snowden lowered taxes, with the declared intention of creating a budget surplus to reduce the national debt. He pursued his free market instincts by abolishing the MacKenna Duties (a wartime measure to protect certain strategic industries), despite objections that it would cost jobs in, amongst others, the motor industry. Notably, he failed to provide the funds required for public works on the scale to make significant inroads into unemployment.

Thus, the budget missed the opportunity to check unemployment. The performance of Sidney Webb's Cabinet team to deal with joblessness was even more lamentable.[20] Tom Jones, assistant secretary to the Cabinet, acerbically recorded Webb's impotence in this regard: 'All Sidney Webb, as Chairman of the Committee, after 30 or 40 years of reflection on the subject, has been able to prescribe is a "revival of trade".'[21]

Pressure mounted on Labour; they had made great stock out of the evil of unemployment in opposition but turned to tired platitudes once in office. In the House of Commons, they were repeatedly reminded of their manifesto pledge that they were 'the only party that could end unemployment'.[22] Shaw declared, to the derision of opponents, that he could not 'produce schemes like rabbits out of a hat'.[23] The Cabinet insider, Tom Jones, captured Labour's dithering in his diary: 'The PM was especially concerned about unemployment, and wanted to be in a position in the middle of July to make a statement of the government's policy which would meet the criticism that they had none.'[24]

To rectify this situation, the Board of Trade appointed the Balfour Committee on 30 July to investigate the export performance of British commerce and industry. On the same day, the Labour government's last unemployment debate in the House of Commons took place. In an astonishing abandonment of Labour policy, Snowden outlined his general hostility to the use of public works schemes to reduce unemployment, asserting that they should be geared to improving the competitiveness of the country. He suggested a major electrification scheme. These plans were hardly original, borrowing much from Lloyd George's proposals.

The Labour government fell because of the divisions within Liberals on whose support it relied and in particular because of Liberal opposition to Labour's Russian policy.[25] The 'Zinoviev letter', a forgery supposedly from Moscow instructing the Communist Party to prepare for insurrection, did not help Labour's case at the polls. Parliamentary opponents and the press seized on the letter to censure Labour over its more sympathetic foreign policy stance towards the Soviet Union. In an atmosphere of press hysteria, Baldwin was re-elected.

Neither the Party nor the electorate viewed the 1924 Labour government as a failure. After all, it was a short-lived minority government, Labour's first taste of office, and it had been hounded by a hostile press. It is true that political opponents had criticised its unemployment policy, but they were themselves largely without constructive alternatives. In an atmosphere of political partisanship, Labour's support was reinforced. Even the ILP pamphlets underlined (and exaggerated) the government's achievements in foreign policy, unemployment and housing.[26] With hindsight this complacency was misplaced. On the question of unemployment, Labour had rejected significant public works and other initiatives to stimulate employment. It continued with existing schemes: the Unemployment Grants Committee, the Trade Facilities Act and Export Credit scheme. UGC expenditure even fell under Labour. For the three years to February 1924, the UGC granted £350,000 a month but, in the first four months of the Labour government, the UGC made grants of only £106,000 a month, with fewer applications and fewer approvals.[27] The Trade Facilities Act grew, even though it was in effect a subsidy to big business marking Labour's shift from public works to hand-outs to British capital. In addition, compromise with the right-wing agenda over the issue of abuse in their Unemployment Insurance Act led to misery for millions of unemployed through subsequent disqualifications. Although Labour's first term in office revealed its weaknesses on the question of unemployment, they went largely unnoticed inside the Party. Instead of re-examining its policies, it robustly defended its unemployment record. In response to accusations of lacking innovation and making exaggerated pledges, Labour published *Work for the Workless* as an official defence of the first Labour government's record. It pointed out that it was a minority government, 'in office but not in power'.[28] It also asserted that the UGC and Exports Credit Schemes which had been set up under Lloyd George, were really the unattributed result of Labour Party thinking. Unwittingly, Labour admitted to creating expectations that, short of the unlikely event of a majority Labour government, it could not hope to fulfil. Nothing was learned. Its 1929 election literature declared it would 'not only set the workless to work, but also by removing the root causes of unemployment, effectively prevent its recurrence'.[29]

Labour's Second Term, 1929–31

The second time around the sharpest economic and political crisis that a British government had faced for years cruelly exposed these flaws. In June 1929, Labour was asked to form a second minority government. At the time of their election the economy was in relatively good shape: unemployment was falling, and GNP and industrial production were growing strongly. It was important for Labour to be seen to be doing something about unemployment as this issue had dominated the election and was, in Labour's own words, 'its acid test'.[30] The new government set up the Morris Committee to investigate the 'procedure and evidence for the determination of claims' or, in other words, to examine the genuinely seeking work clause, which was coming under increasing criticism.[31] The Labour leadership still accepted the largely mythical spectre of abuse. The key spokespersons, Shaw and Bondfield, as Alan Deacon pointed out, 'at no time – or anyone else on Labour's front bench – denied the need for some measure to deter malingering and the leadership remained convinced that the complete withdrawal of the "seeking work" test was politically impossible'.[32]

The Morris Committee, reporting in October 1929, was divided. Employers' representatives insisted on proof of search for work even where employment was known to be non-existent, but the majority argued that disallowance could only follow refusal to accept suitable employment.[33] The majority's recommendations were embodied in the 1930 Unemployment Act, but only after pressure from the Party on the leadership. The Act also reversed the previous government's reduction of state contribution to the unemployment fund (from 50 to 40 per cent). Moreover, it relieved the drain of transitional benefits payments on the Unemployment Insurance Fund by Exchequer funding. Steel-Maitland, Baldwin's Minister of Labour, attacked the Act as the 'endowment of the work-shy'. Snowden, the Labour Chancellor, argued in terms with which the Tories could agree, 'I defended the Bill on the ground that it was not only discharging a humanitarian duty, but was insurance against revolution.'[34] Labour had abolished the 'genuinely seeking work' clause, but it had done so in such half-hearted and apologetic terms that the myth of widespread abuse was to resurface later, to its own disadvantage.

This legislation failed to resolve the unemployment problem. Within months the world economic crisis held the MacDonald government in its clutches. The Labour government was forlorn in the face of rising unemployment figures and was criticised by opposition parties, press and the business community. The Party suffered several worrying by-election defeats. The Labour's answer to the rise in unemployment was visible activity – committees, reports, royal commissions, high-profile economic advisers – giving the illusion of purposefulness, but not masking the government's fundamental confusion and impotence. In January 1930, MacDonald formed the Economic Advisory Council (EAC), which lent him the credibility of expert economic advice. However, Magaret Cole recalled how MacDonald paid little or no attention to her husband, EAC member G.D.H. Cole, Reader in Economics at Oxford.[35] A further problem existed within these bodies. They brought together people with diametrically opposed views, so the socialist Cole and radical Keynes sat side by side with the conservative Lionel Robbins.

MacDonald's Cabinet committee on unemployment also tried to mix oil and water. Jimmy Thomas, preoccupied mainly with ratio-nalisation, would never share Oswald Mosley's radical views, while Lansbury and Tom Johnston, the committee's other members, leant towards Mosley. However, the committee worked to Snowden's and Thomas's unwritten agenda which ruled out credit expansion, protection and subsidies. The team could only formulate a modest programme of rationalisation, colonial development and road-building. Rationalisation would, at least in the short term, aggravate, rather than improve, the levels of unemployment with no guarantees about the future. The need for local authority planning permission and civil service co-operation rendered largely ineffective even the relatively small sums set aside for public works. By June 1930, £111 million of public works had been approved but projects amounting to only £44 million were in progress, employing 64,000.[36] Casting Thomas and Mosley together provoked an episode that threatened both the leadership's economic policy and party unity. By late January 1930, Mosley's impatience at Labour's passivity led him to break with Thomas. He wrote a memorandum proposing to create public works jobs with the help of a new institution that would be able to bypass the civil service and local government. Having gained support from Lansbury and Johnston on the unemployment committee, he unsuccessfully circulated the rest of the Cabinet. Frustrated but undeterred, Mosley read out the memorandum in the House of Commons and on 19 May resigned as junior minister, forcing a debate amongst the Parliamentary Labour Party. Although Mosley lost the PLP vote by 202 to 29, he had exposed a deep-seated disillusion with the leadership's performance on unemployment and was only narrowly defeated at the Llandudno Labour Party conference in October (by 1,046,000 to 1,251,000). Even in December 1930, he was still attempting to rally support for his project within the Labour Party, publishing a manifesto backed by the miners' leader A.J. Cook and 19 MPs. As his expectation of overturning the leadership had been dashed at every turn, he soon abandoned Labour to form the New Party in February 1931. Mosley's revolt revealed the Labour leadership's poor handling of the unemployment crisis and unease over this in certain sections of the movement. As for Mosley, his ambition thwarted, he turned elsewhere for a political vehicle. A.J.P. Taylor commented, 'Mosley was politically ruined. His ideas were ruined with him. Labour drifted on without a policy.'[37] That ruin was compounded by the New Party's electoral failure. These defeats ultimately led him to found the British Union of Fascists in 1932.

In October, whilst Mosley's revolt rumbled on, the government appointed the Royal Commission on Unemployment Insurance. Registered unemployment had risen from 1,222,713 at the end of May 1929 to 2,050,000 by mid-August 1930. Holman Gregory, a criminal court judge, chaired the Commission and of nine other committee members only two were sympathetic to the labour movement.[38] Pressure had been mounting as the UIF debt deepened and unemployment continued to climb. As early as July 1930, the anxious voice of Magaret Bondfield, Minister of Labour, suggested the means test or transference of the unemployed to the Poor Law in order to redress mounting UIF debts. The government envisaged the Royal Commission as a means of gaining parliamentary support from the Liberals and even the Conservatives for unemployment policy. But perhaps more importantly, the Labour leadership wished to quieten opposition to unpopular measures within its own ranks. The government set the inquiry two goals: to sort out relief of the uninsured unemployed and to restore solvency to the Unemployment Insurance Fund. By late 1930, a feeling of national crisis had infected the country. Economic distress and party factionalism caused growing disaffection with the government and parliament. In this atmosphere some newspapers and prominent lobbyists began to push for a national (i.e. coalition) government to overcome party divisions. The government wished to remove unemployment from the political agenda until the authority of the Royal Commission's findings could ease these strains.

It was a vain hope. The new year brought no end to the upward course of the jobless total. Worse still, from the spring a financial crisis gripped central Europe which, by late summer, was threatening sterling. Business was noisily sloganising about the last straw of tax increases and the need for retrenchment, a contemporary euphemism for cuts in the dole. The NCEO was to the fore and the 'Friends of Economy' was set up in January 1931 specifically for this task, organising dozens of public meetings calling for expenditure cuts.[39] The capitalist class, seemingly only an agitator's bogey, revealed its omnipresent influence. The associational culture of the NCEO, FBI, the League of Industry, the Friends of Economy, Chambers of Commerce and the London's exclusive clubs cemented the growing mood of impatience. This agenda was transmitted by various means. Newspapers mounted crusades for retrenchment, for empire protection and of criticism of Labour. Top civil servants in the Treasury supported these calls for retrenchment and helped Snowden and MacDonald in their manipulation of their party. The Bank of England, whose Governor was described by the City editor of the *Daily Herald* as 'a virtual despot and a powerful influence, perhaps the most powerful, influence on the national economic as well as financial policy', pressed the point home with ministers.[40] Abroad, American and French central bankers were warning the government of the effects on sterling if they did not embark on retrenchment particularly if they did not cut expenditure on unemployment.[41] Decisively, the captains of finance and industry were present in abundance on government committees. The principle of 'sound finance' was exorted at every turn and this meant cuts in unemployment benefits. As Labour had criticised their opponents just two years earlier, so too they 'were too much under the thumb of capitalism to apply coercion to their masters'.[42]

Historians who paint the Labour Party as entirely the victim of circumstances are wrong. The Labour leadership, and in particular Snowden, had pursued a policy that precipitated this crisis. In part, this resulted from his economic orthodoxy as he refused to consider three options (tax increases, protection or leaving the Gold Standard) that might have given him more room to manoeuvre. He aimed to sail close to the wind in the budget to force the Cabinet into accepting the cuts that he deemed necessary from the end of 1930 'as unpalatable as it might seem to the Labour Party'.[43] *The Economist* applauded Snowden's budget for not increasing tax (except 2d on petrol) but remarked that he 'has reduced provision for the debt to dangerously low levels'.[44]

In February 1931, the government appointed another committee, this time to investigate public expenditure after Snowden had already ruled out tax increases: 'an increase in taxation in present conditions which falls on industry would be the last straw. Schemes involving heavy expenditure, however desirable, will have to wait until prosperity returns.'[45] *The Economist* described the committee headed by Sir George May (the former head of Prudential Assurance Company), as 'a small, independent, expert committee to advise upon government retrenchment'. Beatrice Webb, the Fabian socialist, did not share this view of its personnel and was closer to the mark in describing them as 'five clever hard-faced representatives of capitalism and two dull trade unionists'.[46] The wording of its parameters were borrowed from the Geddes Committee's (a clear indication that a heavy axe was to be taken to public expenditure). Snowden made its purpose clear in his memoirs: he wanted the committee's 'authority for proposing cuts in expenditure' which would otherwise would have been 'quite impossible'.[47]

Despite the relentless rise of unemployment, the commissioning of reports held Labour's political crisis in abeyance, or more precisely it postponed its date. However, when the commissions reported they dramatically heightened the atmosphere of national crisis. In June, the Royal Commission on Unemployment Insurance published an Interim Report which echoed business clamours for a 'new axe'.[48] The majority report called for a 2 shilling cut in the dole (that is, up to 30 per cent) and the elimination of the so-called anomalies – that is, unemployed seasonal or short-time workers and married women who were claiming benefit. The report also proposed increased unemployment fund contributions from employers and workers. The government responded swiftly. On 19 June, it introduced the Anomalies Act to prevent abuse of unemployment scheme by disqualifying those that the government thought should be ineligible for relief. By March 1932, more than 82 per cent of married women claimants had been disqualified.[49] Ironically, the Act's prime mover was Margaret Bondfield, the Minister of Labour and first woman Cabinet member. She had for some time been keen to see married women struck off benefit.[50] On 13 July, the Macmillan Committee published its report on finance and industry. Having outlined the weakness of sterling's position and the parlous state of government finance, it too called for cuts in the dole.

By late July, after several spectacular Central European bank collapses and German and Austrian currencies crises, the financial storm was bearing down on sterling. In the fortnight to the end of July, the Bank of England lost £32 million in gold reserves, or nearly a fifth of its total. If the next two weeks were as bad, the pound would collapse. On 26 July, the government was forced to secure a £50 million loan from Paris and New York to bolster sterling, but speculative pressures redoubled after publication of the May Committee's report on 31 July. This had an even more unsettling effect than the two preceding reports. It recommended deep cuts: £97 million in retrenchment, of which £67 million was to come from unemployment relief (a 20 per cent cut in benefit). Further savings were to come from reductions in teachers', civil servants', police and the armed forces' pay. The roads budget would also be slashed by £7.8 million, further aggravating the jobless figures. Beatrice Webb was shocked by this 'sensational demand for economy in public expenditure, not merely cutting down what they consider "doles" but also health and education services'.[51] Keynes called it the 'most foolish document I have ever had the misfortune to read'.[52] Frederick Pethick-Lawrence declared it 'designed to shock' and that it led to 'scare descriptions' in the press.[53] The report, ignoring the conventions of budgetary calculation, forecast a budget deficit of £120 million. It included borrowing for the Unemployment Insurance Fund, the Road Fund and full maintenance of the Sinking Fund as budget items. As a result, the deficit appeared to be a sixth of total government revenue and exaggerated the total deficit. One Treasury official secretly told Snowden that the report exaggerated the deficit by £50 million.[54] The Cabinet ignored one obvious solution, which was to delay the National Debt repayments, as the recent Macmillan Report had suggested. In his memoirs, Snowden prided himself on his overriding patriotic goal of rapidly reducing the National Debt. Even if Snowden's goal of debt repayment is accepted, the projected debt was wildly pessimistic. In reality, the government had large budgetary surpluses throughout the 1930s: the surplus for the financial year 1931–32 was £152 million, rising to £174 million the following year. These surpluses were in part paid for by cuts in unemployment benefits.[55] Despite the fantasies of the report, sterling's collapse and the massive withdrawals of gold and foreign exchange from Britain were real enough. On the other hand, the press largely ignored the minority report and Snowden scornfully remarked that it 'showed no appreciation of the gravity of the national financial position, and generally followed the lines of ordinary socialist propaganda'. The two trade unionist representatives on the May Committee reasonably argued that there should be an 'equality of sacrifice' based on 'capacity to pay', and that the cuts should not be borne by the unemployed disproportionately. Unfortunately, they were unable to challenge the majority report's most vulnerable aspect: the estimated deficit.

The report deepened sterling's difficulties and it became clear that either another foreign loan or exit from the Gold Standard was necessary. On 5 August, Keynes advised MacDonald to leave the Gold Standard, but this move was rejected because it was unacceptable to the City of London. On 12 August with the financial crisis mounting, a 'Cabinet economy committee' was formed and recalled from holiday to discuss the emergency. MacDonald and the Bank of England then requested the leaders of the opposition parties return to London. Threefold parallel negotiations which followed were linked only by Macdonald and Snowden, these were: Cabinet deliberations, meetings of the Party leaders and the dialogue between the Prime Minister and Chancellor and the banks. On Wednesday, 19 August, the Cabinet economy committee agreed to a £78 million cut and the full Cabinet to a £56 million cut, but there was no agreement on a cut in the dole.[56] The next day, the Labour Party executive and the General Council of the TUC met to discuss the crisis. Despite Snowden painting a frightening alternative of economic ruin and 10 million unemployed, the TUC leaders opposed any cuts in the dole. They had lost patience with a government that had excluded them from policy formation too often. Neither did they all fear devaluation.[57]

Friday's Cabinet discussions were unable to resolve the matter, but the need for a loan from abroad was obvious to all. The following day, MacDonald duly contacted the J.P. Morgan Bank of New York to discuss the terms of a loan. The Bank's reply stated that a loan would be forthcoming if Labour imposed a cuts package that was agreeable to both the Bank of England and the City. Beatrice Webb's memoirs recorded how MacDonald also dined with opposition leaders, at which time he

> suggested another compromise (Sidney said that J.R.M. was not authorised to do it), which Chamberlain accepted, *assuming the City agreed*. It was left to the bank of England (vice-chairman) to consult the Federal [Reserve] Bank of the U.S.A. whether they would back such a governmental policy, and their decision will be reported today (Sunday) when the cabinet meets at seven o'clock. So it is financiers, British and American, who will settle the personnel and policy of the British government.[58]

Hence the full ideological and economic weight of the capitalist class at home and abroad was bearing down upon the Labour Cabinet. There were also suggestions once again that a national government could overcome the crisis.

On 24 August, the Cabinet had to decide. Tom Johnston, the Lord Privy Seal, recalled the Cabinet waiting on 10 Downing Street's lawn that evening for a telegram from New York 'as to whether the pound was to be saved or not, and whether the conditions would be insisted upon that the unemployed would be cut 10 per cent'.[59] A slender Cabinet majority voted in favour of the cuts package, which included the 10 per cent reduction of unemployment benefit and the reintroduction of the means test. However, MacDonald wanted wider backing from his Cabinet and went to the King to tender his resignation. The following morning, the King interviewed opposition leaders and invited MacDonald to form a National government.

On 28 August, the cuts package was unveiled. This would supposedly save the nation from the financial and political abyss of sterling quitting the Gold Standard. Ten per cent was to be cut from standard rates of benefit, a household means test imposed on transitional benefits and there was to be a 10 per cent cut in the pay of the armed services, police, civil servants and teachers. Ironically, within a month, despite these cuts, sterling left the Gold Standard. Labour had not even considered such a move. As Lord Passfield (Sidney Webb) said later, 'No one ever told us we could even do that.'[60]

The Aftermath

We're going to hang Ramsay Mac from the sour apple tree,
We're going to hang Snowden and Thomas to keep him company,
For that's the place where traitors ought to be.[61]

This popular ditty aptly demonstrates the Labour Party rank and file's bitterness at the great betrayal. However, the crisis of 1931 should not be seen in terms of the personal failings of MacDonald or the failure to adopt some new ideology, but as a failure of Labour Party reformism. Sidney Pollard, the economic historian, summed up the record of the second Labour government as 'totally committed to reviving capitalism rather than burying it', arguing that 'such an attitude became an escape from the reality rather than a blueprint for a realistic policy: the belief in ultimate socialism became an excuse for not doing anything meanwhile'.[62] R.H. Tawney, in a brilliant essay on the 1931 collapse, pointed out that whilst the Labour Party thought of capitalism as an onion to be peeled layer by layer, it was in reality a tiger which could not be skinned paw by paw, because 'vivisection is its game. It does the skinning first.' He went on to argue that the Labour Party had ignored both the inevitable capitalist resistance to its goals and the need to steel, educate and mobilise mass support. Whilst many had blamed Labour's failure on the lack of a parliamentary majority, Tawney countered that this ignored the fact that the most signficant pressures came from outside parliament (i.e. from the press, business and the banks). Its principal failings were that it had acted as an 'obsequious apprentice' to capitalism in office and it had failed to mobilise supporters to its defence: 'it often did the opposite. It courted them with hopes of cheaply won benefits, and if it did not despise them, sometimes it addressed them as though it did.'[63]

After the débâcle of 1931 the Labour Party seemed to undergo a fundamental transformation. The catastrophic electoral defeat left the ranks of the Parliamentary Labour Party decimated. Although their vote had fallen by 2 million (with a fall from 37.1 per cent to 30.6 per cent of the vote), the number of sitting MPs fell from 288 in 1929 to just 52. Much of the PLP leadership was lost in this way or through defection. The ILP voted to leave the Labour Party in 1932. The electoral disaster resulted principally from the Labour government's failure to cope with rising unemployment. It was found wanting both in terms of ideas and political power in the face of the persuasion and financial muscle of the Bank of England, the City of London and international finance houses. Internally, in the aftermath of 1931, the Labour Party was in a state of flux. Some moved to the left, the Socialist League was formed inside the Labour Party to rethink Party policy in the light of the events of 1931. The most notable figure of the Socialist League, Stafford Cripps, shifted dramatically to the left in 1931. His battles with the leadership of the Party led to his eventual exclusion in 1938. After short spells of leadership from Henderson and Lansbury, a compromise candidate, Clement Attlee, emerged as leader in 1935. Perhaps the most significant changes to the Party were organisational, with the increased power of the National Council of Labour (which brought together Labour Executive, Parliamentary Labour Party and TUC General Council members) and the growth of the constituency parties membership to 400,000 by 1935.

The Labour Party, in a decade remembered for the hunger marches, staged only one national demonstration against unemployment, on 5 February 1933 in Hyde Park. The huge attendance made it a striking success and this was followed by equally impressive provincial demonstrations the following week. The Hyde Park demonstration highlights the wasted opportunity for a movement against unemployment with clear official backing. The Hyde Park demonstration also revealed the trade union bureaucracy's sloth and tailing of events. Its initial preparations were over two months after the Determination of Needs Act had softened the means test and after the wave of unemployed agitation of autumn 1932.[64] For the most part, the Labour Party ignored unemployed struggles and their main organisation, the NUWM, because of its communist links. From 1930, the Labour Party and TUC repeatedly mailed 'black' circulars warning local bodies against co-operation with the NUWM and hunger marches.[65] Wal Hannington encapsulated its attitude as 'distant aloofness or open discouragement'.[66]

Admittedly, the sectarianism of the Communist Party (CPGB) during the 'third period' (1928–34) returned that hostility with interest, but during the later 1930s a more complex relationship developed. For example, the NCL, the PLP, the London Labour Party and Trades Council supported the reception demonstration for the 1936 National Hunger March (as long as no communists spoke from the platform) although not the march itself. The NUWM received greater rank-and-file support and participation from Labour Party members and bodies. They also found more MPs willing to work with them. Having said that, the Labour Party was basically isolated from unemployed struggles, a fact that stemmed from the labour movement's very make-up. Trade unions were primarily concerned with their working members rather than with the unemployed and Labour sought reform and parliamentary representation. Hence the extra-parliamentary activities of the unemployed were a double blind-spot. Powerful movements of unemployed agitation of late 1932 or early 1935 left the Labour Party leadership sidelined and confused as to how to respond. For the Labour Party, Margaret Cole pithily observed, the unemployed were 'tiresome creatures' who should join their trade union and 'who had certainly no business to be organising and demonstrating on their own as though they needed special attention'.[67] By contrast, the spontaneous upsurges in unemployed activity naturally drew in the Labour grass-roots in areas such as South Wales or Scotland where Labour Party strength and unemployed militancy coincided.

Prompted by the fact that trade unionists were joining the NUWM or setting up their own associations not connected to the official movement, the TUC did attempt to organise the unemployed. In 1932, the TUC General Council called on local trades councils to set up unemployed associations (after the Labour Party had passed the buck to them). The rationale was that membership of an Unemployed Association might lead a young unemployed worker to join a trade union on finding work. By 1934, there were 123 unemployed associations which had sold 54,000 membership cards in the year. They were mainly recreational centres for sport and socialising, and provided representation for claimants. They did not involve themselves in agitation or self-help work such as boot-repairing as this was seen as a challenge to those in work. Only roughly half the country's trades councils set them up. They were smaller in number than the unemployed clubs of the charitable National Council of Social Services and less influential than the NUWM which the TUC leadership sought to undermine.[68]

The Labour Party's unemployment initiatives were largely restricted to parliament. Up to 1937, only four pamphlets with 41 pages in total had been written about unemployment.[69] Even Hugh Dalton's impressive enquiry into the Depressed Areas came from a conference debate at which the report was counterpoised to action. The ultimate outcome of Labour's *Programme of Immediate Action* borrowed from the programme of the Socialist League but continued to ignore the question of the resistance they had faced in 1924 and 1931 with no mention of the Socialist League's proposal for an Emergency Powers Act. This programme called for nationalisation (of the Bank of England, rail, coal, electricity, gas), a National Investment Board, progressive taxation, action for the distressed areas (to which would be added Lancashire), a 40-hour week and the raising of the school-leaving age.[70] Labour had developed a more detailed formal commitment to planning and nationalisation, but whether this constituted real progress on previous programmes is highly dubious for the reasons that Tawney had identified in 1932: it ignored resistance from the banks, the City of London and big business. Also, experience had proved that Labour's manifesto commitments and policy once in office were two quite different things.

Unemployment continued to feature prominently in the Labour Party's electioneering. In 1935 election leaflets asserted, 'Unemployment is the real issue ... Support Labour and help end poverty' and 'The National government attacks on the unemployed ... If you want fair play for the unemployed vote Labour.' At the same time they continued to defend the achievements of the second Labour government which was associated with the depths of the depression and the disaster of autumn 1931. The National Government simply pointed to the fall in unemployment and strenuously promised measures to deal with the 'Special Areas' of chronic unemployment. For many parts of Britain and especially the middle class, economic recovery was bringing prosperity. In addition, working-class confidence was only just beginning to recover from the triple shock of the defeat of the general strike, mass unemployment and the collapse of 1931. In the 1935 election Labour pulled back from the disaster of 1931 with 154 seats but it continued to be far from its 1929 level of 288 (although it polled a marginally higher percentage of the vote). However, Labour's electoral recovery was uneven and mass unemployment did not necessarily translate into Labour seats. In English towns with the highest unemployment (Sunderland, South Shields, West Hartlepool, Tynemouth, Middlesbrough, Gateshead and Newcastle) Labour lost every seat in 1931 and only gained two seats out of 12 in 1935.[71] Although resulting more from luck than judgement, the Conservative or 'National' recipe of devaluation, economic recovery and appeasement was working for them electorally.

Despite the impression given in political memoirs, the Labour Party in the 1930s was not the womb in which the postwar consensus of Keynesian full employment and welfare state gestated. The Labour Party's conversion to Keynesianism was late. John Maynard Keynes was a Liberal by political persuasion, was closest to Lloyd George's faction of Liberals and had done battle in the 1929 election for the Liberals against Labour. None the less, he briefly attempted to court the Labour Party after the 1931 election through his relationship with Francis Williams, the *Daily Herald* editor. Keynes' efforts were frustrated by his barely concealed disdain for many of Labour's leaders. Keynes' hostility to nationalisation and the conversion of a small number of notable Tory MPs (such as Macmillan and Boothby) to Keynesianism also made Labourites suspicious. Sections of the Labour Party had an alternative radical economic strategy in the shape of under-consumptionism. Many in the party combined this theory with the goal of widespread nationalisation. It was precisely the party leadership that was most resistant to the creeping Keynesianism within its ranks. Thus, during the whole of the 1930s, no official policy document made mention of the defining feature of Keynesian policy: deficit-financing. This is not to say that there were not those who were warming to his views even in the early 1930s. G.D.H. Cole edited a volume entitled *What Everybody Wants to Know about Money* in 1933 which was clearly influenced by Keynes. The penetration of such ideas was aided by the formation of groups designed to put Labour thinking on more solidly researched ground. The New Fabian Research Group and the XYZ Club (which attempted to build links with sympathetic parts of the City of London) both created forums in which Keynesian ideas could be transmitted, but, by the outbreak of war, Keynesianism was still not official Labour policy.

Labour was transformed in the 1930s but mainly in organisations terms. Whilst it is true that the level of economic debate had improved, it produced no original insights. Its programmes had been modified, but in essence differed little from *Labour and the New Social Order* written in 1917. It continued to make great capital out of unemployment, but there was no reason to believe that Labour would be any more effective in dealing with it in office than it had before. Above all, Labour turned its back on workers' and unemployed struggles as a means of winning concessions and continued to focus almost exclusively on elections and parliament.

Meanwhile, the real impact of unemployment was felt, not in the Cabinet or trade union head offices, but in the homes and on the streets of working-class communities up and down the country. Here, amidst the blight of despair, a struggle ensued which undermines the myth of consensus and the idea that protest was marginal and limited. It is to this phenomenon that we now turn.

5   Unemployed Struggles

> The Jarrow March which took place at the same time as ours equally was of significance, but over the years the media and the establishment have put it to the fore and have virtually ignored the NUWM march.
>
> John Lochmore, Scottish hunger marcher[1]

> There was never any concession by way of improved scales of relief or better administration of unemployment insurance and poor law relief which has not had to be wrung from the governments ...
>
> Wal Hannington, *Problem of the Depressed Areas*, 1937[2]

The received wisdom suggests that the Jarrow March epitomised the unemployed struggle during the 1930s: 207 rain-soaked men backed by all-party local support organised by Jarrow town council, staging an apolitical local protest, drawing media sympathy but having no impact on government. Sir Bernard Ingham, Margaret Thatcher's former-press secretary, presented a three-part BBC documentary, the *Road to Jarrow*, which insisted on this view. Alan Travis confidently asserted in the *Guardian*: 'The 1930s saw failed attempts to create mass movements to highlight the plight of the unemployed with the most successful being the Jarrow Crusade in 1936.'[3] This confirms the enduring the myth of British history that extra-parliamentary action is symbolic and marginal rather than agitational and effective. The idea that change is gradual, peaceful, conducted from on high and centres on parliament serves the Labour and Conservative Parties' own views of history. All this is highly misleading because more typical and 'most successful' were the hunger marches and protests of the National Unemployed Workers' Movement (NUWM), an organisation with a communist leadership that addressed unemployment from an agitational and extra-parliamentary direction.

Rather than retelling the NUWM's history, this chapter concentrates on an assessment of its role and an account of its major unemployed struggles in the light of contemporaries' and historians' reactions.[4] These events allow us to probe the character of unemployment and to compare experiences of unemployed political action internationally. After 1923 and 1936, the NUWM suffered periods of deep malaise and, in the latter case, disintegration because of the difficulties of sustaining a movement based on the unemployed. These periods are much easier to explain, as they conform to the consensus of contemporary social psychologists that unemployment led to apathy and resignation.

The National Unemployed Workers' Movement and its Major Battles

The National Unemployed Workers' Committee Movement, as it was called until 1929, was established on 15 April 1921 amidst agitation of unemployed ex-servicemen and engineers. This unrest initally centred on London, but at the NUWCM's launch, unemployed groups from 50 towns were represented. There were two major phases of unemployed agitation: 1919–22 and 1931–36. These two periods saw very rapid growth in membership and the ability to mobilise on the streets. While the national hunger marches, which it organised in 1922, 1929, 1930, 1932, 1934 and 1936, are the feature most deeply etched into popular memory, its activities were considerably wider than that. The organisation also led local protests outside local authorities charged with setting the rates of relief, physically prevented evictions, won rent reductions, played a role in industrial disputes such as the engineering dispute of 1922 and the General Strike of 1926, and even, on a few occasions, raided factories where overtime was being worked. As one NUWM activist from North Shields remembered the response to an eviction notice: 'The family asked the NUWM for help. When the bailiffs arrived members of the NUWM were waiting. They told the bailiffs that if they went into the house their van would be turned over. The bailiffs left.'[5]

In addition, the NUWM played an important role advising and representing the unemployed. The movement took part in over 2,000 appeals tribunals for those threatened with disallowance or reduction in benefit, of which a third were successful. Many members were expert in the bewildering unemployment regulations and sold pamphlets detailing changes to unemployment rules.[6]

1919–23

The NUWCM was formed out of postwar unemployed militancy. By the end of this first phase of unemployed unrest the movement had undisputed leadership of unemployed protest. Harry McShane remembered the unemployed of Glasgow in January 1921 chasing

T.J. MacNamara, the Chancellor of the Exchequer, round the town, with Jimmy MacDougall demanding, to the delight of the crowd, a 'million pounds or bloody revolution'. Two months later, 2,000 'really wild' unemployed men, some, according to McShane, armed with hand grenades and guns, angrily received the Prince of Wales.[7]

In the summer of 1921, the London-based organisation was able to stage a march to the Labour Party Conference. Agitation amongst the unemployed had grown as their numbers mounted. The government *Reports on Revolutionary Organisations* record unemployed protests across nearly every industrial area of the country. The London District Committee of Unemployed and George Lansbury (the leader of the rebel Poplar council) urged the unemployed to 'Go to the Guardians' to put pressure the local administrators of poor relief to increase their scales, give outdoor relief and forgo task work. For example, when the Wandsworth Poor Law Guardians imposed application to the workhouse as a criterion for receiving relief, the unemployed of Wandsworth tramped to the workhouse *en masse*, forcing the Guardians to abandon their plans. John Marriot, in his study of London's East End, noted that unemployed agitation brought uneven but clear concessions in relief and lenient conditions from the local Board of Guardians.[8] The campaign against the Guardians continued as the NUWCM designated the second week of October as a national week of action, drawing hundreds of thousands in London and the provinces. On 13 October, regional demonstrations coincided with a NUWCM delegation to the Ministers of Labour, Health and Agriculture. Official sources spoke of 59 demonstrations with 50,000 participants.[9] Five days later, dependants' allowances were established and uncovenanted benefit extended to shield the Guardians from pressure from the unemployed.

Many urban centres became the scene of unemployed activity, sometimes only briefly. George Garrett detailed the development of the unemployed militancy in Liverpool in 1921 and 1922. In the inital stages, begging gave way to demonstrations of ex-servicemen led by an ex-police striker, a parson and left-wingers. From September 1921, large local demonstrations of up to 20,000 pressed the Poor Law Guardians, parading around shopping centres and the Art Gallery. On several occasions they were baton charged and activists were hauled before the magistrate. His account reached its climax with the departure of the Liverpool contingent of hunger march of 1922.[10]

The NUWCM was able to hold its first national conference in November 1921. The rowdiness of the assembly testified to the temper of the unemployed at this time. Meanwhile, agitation continued with the slogan 'Go to the Factories'. The unemployed would occupy factory premises where it was known that large-scale overtime was being worked. They would argue that overtime should be cut so that more workers could be taken on. After some initial successes this campaign petered out. In the new year the movement faced two major challenges: the engineering lock-out and the 'gap'. The engineering employers locked out their workers in an attempt to cut wages. The industry provided many of the recruits to the NUWCM and was a former stronghold of the shop stewards' movement. Despite the ultimate defeat of the engineers, the NUWCM helped picketing and presented a successful argument amongst the unemployed against scabbing. In April 1922, the government introduced a five-week gap to the right to unemployment benefit once a worker had exhausted covenanted benefit. After sustained agitation in the summer, the gap was reduced from five weeks to just one.[11]

This first period of activity culminated in an unplanned but very significant development: the NUWCM's first national hunger march. Contingents arrived in London during the winter of 1922–23. By 1923 the NUWCM was recognised as the national organisation of the unemployed and the TUC General Council sought its co-operation in the organisation of a national demonstration against unemployment.

1931–36

The second major phase of unemployed activism resulted from the crisis and fall of the second Labour government in the autumn of 1931.[12] The National government of Ramsay MacDonald's introduction of cuts in the dole, transitional payments and the household means test provoked demonstrations throughout the industrial areas. Though continuing to suffer from a high turnover, the NUWM membership grew at the rate of over 2,000 a week.[13] Even the crushing electoral defeat for Labour did not quell unemployed activity.

1932 began with violence when in January unemployed demonstrators clashed with police in Rochdale and Glasgow. Outside Keighley Town Hall on the 15th, both police and the Territorial Army confronted an unemployed demonstration and twelve were arrested in the fracas that ensued. Three days later, the cases of 13 Glasgow unemployed who had been arrested on an earlier march were heard. Baton-wielding police attacked the thousands who assembled outside in protest but, to the crowds delight, the accused – Harry McShane and his comrades – were found not guilty. Late February saw more unemployed struggles with the 1,500-strong

Scottish hunger march descending on Edinburgh. The unemployed did battle with police in Parliament Square and 15,000 unemployed fought the police in Bristol. These actions spilled over into March, with large demonstrations in Dundee on the 3rd and Newcastle on the 14th, the latter attracting some 100,000.

The NUWM then made considerable efforts for the National Day of Demonstration against the means test scheduled for 3 April, with protests organised in several major towns. At this point the NUWM focused its activities on a petition against the means test (which gathered a million signatures) as their agitation continued and bitterness intensified. During a July protest in Castleford, Arthur Speight, one of the demonstrators, died and subsequently local NUWM leaders were imprisoned. It was not until September that the struggle of the unemployed was to surpass the early months of the year with the events in Birkenhead and Belfast.

In Birkenhead, from 13 September, there were five days of demonstrations, rioting and vicious police raids on working-class areas. A protest outside the Public Assistance Committee, demanding more generous relief, boots, coal and work schemes, triggered the events. Baton charges against the demonstrators provoked fierce fighting, with 37 civilians hospitalised on the night of Thursday, 15th, four with fractured skulls.[14] Three nights of police raids in working-class areas of Birkenhead followed, on the pretext of looking for looted goods. During these operations, the police pulled people from their beds, beat them and flung them into police vans. Over 100 were hospitalised with injuries including broken ribs, arms, legs and pelvis. One eyewitness described the scene of police smashing down doors, beating victims and abusing women and children.

> Twelve police rushed into the room and immediately knocked down my husband, splitting open his head and kicking him as he lay on the floor ... When I tried to prevent them hitting my husband they commenced to baton me all over my arms and body; as they were hitting my husband and me the children were screaming, the police shouted: 'Shut up you parish-fed bastards!'[15]

The pitched battles with the police continued until the 18th. Over the weekend, 65 were admitted to the General Hospital – 45 civilians and 20 police. On Monday, 19 September, despite the arrest of the NUWM leaders, 20,000 assembled outside the meeting of the PAC and were joined by workers from Cammell Laird's who had downed tools in sympathy. Three facts bear witness to the determination of the people of Birkenhead. First, the mayor and Chief Constable were considering military intervention. Second, the Tory council raised PAC scales of relief by 3s 6d, promised £170,000 for public works schemes and sent a message of opposition to the means test to the government.[16] Third, the House of Commons reverberated with the din made in Birkenhead when the events were debated on the 18 October.

The situation in Birkenhead signalled an upsurge in unemployed militancy and NUWM membership.[17] It fuelled further clashes with the police and the national hunger march of 1932. Three days after the end of the Birkenhead events fighting broke out in Liverpool between the police and 20,000 unemployed. A week later, a similar number of unemployed in West Ham were involved in fierce fighting with the police, which reignited a few days later. The unemployed of North Shields followed suit when police baton-charged a demonstration of 3,000 *en route* to the Public Assistance Office. Running battles with the police ensued before eight 'evilly disposed persons', as they were described by the prosecution, were arrested, seven of whom were imprisoned for between six and 12 months.[18] The rising tide of struggle reached new heights in Belfast, where the longest and most serious violence and rioting occurred from 5 to 14 October. Initially, 2,000 relief workers went on strike. The strikers organised protests, marches and rallies, which brought clashes with the police and spread the movement to Derry. By the 10th, the Relief Workers Strike Committee was organising a rent and school strike. Indeed the authorities raised the stakes by drafting in police reinforcements and by calling on the army to suppress the unemployed who were increasing taking recourse to street-fighting to defend themselves. The British state deployed armed police, armoured cars and even machine guns against the unemployed. On several occasions, the police opened fire on the protesters, killing two. In response, barricades were thrown up across Belfast in the Falls Road and the Shankill Road areas; in the former, pavement was torn up and trenches dug. The mood of resistance spread to those in work. Three thousand workers at a Belfast linen factory voted for sympathy strike action with the relief workers, and the Belfast Trades Council voted for a general strike. The state was only able to diffuse the movement by a combination of repression and concession. There were waves of arrests and massive mobilisations of police, B-specials and army. At the same time, relief scales were raised considerably, doubling the relief for an unemployed family of man, wife and one child.[19]

The events of Belfast and Birkenhead provided the backdrop for the 2,000-strong hunger march to London. Its first contingent set off from Scotland on 26 September and converged on London on 26 October. At the journey's end they were to present a 1 million-signature petition against the means test. As with the other hunger marches, they were met on the way with a mixed reception from the local labour movement. In many places, they received support from the local Labour Parties and trades councils; others, such as Stratford-on-Avon Labour Party, following the advice of the official leadership and press, shunned them. The marchers also had to contend with inconsistent treatment from local authorities when they were forced to sleep in the workhouse. They would demonstrate against the imposition of casual conditions (that is, being treated as vagrants and therefore having their possessions confiscated). These marchers also faced police violence on several occasions so that, by their arrival in London, there were many wounded among their number. In an attempt to discredit the marchers, the press printed police advice to shopkeepers that they should board up their premises on the hunger march route. Once they had arrived in London, ten days of intensive agitation followed. The NUWM leadership attempted to organise the various contingents in a series of demonstrations that would have culminated in the presentation of the petition to the House of Commons and these marches resulted in several clashes with police. Mass demonstrations were held in Hyde Park and Trafalgar Square, Hannington putting the number on the second protest, on Sunday, 30 October, at 150,000.[20] On both occasions demonstrators skirmished with the police; at the former there were 12 arrests, and 19 police and 58 civilians injured.[21] On 1 September, Special Branch arrested Hannington, bringing the unemployed onto the streets in protest. The hunger marchers finally left London on 5 November.

This agitation coincided with the first year of Ramsay MacDonald's National government. The activities of the NUWM combined with and channelled the spontaneous anger of the unemployed, who were facing cuts and uncertainty at a time when the Labour Party was in disarray. Despite the press slander, the movement was able to mobilise large numbers when the British working-class movement was at its most despondent for many years. For a time after the 1932 hunger march, unemployed activism quietened down. There were no more explosions on the level of Birkenhead or Belfast, and NUWM branches returned to more routine matters. Then in June and July 1933, regional hunger marches took place notably in Lancashire and Scotland. A national hunger march was organised to arrive on 24 and 25 February 1934. Again, this brought a massive demonstration in Hyde Park on the 24th. The marchers demanded the abolition of the means test and the restoration of the 10 per cent cuts of October 1931. They persistently demanded a hearing in the House of Commons, ignoring police bans and making their way into the House to protest at MacDonald's refusal to receive them. When the House debated this large numbers of Labour MPs were now in favour of receiving the marchers' delegates. Although the Commons motion to allow the marchers a hearing was lost, the latter focused the public eye on the cuts and considerable pressure for the restoration from several quarters mounted. In the light of this, the NUWM called a demonstration on the Sunday before the budget. Despite shunning the marchers and repeatedly stating that the cuts would not be restored, the government retreated in the April 1934 budget.[22]

The new Unemployment Act of 1934 precipitated the strongest torrent of unemployed protest across the country. The Act resulted from the 1932 *Final Report of the Royal Commission into Unemployment Insurance*, which recommended a reorganisation of unemployment insurance and the creation of an Unemployment Assistance Board to relieve all the unemployed who did not qualify for insurance.[23] The UAB brought cuts, national scales of relief rather than the local rates of the PACs, and intricate rules for the calculation of benefit which reinforced the role of the detested means test. Despite becoming law in May and its operation beginning in July 1934, its provisions were introduced over an extended period. In October, rumblings of discontent produced local demonstrations demanding winter relief from PACs in Forfar, Glasgow, Rhondda and Newport. Part II of the Act passed the relief of all unemployed not eligible for unemployment insurance benefit to the UAB. Its scales of relief were announced in December and were to be implemented from the 7 January 1935.[24] The scales and their imposition sparked furious protest.

By January, broad opposition to the UAB was developing. The South Wales Miners Federation (SWMF) called a regional conference to organise resistance. The new scales found critics amongst doctors, Public Assistance Committees and even some local councils. As the UAB scales were implemented in early January, hundreds of thousands faced benefit cuts or disallowances. The means test under the UAB was now much harsher than had been expected and forged a militant movement of opposition. On Sunday, 21 January, 60,000 marched on Pontypridd, and 40,000 descended on Merthyr the following day. Miners' branches in the area were discussing strike action against the UAB. The demonstrations gathered force as 20,000 turned out in both Glasgow and Pontypridd on 23 January. On the Saturday, 1,600 delegates met for the All-South Wales Conference against the new Act. The Cambrian Combine miners of the Rhondda declared they would strike if Part II of the Act was not withdrawn by 25 February.

On the 30th, after heated debates in the Commons, the MacDonald government responded with small concessions over the strictness of the means test and the scales for larger families, but this was not enough to halt the growing movement of opposition. On the 31st, 10,000 marched to the docks in North Shields in an attempt to persuade the dockers to strike and then went on to the Council. The greatest demonstrations took place on 3 February, with the *Manchester Guardian* estimating 300,000 on the streets of South Wales. The following day, women and children marched on the Merthyr UAB to protest at the difficulties of trying to feed a family on the new scales, and there were demonstrations across Britain, with a protest of 30,000 on Tyneside.

On the 5th, desperate to quell the storm of protest, the government announced it would withdraw the cuts brought about by the new regulations. The following day in Sheffield, in the face of opposition from the local Labour leadership, 40,000 called for the immediate withdrawal of the cuts. The police tried to disperse the crowd and two hours of street fighting ensued, with 26 arrests and 9 police injured.[25] Three participants recalled the events. Herbert Howarth remembered:

> And I looks back and the next lot were ... coming round the corner and the bloody police charged – no question, just charged them. And for the two and a half hours there was bloody pandemonium, fighting like bloody tigers – and all the bloody Town Hall officials were out on the bloody balcony watching us.

George Fradley witnessed:

> The demonstrators broke every banner and used every form of missile that they could and fought the police until ... the police were absolutely beaten ... we went back to Barkers Pool and held a meeting and decided that unless the cuts were restored [at once] we would have an even bigger demonstration.

Another, Sid Bingham, related, 'If ever I've seen fear on men's faces it was on some of the policemen's faces.'[26]

Sheffield councillors travelled to London in a state of alarm. They requested the immediate reversal of the cuts and the government yielded. This concession spurred protest up and down the country on 9 February, as others areas pressed for the same treatment as Sheffield. In the days that followed there were violent demonstrations in Maryport, Cumberland and Dundee. Harassed and unable to control events, the government dramatically retreated by introducing the Standstill Act on 15 February. Many, but not all, unemployed had lost out with the switch from the old transitional benefits to the UAB scale. Faced with this confused situation, the government granted each unemployed individual whichever benefit scale was the higher for them. The unemployed, the NUWM, the ILP, the CPGB (and the sections of the Labour movement that had participated without official sanction) had secured a major victory over the

National government. The campaign against the UAB was the high point of unemployed activity and secured by militant means a major concession and an embarrassing government U-turn. An NUWM circular underlined its significance:

> We have scored one of the greatest victories in the history of the British working class movement. The National government, in the face of the tremendous storm of working class demonstrations and mass action, led by the NUWM, has been compelled to make a humiliating retreat to restore the cuts that were imposed under the new scales and to suspend part II of the Unemployment Act.[27]

The activity soon died down, but was rekindled in autumn 1936, the last significant phase of unemployed protest. On 10 July 1936, the government announced that new national UAB scales were to be introduced in mid-November. These were to be more generous than their predecessors and they were prepared with utmost caution. Cabinet minutes recorded: 'Every sentence had to be examined as presentation of the case was all important.'[28] From the announcement the CPGB and the NUWM swiftly set about building alliances for a hunger march. The National Hunger March of 1936 and its London Reception Committee (which included five Labour MPs) signalled the broadest unity in action the NUWM had ever achieved. In South Wales, a Council of Action was set up, which included the South Wales Miners Federation, the Welsh TUC and the Labour Party. The Labour Party leadership was worried that, as in January 1935, it would be sidelined by mass opposition to UAB scales. A Labour Research Department pamphlet, *Standards of Starvation*, expected a repetition of the events of January 1935.[29] Despite the National Council of Labour's attempts to stage a moderate campaign, the National Hunger March seized the imagination of the labour movement. In these circumstances, the NCL backed the National Hunger March's reception demonstration in Hyde Park, whilst continuing the 'black circular' policy with regard to the march itself.

The government faced not only the National Hunger March, but also the Jarrow Crusade and the Blind Marchers (who sought amendments to the Blind Persons Act). While the National Hunger March worried the Cabinet the most, they adopted the same hostile attitude to all three marches, publishing a press release denouncing the protests and stating that they caused 'much hardship to many of those taking part in them and are only a method of exploiting the unfortunate without bringing any real advantage'.[30] Although the Jarrow Crusade received the most publicity (though this has subsequently been exaggerated), the newspapers followed all three marches with interest. While October–November 1936 was no repeat of January 1935 and there was no spontaneous local protest on a comparable scale, the events of the previous year had only begun in earnest after the implementation of the new scales. The National Hunger March Hyde Park demonstration was massive – with the *Daily Herald* claiming a quarter of a million. This, combined with the press spotlight and questions in the House of Commons, led the National government to postpone the new scales.[31]

The Record of the National Unemployed Workers' Movement

The NUWM provoked sharply polarised views among contemporaries and continues to divide historians. George Orwell toured the depressed areas via a network of NUWM members while writing *The Road to Wigan Pier*. In that book he was disparaging of the Left and in his diary described an NUWM public meeting at which Hannington's speech was 'all padding and cliché'.[32] Judge Justice Charles, presiding over the case of the Birkenhead NUWM leaders, described them as the 'very worst friends of the unemployed'.[33] Mainstream newspapers, not averse to red-baiting, were wholly unsympathetic to the NUWM and alerted readers to its Moscow links. The Labour Party and its press denounced the organisation in similar fashion. Not all contemporary commentators were so negative though. E.W. Bakke, the American sociologist, in his study of London's unemployed, wrote that though 'unpleasant to the rest of society' and though the unemployed were drawn into its influence because of the 'hardness of their circumstances or flaws in their own character', he believed that 'these demonstrations are crude but eloquent testimony that human nature is not yet demoralised to the brute level of existence'.[34]

Historians have disagreed over the size, importance and impact of the organisation. The liberal historians, Stevenson and Cook, argued that the demonstrations and marches of the NUWM 'achieved very little and faded into obscurity'.[35] At its height in the early 1930s with some 3 million unemployed, the NUWM had 40,000 members. The obvious conclusion is that the minute fraction of the unemployed who joined the movement showed how marginal it was to the experience of the majority of the unemployed. But this bald statistic is misleading as it assumes that a mass organisation of the unemployed was a viable possibility and that the NUWM failed in the task of forming one. Comparison with the other working-class organisations shows the weakness of such an assumption. If the implicit comparison is between the NUWM and union density of 23 per cent in 1933, then the unemployed movement failed. But organising unions in the workplace is entirely different from organising the unemployed, and the NUWM could not rely on the collective routine and conditions of the pit or factory. Numbers constantly flowed in and out of unemployment, they were subject to different schemes of relief and experienced domestic and sometimes geographical isolation. Alternatively, comparison of the NUWM with working class party membership is more flattering. The Labour Party in 1935 had 400,000 members and claimed to represent the working class, which comprised the larger part of the population. Given the uncertainties of unemployment and the insistence on the payment of membership dues from the unemployed, the peak figure of 23,000 paid-up members with at least 400,000 who at some time or other had been a member of the organisation is in itself impressive.[36]

As it is misleading to compare the NUWM with trade unions or political parties, unemployed movements should be judged in their own terms, that is, by the broader historical experience of hunger marchers and unemployed movements. The record of the NUWM stands up favourably to such scrutiny. Most obviously, despite half-hearted attempts to create alternatives to the NUWM by Sylvia Pankhurst and the TUC, there was never a serious rival to the NUWM as a national organisation of the unemployed. Caution should be sounded when the Jarrow Crusade success is counterposed to NUWM failure. It is doubtful whether the Jarrow hunger march would have been conceived without the precedents set by the NUWM. Wal Hannington advised Ellen Wilkinson on four separate occasions on how to organise the march and the NUWM organised the reception demonstration for the Crusade in London. According to Wilkinson, the Jarrow marchers viewed them not as competitors but as comrades, 'To them, these other marchers were a welcome sign that other men felt the same as they did, and they were kicking too.'[37] Harry McShane, heading the Scottish contingent of the 1936 NUWM hunger march, echoed these sentiments.[38] If we compare the NUWM with the experience of unemployed movements before and after, its size and ability to mobilise exceed the efforts of the ILP and SDF in the late 1880s and 1890s or the Right of Work Campaign or People's March for Jobs of the late 1970s and early 1980s. Contemporary international comparisons are also instructive. Although the struggle had greater intensity in Germany in 1930–31 this was largely because unemployment was a much more catastrophic experience there and the German Communist Party (KPD) was much larger than the CPGB.[39] The NUWM had a greater permanence and more concrete achievements than the European and American unemployed movements of the interwar years.

Furthermore, the NUWM should not be judged simply in terms of its membership figures as these show only those who were able to pay their dues and ignores the numbers passively sympathetic or actively drawn into NUWM-inspired agitation. It is impossible to know how many of the unemployed were sympathetic to the NUWM as most contemporary social investigators of unemployment dodged this question. A Pilgrim's Trust investigator noted that 'the majority of those who spoke about it evidently valued it', despite the investigator's prejudice that it tended to encourage men not to find work.[40] The demonstrations organised by the NUWM could attract very large numbers, some one hundred or so thousand on occasion. Though contradicted by police sources (and historians who use these as evidence), numerous eye-witness accounts confirm such figures. The NUWM membership was in effect a minority that was able to engage with and agitate amongst much greater numbers of those without work. The success and impact of this agitation is a much better gauge of the movement's success or failure than its membership figures. Harry McShane, the Scottish NUWM organiser, remembered:

> We were very careful that only those with membership cards could vote at our meetings, but our activities were never confined to our membership. We constantly organised mass activity in which most of the people demonstrating were not actual paying members.[41]

Max Cohen, who was unemployed for long spells, mentions the movement twice in his memoirs, *I Was One of the Unemployed*.[42] He was drawn into an unemployed demonstration in his native 'Forgeton' and makes reference to the advantages of being represented by someone from the 'unemployed organisation' at the Courts of Referees. This is probably a typical experience of hundreds of thousands of unemployed workers: Cohen, though not a member, knew the NUWM did good work and had participated in one, perhaps more, of its demonstrations.

Harry Harmer has examined internal Communist International criticism that the NUWM failed to build a mass revolutionary organisation of the unemployed and argues that the NUWM was a peripheral organisation that met with little success.[43] The relationship of the NUWM to the Communist Party of Great Britain and the Communist International does raise important insights into its character and development. Whilst the press repeatedly stressed these links in the campaign against the NUWM, and the Home Office and Scotland Yard treated the organisation as an agent of a foreign power, the NUWM was not a creature of the Comintern.

Initially, the NUWM developed from spontaneous agitation amongst the unemployed. Thus began amongst ex-servicemen's organisations or independent socialist groupings such as John

MacLean's Tramp's Trust Unlimited in Glasgow and when unemployed agitation began, the British Communist Party was only in the process of forming. Only later did the NUWM come under communist leadership and even then, the NUWM was able to retain a degree of independence from the CPGB, which caused serious tensions between Hannington and members of the Communist Party Central Committee (CC), especially from 1928 onwards. The leadership of the CPGB itself was divided between the 'Young Turks', who sought slavish implementation of the Comintern line – now firmly under Stalin's control – and more experienced working-class activists such as Hannington.[44] There were two attempts to unseat Hannington from the CC, in 1929 and again 1933, with the latter being successful.[45] Hannington and McShane's objections in December 1933 to the hasty preparation, at the CPGB's initiative, of the 1934 Hunger March (they were defeated on this issue) provide another example of these tensions.

Within certain limits, the NUWM was also able to develop a policy that was at odds with Executive Committee of the Communist International (ECCI) instructions. One of the key questions here was over the nature of the organisation itself, so that whereas the NUWM based itself on a dues-paying membership, the Communist International and the Communist Party insisted on several occasions on a wider membership. This reflected the German Communist Party's (KPD) practice, which established broad committees at Labour Exchanges. The KPD was the largest Communist Party outside the Soviet Union and had enthusiastically adopted the social fascist line (even calling on Communist Party children to attack Social Democrat schoolmates: 'Chase the young Zorgiebiels out of the playground!'). At the International Congress on Unemployment which the Communist International called, it was Walter Ulbricht, the German Communist, who delivered the presidential address calling for the German type of organisation, instructing the English Communists to abandon subscriptions as the criterion for membership.[46] NUWM leaders such as Hannington and McShane came in for criticism within the International but were able to weather it. The adoption of the popular front line was another such occasion. For Harry Pollitt and Will Gallagher, the people's front meant the unification of the NUWM and the TUC unemployed associations under TUC control. At a January 1936 CC meeting, Pollitt rounded on the two NUWM leaders:

> We cannot be satisfied with the speech of comrade Hannington and the speech of comrade McShane. Why? Because these are comrades who say they are in agreement with the new turn that Party wants to make in relation to the unemployed, but their

speeches were devoted 1 percent to agreeing with the line, 99 per cent to explaining difficulties in operating the line ... We expect there will be no further doubt or hesitations on this question.[47]

As McShane recounts:

In the NUWM we didn't always work according to the party line, and Hannington and I were put on the carpet a number of times. We got away with being unorthodox because the NUWM was the only mass organisation the party had and Wal Hannington had great personal standing within the party.[48]

The sheer impracticality of many Comintern suggestions aided Hannington and McShane's room for manoeuvre, a fact that must have been apparent to rank-and-file CPGB and NUWM members alike.

Despite Hannington's degree of autonomy, Communist Party links profoundly affected the NUWM. There was a near constant pressure on the NUWM to move in the direction of the Comintern policy, and the strategic inadequacies of ultra-leftism (1928–34) followed by popular frontism (1935–39) certainly damaged the NUWM. In the former period the vicious attacks that were concentrated on the Labour Left weakened their ability to mobilise, but it would have been a greater mistake to fudge criticism of the Labour government and those who defected from Labour to the National government. Also, the NUWM was never as sectarian as the CPGB. The popular front period coincided with the decline of unemployed militancy and left-wing eyes turned to Spain. In these circumstances the NUWM virtually abandoned mass activity in favour of stunts involving small numbers such as carrying coffins, protests at high-class hotels and the like.

Despite the deficiencies of Stalinism, the Communist Party's network of sympathisers and cadre did allow the NUWM to survive through the ups and downs of unemployed struggles. Having gained organisational skills and experience as shop stewards or within the Minority Movement, Communist Party recruits who then lost their jobs would join the NUWM, with both organisations reaping the benefits. With the growth of unemployment in the early 1930s a situation of mutual dependency developed so that in 1931 49 per cent of the CPGB were unemployed as were 60 per cent in 1932.[49] The unemployed who joined the party and stayed cut their teeth on unemployed struggles and would later go to Spain or rebuild the unions. Jack Dash, the famous dockers' union activist, was recruited to the CPGB via the NUWM. Will Paynter, who was to become a

South Wales NUM official, noted the importance of NUWM work was to his development:

> I joined this movement and there was hardly a Wednesday or Friday, the days when we were required to sign on to qualify for benefit, when we did not hold a meeting, and it was this I believe that helped me more than anything to turn me into a fairly good speaker, but it took a fair time.[50]

These skills played a crucial part for a generation of engineering shops stewards in Manchester, Coventry, London, Sheffield and elsewhere, who rebuilt trade union confidence in an age of rearmament and war.[51]

Elections highlighted some of the limitations of the NUWM. There is no evidence to link its activity with advantage for Labour or other candidates of the Left, and the high-points in unemployed protest coincided with the Labour catastrophes in 1931 and 1935. When the NUWM did field candidates, or NUWM members stood as Communist Party candidates, they had very poor showings at the polls. Even Wal Hannington could muster only 9.5 per cent in the June 1934 Merthyr Tydfil by-election; in the 1929 election he stood in Wallsend and did even worse. The NUWM made even less impact on high politics which the 'Baldwinite consensus' dominated from 1922 to 1940.

The weakness of the NUWM can also be seen in terms of its press. Though they tried on several occasions, the unemployed workers' movement failed to establish a stable regular paper for financial reasons. Some papers achieved partial success during the peaks in activity – the fortnightly *Out of Work* (1921–23), for example, achieved a readership of 60,000. Again, from July 1932 to November 1935, a regular paper, the *Unemployed Leader* (though it was called *Unemployed Special* for its first four issues) attained a circulation of 15,000–19,000. On other occasions the launches of unemployed newspapers, such as the *Unemployed Worker* or *Unemployed Charter*, failed.[52] This experience proved that it was only possible to establish a self-financing press based on sales to the unemployed when the movement was strong. The dynamic of unemployed protest rested on external factors (new government regulations or increasing unemployment) which brought short-lived surges in unemployed activity. Building a stable organisation and a stable press in such conditions was an impossibility, as the reports of the other unemployed movements demonstrated. After a monthly circulation of 485,000 in June 1931, most of the German unemployed papers folded within months and the same was true of unemployed newspapers across Europe.[53]

Stevenson and Cook argue that mass action occurred only in exceptional local circumstances and challenge the idea that the NUWM was nationally coherent in any meaningful sense. Its implantation was regionally uneven, with strong representation from engineering and mining areas of South Wales, Scotland, Coventry, the North-East and South Lancashire. In the 'little Moscow' of Mardy, for example, there was a branch of 1,500, with half paying regular dues.[54] Relatively large towns would have no NUWM until the height of activity, as Hannington noted, when several new branches formed in 1932. The NUWM appeared to have several faces. Harry McShane described how the NUWM in Edinburgh devoted itself almost exclusively to casework at Courts of Referees, while Glasgow branches saw this as secondary to agitation; and unlike Glasgow, Dundee UWM needed a prod from the outside to challenge a local police ban on demonstrations. Likewise, Richard Croucher recognised considerable variation in the outlook of local branches, which ranged from the non-militant 'self-help' approach of kids' parties, advice and public meetings of Bury St Edmunds to the regular agitation and militancy of the Tyneside or Clydeside branches. However, the extremes belie a common but uneven experience because national changes in provision (the means test or the UAB scales) or the nationwide effects of major, often local, struggles such as Birkenhead, Belfast or the hunger marches bound the unemployed together in a shared experience.

The contrast between casework and agitation should not be drawn too sharply as the two were mutually beneficial. Whilst Harmer urged that casework was the only significant success of the movement and its only real attraction for the unemployed, NUWM did not carry out casework in the spirit of the trade union legal departments which conducted comparable work and saw regulations as immutable boundaries which could only be challenged in Parliament. Frank Stillwell, head of the TGWU legal department, wrote to the chair of the North region stating, 'We have been inundated with claims arising out of the Anomalies regulations', but that it was 'hopeless to appeal' because of 'very close fencing which has been established under the ... Act'.[55] The NUWM combined protest and casework in the hope of breaking down such fencing. After all, the Umpire had recognised the NUWM in 1930 as a legitmate representative of the unemployed in the disqualifications and appeals procedures.

The NUWM's achievement were made in the face of very adverse conditions. The Ministry of Health, the Ministry of Labour and the police all tried – and failed – to prevent the hunger marches and settled for continually harassing them. The 1922 hunger marchers were refused the right to sign on for benefit outside their home town and the Ministry of Health treated them as vagrants when they entered the workhouse for accommodation, but the marchers became adept at protesting against the imposition of such conditions, usually making workhouse governors concede.[56] The police found various ways to make life difficult for the organisation. They drew their truncheons against the marchers on several occasions, such as during the 1932 march in Stratford-on-Avon. Special Branch infiltrated the last three hunger marches and the NUWM leadership, and plain clothes police tailed NUWM leaders.[57] They often imposed local bans on demonstrations or street meetings, but the movement usually defied these bans and reclaimed the right of assembly.[58] The movement was also subject to arrests. In 1932 alone, the police arrested 400 NUWM members; in that year, several leaders were imprisoned – Wal Hannington for three months, Sid Elias for two years, Emrhys Llewellyn and the 75-year-old Tom Mann for two months.[59] Some of the movement's leaders had several brushes with the courts and spells in jail: the authorities jailed Hannington five times in ten years.

At times, parliament and the press chose to ignore unemployed protestors. Prime Minister Bonar Law refused to meet a marchers' delegation and this established a pattern that was to be repeated time and again. Successive prime ministers refused every hunger march, including the Jarrow Crusade, a hearing. The labour movement refused the NUWM affiliation or official recognition, although briefly in the mid-1920s there was a joint advisory committee between the TUC General Council and the NUWM to raise the question of unemployment. Even at this time, the TUC still denied NUWM affiliation to its ranks because it believed the unemployed should remain in their former unions and this joint advisory council broke down in 1925 because the TUC wanted to distance themselves from militant protest.[60] The TUC not only refused to support all the NUWM national hunger marches but also the South Wales unemployed miners' march of 1927 and even the Jarrow Crusade. The General Council circularised local trades councils against supporting the latter, with the result that the Conservative Party put the marchers up in Sheffield, Chesterfield and Nottingham. The record of the Labour Party was, if anything, worse. In February 1930 the Labour Party issued the so-called black circulars banning Labour Party members from joining the NUWM (or the Minority Movement, Friends of Soviet Russia because of their links with the CPGB). The Jarrow Crusade was denounced from the platform of the 1936 Labour Party conference for sending hungry, ill-clad men across the country to London. Any balance sheet of unemployed protest should take account of such serious obstacles. The historian Maureen Turnbull contends that in the face of such persistent disruption from the authorities, 'The fact that the marches took place and reached their destination is in itself no inconsiderable achievement.'[61]

Local and national concessions provide another measure of NUWM success. While unemployed protest was wider than the NUWM, they were the organisational focus of much of it. In assessing the impact of the NUWM, we have to consider the wider threat that the unemployed posed to the authorities. Many concessions over the rates of poor relief or against the imposition of task work were extracted locally from the Boards of Guardians (or in Scotland, the parish councils) who administered the Poor Law until 1929 and the Public Assistance Committees thereafter.[62] Unemployed protest was, at least in part, responsible for national concessions, most obviously with benefit increases to 1922, the restoration of the cut in 1934, the Standstill Act of 1935 and the extremely cautious implementation of new scales in November 1936. Though these improvements have been seen as 'minor' they could mean the difference between having food on the table and coal in the hearth or not.

The movement's activity was never persistent enough to wrestle the long-term initiative from the authorities or set the political agenda in relation to unemployment. The *Royal Commission on Unemployment Insurance* ignored their recommendations and their broader demands such as work or full maintenance were never achieved. Rosa Luxemburg, the Polish-German Marxist, described the fight for reform as the task of Sisyphus, a figure of Greek legend who repeatedly pushed a great stone up a hill only to see it roll down each time.[63] Every hard-fought concession was sooner or later eroded or called into question by a new measure. Whilst this was true, over the long run the provision and coverage for the unemployed were improving and there were also important limits to retrenchment which the government dared not cross. In 1931 the National government cut the benefit by 10 per cent (which reduced the weekly standard benefit from 17 shillings to 15 shillings for an adult male), rather than 25 per cent which the May Committee Report or the 33 per cent which the NCEO called for, (the latter would have left an adult unemployed man with 11s 8d benefit). This was a cut that it was later forced to restore. Over the long term, the government came to defend its scales of relief in nutritional terms, indicating a partial acceptance of the principle of maintenance, an important ideological concession to the demand of 'work or maintenance'.

The hunger marches also had a more subtle effect. Not only were policy reversals important, but also the ideological impact of the NUWM and hunger marches was significant. The Baldwin–Chamberlain consensus finally collapsed after Dunkirk. Whilst there was little electoral indication of its disintegration before the outbreak of war, there were important breaches in this consensus which resulted from a combination of factors, one of which was the action of the unemployed. These flaws in the ruling ideology were exposed in a number of ways. The NUWM ensured that unemployment was a very visible problem, one that could not be forgotten amidst the prosperity of many. The government also became more sensitive to the question of working-class health. Unemployed agitation played its part in pricking middle-class opinion with slogans such as 'We refuse to starve in silence' and 'Stop this starvation of mother and child' and protests for free school milk and children's boots and clothes. Even government encouragement of the voluntary sector, which was an attempt to marginalise the NUWM, partly backfired as it further focused attention on unemployment and the depression. Nutrition and maternal mortality became matters of public concern and debate. Sections of the medical profession, in particular after the threat of cuts, became openly critical of the government's record on health.[64] Pressure groups, the Committee against Malnutrition and the Children's Minimum Campaign, were established. These straddled the medical profession and middle-class reformers. Perhaps most importantly, notwithstanding the persistent view of employers' organisations and the Right that unemployment insurance was open to abuse and too expensive, the mass of the unemployed were not forced onto the Poor Law. The cry 'Work or full maintenance!' shook the old associations between relief and the malingering, feckless, undeserving pauper. Consequently, there was less stigma attached to applying for benefits. Workers viewed unemployment relief as a right and a matter for public discussion, not the prerogative of Poor Law Guardians concerned about the burden on ratepayers. The NUWM acted as a catalyst to these ideological changes. Arthur Horner remembered:

> Previously it had been a shameful thing to apply for relief to the Guardians. Miners and their wives would starve rather than submit to the indignity. But we insisted that in the new circumstances it would be a point of honour to demand from a country which was denying us the right to a living wage, and in an increasing number of cases the right even to a job.[65]

Revisionist historians have argued that the NUWM's militant methods were ineffective.[66] The interpretation that the Jarrow Crusade was the most successful unemployed protest and that the Standstill Act was introduced because agitation against the UAB was led by trades councils and local Labour Party branches attest to this view. The chief proponents of the view write:

Though the NUWM played an active role in the demonstrations against the new regulations, the campaign's effectiveness derived primarily from the broad basis of opposition to the government. It was essentially a respectable opposition which drew upon the middle ground in the country and Parliament. Because moderate opinion was mobilised and violence kept to a minimum, agitation proved effective.[67]

Revisionists also contend that the violence of the NUWM marches and demonstrations was counter-productive, drawing adverse press – such as the accusation that Moscow was in control – and that this inhibited mobilisation of the unemployed. However, this misunderstands the nature of the violence, which usually resulted from the authorities' desire to disperse a crowd or block a desired route. In this respect the lack of violence in the campaign against Part II of the 1934 Unemployment Act was not a consequence of the tactics of the demonstrators but because of the scale, speed and militancy of the movement and the breadth of local participating organisations. The movement against the cuts in 1935 did witness violent confrontations with the police in Sheffield, which provoked both local and national governments to backtrack, and in Maryport. If anything then, this campaign vindicated the NUWM argument that the self-activity of the unemployed and workers was the most effective strategy rather than 'official channels' and parliament. The NUWM's isolation resulted not from violence or sectarianism but from the labour movement shunning extra-parliamentary activity against unemployment. Even during the UAB campaign the official line of the leadership of both the TUC and the Labour Party was to condemn the movement. The UAB campaign may have brought the most dramatic retreat, but it was not the only notable government concession. The struggles of the unemployed cannot be judged as if they existed in a political vacuum since the greatest mobilisations of the unemployed – 1931–32 and 1934–35 – coincided with the darkest days for the British working class which was still smarting from the defeat of the General Strike and the collapse of the second Labour government.

In order to understand these unemployed protests, we require a wider appreciation of the confidence of the working-class movement. Historians who conceive of unemployed action as separate from the struggles of waged workers miss the relationship between the confidence of the militant in the workplace and the activity of the unemployed. Unemployment fundamentally transforms the bargaining position of labour, with workers knowing that 'there are hundreds out there that will do your job'. Whilst the lack of confidence and legacy of defeat limited the scope of the NUWM and

Left in the 1930s, the NUWM significantly contributed to the recovery of the working-class movement in the late 1930s by keeping the flame of working class opposition alive on the level of ideas, activity and personnel. Though slow, the recovery was real and reflected in the development of admittedly small rank-and-file movements, growth in union organisation, key defeats for company unionism and popular anti-fascism. From this perspective the NUWM was an impressive, even unique, achievement on the part of its activists, albeit within the obvious limitations and difficulties of organising the unemployed.

INTERNATIONAL COMPARISONS

6 The Unemployed in the United States

We thought American business was the Rock of Gibraltar. We were the prosperous nation, and nothing could stop us now. A brownstone house was forever. You gave it to your kids and they put marble fronts on it. There was a feeling of continuity. If you made it, it was there forever. Suddenly the big dream exploded. The impact was unbelievable. I was walking along the street at that time, and you'd see the bread lines. The biggest one in New York was owned by William Randolph Hearst. He had a big truck with several people on it, and big cauldrons of hot soup, bread. Fellows with burlap on their shoes were lined up all around Columbus Circle, and it went for blocks and blocks around the park, waiting.

> E.Y. Harburg, composer of 'Brother,
> Can you Spare a Dime?'[1]

We oppose the enactment of compulsory laws which give to the individual a right to payment while unemployed from a fund created by legislative order and subject to continuing political pressures for increases without relation to periods of employment and contribution. Experience demonstrates that public doles tend to continue and exaggerated the evil by subsidising uneconomic factors in industry.

> The National Association of Manufacturers,
> *The Platform of American Industry*, 1932[2]

Britain and the United States

Current ideas of welfare reform in Britain have taken the US example as their starting point. Today's rhetoric of welfare 'reform' – the 'welfare queens', dependency culture, the underclass, workfare – is derived from the United States. In the 1980s, the US became the adopted home of the New Right with the Reagan–Bush administrations, the social policy of Charles Murray and the Chicago School of economists. Charles Murray has been the major figure in the development of the idea of the underclass in the US, before turning his attention to the UK.[3] Welfare reform proposals are also based on US welfare practices such as workfare. Quite different welfare traditions underpin these practices and ideologies for which 1930s and 1940s were a crucial formative period. The transatlantic dialogue about welfare has deep roots, beginning with the fact that the old Poor Law in the US was modelled on the English Poor Laws. Between the introduction of British unemployment insurance in 1911 and and its adoption in the US in 1935, the American debate over unemployment insurance centred on a discussion of the British example. Historians have also probed the importance of the US–UK comparison. For instance, the monetarist historians Matthews and Benjamin warned of the supposed follies of both New Deal employment-creation and British unemployment insurance.[4] On a less polemical note, King and Ashton have both written comparative studies of unemployment in these two countries.[5] David Englander edited an important collection of essays which also makes the connection between the US and the UK and, in another such collection edited by Clive Emsley, there is a section comparing US–UK welfare and citizenship.[6] This chapter will outline the development of social policy and the experience of the unemployed in the US which allows the consideration of unemployment in a very different context to that of Britain.

The Great Depression's impact was worldwide. Millions of people on both sides of the Atlantic lost their jobs. Both Britain and America were forced to reform their provision for the unemployed. In both, bourgeois democratic political systems survived the traumas of the 1930s. Here the similarities end. In Britain, agriculture accounted for only 9.6 per cent of the occupied population, whilst in the US the figure stood at 27.9 per cent. Whereas the American banking system was based on thousands of small banks, in Britain branch banking and amalgamation had established the Big Five as the dominant force. American industry was more concentrated and more convinced of the merits of scientific management. Britain had already introduced a system of compulsory unemployment insurance in 1911, whereas in the United States, this was only achieved in 1935.

The effects of the economic crisis were both broader and deeper in the US than in Britain. Whereas between 1929 and 1932 industrial production fell by 9.3 per cent in the UK (and 11.6 per cent in Germany), in the US it plummeted by a staggering 44.8 per cent. The statistics bear witness to the horrifying scale of the depression in the US. Whereas in 1929 14.3 million were employed in agriculture, mining, manufacturing and building, three years later there were only 8.8 million. In 1932, 2,652 firms were going bankrupt each month. Between 1929 and 1932, car production – the very symbol of the

Roaring Twenties – slowed from 5.3 million to 1.4 million units. Unlike Britain, a combination of droughts, falling prices, soil erosion and overproduction ravaged agriculture. Millions of American farmers were driven to desperation as farm incomes dropped by two-thirds from $7,200 million in 1929 to $2,300 million in 1932. Farm prices fell by 56 per cent between 1929 and 1932, wheat prices by 63 per cent and cotton by 68 per cent.[7] As a result, the number of agricultural holdings declined from 11,805 to 6,383. Whilst both countries faced financial crisis and were forced to leave the Gold Standard, the US banking system lacked the stability of the UK's Big Five banks. The stocks on Wall Street lost 85 per cent of their value (or $74,000 million) before they began to recover. The Crash also brought down the US banking system. Between August 1931 and January 1932 1,860 banks failed. In March 1933, 34 governors were forced to close the doors of the banks in their states. Only after a national bank holiday and new federal regulation in the form of the Emergency Banking Act of March 1933 did confidence begin to return to the US banking system.

Individualism, Welfare Capitalism and the Problem of Unemployment

Unlike the United Kingdom where there was high unemployment throughout the 1920s, the American economy underwent an impressive boom. Productivity soared and mass consumer markets for cars, radios, vacuum cleaners, electric irons, refrigerators and washing machines burgeoned. From 1920 to 1929 industrial output per person hour increased by 63 per cent. These conditions allowed for the development of 'welfare capitalism'. With much fanfare, employers undertook various schemes to ensure the welfare of their employees. These included high wages, inducements to buy company shares, home-ownership plans and compensation or insurance (for illness, accidents, old age, unemployment and death). Welfare capitalism sprang from the teachings of scientific management whereby big business realised that the improved treatment of workers and reductions in labour turnover could enhance efficiency. They also hoped that such a project would win the loyalty of their workers and prevent unionisation. One central aspect of welfare capitalism was the introduction of employee representation structures within the firm. By the end of the 1920s, 1.5 million workers, mainly in large firms, were covered by employee representation.[8]

Welfare capitalism conformed to the American notions of rugged individualism and minimal state intervention. It was the paternalistic responsibility of the employer to provide for the worker rather than the duty of the state. Despite the self-publicity of the welfare capitalists, these schemes only ever provided for a minority of American workers.

American business viewed the British model of unemployment insurance as an unnecessary intrusion and a socialist menace. The National Industrial Conference Board castigated it as an impediment to labour mobility and wage flexibility. The Board stated that the British scheme was open to abuse and encouraged idleness. It was

> subject to constant and irresistible pressure to increase the benefits, extend the limits of coverage, relax the safeguards, and thus expand the plan from a limited self-supporting insurance system to a general relief scheme supported by public funds and, in the end, paid for by taxation.[9]

As we have already seen, British employers were making similar objections.

The American way, the welfare capitalism response to joblessness, was for the firm to regularise work, to prevent unemployment and, in some cases, to introduce their own company unemployment insurance schemes. The advocates of the 'regularisation' or 'stabilisation' of work as a means to prevent unemployment cited a number of examples where schemes had been successfully established. These included Dennison in Massachusetts, Hill Brothers in Philadelphia, Proctor and Gamble in Cincinnati and Eastman Kodak in Rochester. There were many major employers, like Henry Ford, who dissented from this view; they wanted less intervention in the industrial system not more.[10] The advocates of unemployment prevention through regularisation ignored the particular circumstances which allowed a handful of firms to operate such policies. The discrepancy between rhetoric and reality was greatest with unemployment insurance as there were only eleven company unemployment insurance plans for 8,500 employees in 1928. A further 63,500 were covered in 22 joint employer–union plans (mainly in clothing) and 34,723 came under union unemployment insurance schemes. But these numbers, a total of 106,723 for 1928–29, were a tiny fraction of the US workforce at that time. Two years later, the Bureau of Labor Statistics discovered little change in the situation with only 116,000 in voluntary unemployment insurance schemes.[11]

Government and the Emergence of Mass Unemployment, 1929–32

In the United States, there was no state or federal assistance for the unemployed, so help was based on charity, the workhouse and local poor relief. In the recessions of 1893–94, 1914 and 1921, reformers had failed to achieve congressional majorities for federal unemployment relief. Traditionally, the frontier and self-help networks of family and neighbours had provided poor Americans with strategies for dealing with hard times, but the very scale of the Great Depression, with a staggering 15 million unemployed by spring 1933, rendered these strategies inadequate. Before the industrial revolution, in Britain, the Poor Law had been tailored to deal with the extensive problem of the impoverished (and landless) agricultural labourer. The American family farmers found themselves in very different circumstances, being capable of both subsistence and commercial activity. In the USA, the idea that poverty was an individual and moral failing rather than the result of economic failure was consequently more pervasive than in Britain and the stigma of charity or relief was even greater. The notion of independence and individualism went to the very heart of the national identity, of what it was to be an American. Unemployed workers and ruined farmers suffered particularly sharply from the indignities of accepting charity, the means test or being 'on the county'. But as existing relief measures gave way during the Great Depression, so too did this set of ideas and attitudes to poverty and unemployment.

With no federal insurance or relief system, provision was local, and varied from place to place. Given the scale of the hardship, relief was both insufficient and punitive throughout the country. At the beginning of the depression in some places, including Philadelphia and New York, the workhouse was the only option for the able-bodied unemployed, and in 14 states paupers were still ineligible to vote. Elsewhere, the practice of auctioning paupers as indentured servants persisted.[12] Under this arrangement, the law forced the pauper to work for one master for a fixed period in return for his or her keep. For a time, the unemployed relied on the traditional means of getting through hard times without assistance: migration, support from family and neighbours, savings, credit with the local store and rent arrears. But with the catastrophe of mass unemployment, these thumb-in-the-dyke strategies were bound to fail.

Herbert Hoover, the President, appeared as confused as everyone else. Initially, he stuck to formulaic announcements designed to restore business confidence and halt the collapse in share prices. His cheery statements that recovery was 'just round the corner', that the 'fundamental strength' of the economy was 'unimpaired' or that the drought had 'officially ended' were grotesque. As the flow of unemployment increased, Hoover asked American citizens to redouble their local charitable efforts. He did not convene the Emergency Committee for Employment and appoint Colonel Arthur Woods as its chair until October 1930. Even then, Hoover ignored the

Committee's recommendation for federally financed public works. He appointed a second committee, the President's Organisation on Unemployment Relief (POUR), in August 1931, when unemployment stood at around 9 million. A wealthy businessman, Walter Giffard, the President of AT&T and the Chair of the New York Charity Organisation Society, was appointed as its head. However, POUR was concerned only with the co-ordination of local relief and the encouragement of charity. Hoover blocked proposals in Congress to stimulate employment through the United States Employment Service and public works. The meagre achievements of these two committees consisted of a campaign to encourage householders to provide odd jobs to 'spruce up' their properties, fund-raising drives for community chests and the Red Cross, and a 'Spread the Work' campaign. Their impact was minimal.

President Hoover reflected the attitudes of American big business. He had close contacts with business opinion through government committees, business associations, conferences on unemployment and the Republican Party. His programme of employment stabilisation, hollow optimism and opposition to federal relief was essentially their programme. Hoover's first response to unemployment after the Wall Street Crash was to convene a conference of business leaders on 5 December 1929. Its proposals – better business information, work stabilisation and an undertaking to maintain employment levels – were at best naive. Business associations, such as the US Chamber of Commerce and the National Association of Manufacturers, exerted a continual pressure on the administration. On 9 February 1931, Mr Rogers of the US Chamber of Commerce (USCC) prematurely asked the unemployment committee to '[let] up on the propaganda on unemployment' because of the 'upturn in business'.[13] A USCC membership survey found 2,534 chambers of commerce against and only 197 for federal unemployment relief. The organisation then wrote to the congressional sub-committee on unemployment relief stating its determined opposition to any such move. Silas H. Strawn, the USCC President, encouraged his members to participate in local organisations of the POUR 'to counter the persistent campaign for federal aid'.[14] For Henry Ford, even stabilisation was a foolhardy interference in the workings of the market; the basic problem was that workers were over-reliant on employers providing work for them rather than creating opportunities for themselves.[15] There were signs that some business leaders were growing impatient with Hoover. Already by 1931, a number of the 'progressive' employers were suggesting reforms that Hoover was unwilling to countenance. These particularly focused on the revision of anti-trust laws and for employers to form cartels to cope with the effects of depression. For others, such as Gerard Swope, a much wider programme, which included unemployment insurance, public works, relief and even deficit spending, was envisaged.[16]

The mounting crisis in local government finances with the failure to pay public employees and the closing of relief stations precipitated Hoover's downfall. In San Francisco, for example, the public and private local relief bill had mushroomed from $487,000 in 1929 to $4,321,000 in 1932.[17] In Washington State, tax receipts fell from $70.5 million to $51.4 million in 1932; at the same time public welfare expenditure rose from $1.8 million to $7.3 million.[18] This combined with growing unemployed unrest and provoked a sharp change in business thinking. On 4 June 1932, Mayor Cermak of Chicago sent a telegram 'representing the business interests in Chicago' asking for emergency federal aid. Amongst the signatories were leading bankers, over a dozen executives with top firms (including the Pullman Company, Colgate-Palmolive Peet Company, Illinois Bell Telephone Company) and the President of the US Chamber of Commerce, Silas H. Strawn.[19] Several Republicans broke ranks in Congress in July 1932 over the Emergency Relief and Construction Act despite Hoover's opposition and attempted veto. By the summer of 1932, Hoover's attempt to deal with the depression was in tatters and his constituency was fragmenting. His very name had become a by-word for the misery of unemployment and the callousness of the rich: the shantytowns were dubbed Hoovervilles and the unemployed complained of having plenty of 'Hoover time' on their hands.

New Deal Reforms and the Unemployed, 1933–40

In the 1932 presidential election, Roosevelt promised Americans a New Deal. His programme centred on restricting agricultural output to protect prices, regularising industrial production, federal public works, federal relief for the unemployed and unemployment insurance. Millions of victims of the depression joined the Democrats' traditional vote, resulting in the most dramatic turnaround in US electoral history. Having won with the largest vote since 1864, FDR's presidency began with considerable élan. The Economy Act, Civilian Conservation Corps (CCC), Agricultural Adjustment Act, Tennessee Valley Authority Act and the National Industrial Recovery Act passed through Congress within the first 100 days of his presidency. In addition, the dollar left the Gold Standard on 19 April. The Emergency Relief Act, which established the Federal Emergency Relief Administration (FERA), was the most audacious step. Of the New Deal reforms, the emergency relief, various forms of work relief and the Social Security Act specifically addressed the problem of unemployment.

The FERA operated from May 1933 to June 1936 and dispensed $3 billion in direct federal relief. It broke with existing American practice and ideology of relief in several ways. It targeted the unemployed (not just the so-called deserving poor, such as orphans or widows); it was a federal response to poverty, overturning the tradition of federal non-intervention; and it broke with the past because of its sheer scale. By the winter of 1934, this scheme was assisting 20 million Americans, and as one relief recipient observed in 1934, 'People don't think the same about welfare as they used to. I would have starved before applying three years ago. I wouldn't apply if so many others didn't.'[20] State not federal government administered the FERA, allowing a degree of local autonomy in the distribution and scale of relief. In addition to the direct grants to the localities, supplementary funds existed that could be secured if they were matched by local funds. As a result, the FERA's impact varied between states, either because of conservatism or lack of state funds. In late September 1933, a FERA investigator reported confidentially on Calais which was typical, she said, of small towns in Maine:

> The town has never had any state or federal aid. It won't ask for it, even though at the last town meeting there was strong agitation for it. The people on relief in that town are subjected to treatment that is almost medieval in its stupidity. The mayor was actually proud of the fact that he had managed so far to pull through without asking for help.[21]

In the initial round of reforms, the Roosevelt administration established two rather limited work relief projects. The CCC provided for about 200,000 unemployed in work camps in the national parks. They were engaged mainly in forestry work under the supervision of the army. The Public Works Administration (PWA) was a public works scheme based on large-scale civil projects; as such it was slow to make an impression and did not set out to hire the unemployed.

In February 1934, FDR declared that the government was 'quitting the business of relief'. With the FDR administration favouring work relief, the FERA was finally wound up in June 1936. In an article in *The Nation*, Isidor Feinstein asked why, with the conservatives so isolated, should relief be cut. In a White House statement, Roosevelt explained:

> They [the unemployed] very properly insist upon an opportunity to give the community their services in the form of labour in return

for unemployment benefits. The Federal government has no desire to force upon the country or upon the unemployed themselves a system of relief which is so repugnant to American ideals of individual self-reliance.[22]

Roosevelt's replacement of direct relief with work relief was on the grounds that there was a danger of eroding self-reliance, or in other words, the menace of dependency.

Since Malthus's day, the threat of creating a dependent poor has been the leitmotif of conservative thinking on social policy. Work relief may have been popular with the unemployed and it may have been relatively expensive, but it should not be seen as a progressive expansion of welfare as liberal historians claim.[23] Though more costly, the works schemes paid wages lower than market rates and accrued considerable economic, especially infrastructural, benefits for the American political and economic system. Work relief was also an ideological concession to the conservatives, it perpetuated certain aspects of Poor Law ideology and it fell short of the ideal of an universal modern welfare state.

The FERA and local relief had funded some work relief, but the distinctive shift from direct relief to work relief came in the shape of the Civil Works Administration (CWA). Created in November 1933 under the leadership of Harry Hopkins, by mid-January 1934 it had a workforce of 4.2 million. These workers were engaged mainly in public works projects such as building roads, schools, parks and airports. Average weekly wage rates were about three times the average relief payments and reflected the value of the work being carried out. The costs of the scheme led to criticism from business and the conservatives. They implausibly accused the CWA of creating labour shortages. Concerns about the budget led Roosevelt to clash with Harry Hopkins over the CWA and on the advice of conservative aids – such as Director of the Budget, Lewis Douglas – the President ordered the CWA's termination by spring 1934.

Despite the CWA's early demise, another work-creation programme, the Works Progress Administration (WPA), soon took its place. The latter paid lower average wages and the numbers on its rolls were never as large as the CWA peak, but it did take a higher proportion of its workers from relief rolls (90 per cent rather than 50 per cent) and lasted until 1943. Like the CWA, most of WPA expenditure went on construction projects such as road-building, schools, parks, and the like. The WPA also sought to create work to match the skills of the large numbers of urban professionals ruined by the depression: doctors, writers, artists, technicians, teachers and nurses. It tried to tackle the question of women's unemployment through school meals projects, clothes-making programmes and nurses' jobs in immunisation campaigns. Whilst work relief was more popular with its recipients than direct relief, conservatives, business and the newspapers lambasted it for amounting to little more than leaf-raking or 'boondoggling'. By 1943, however, the WPA had chalked up considerable achievements. It had employed over 8 million; between 1935 and 1940, its workers had constructed or repaired 200,000 buildings and 600,000 miles of road; in New York, 60 per cent of all construction in 1937 was under WPA auspices. At its peak, it employed 3.24 million in November 1938; and between 1936 and 1941, its lowest figure was 1.45 million in September 1937.[24]

Unlike the WPA, the Social Security Act, which passed through Congress in April 1935, was a permanent legacy of the New Deal. The Act constituted the cornerstone for the future American welfare system and consisted of three reforms: federal aid for the economically inactive poor – the old, widows and orphans; an old age pension based on wage deductions and a payroll tax; and compulsory unemployment insurance based on a payroll tax. This was a major achievement, as American employers had steadfastly opposed these reforms for decades. In the 1920s, the National Industrial Conference Board lamented and warned of the 'malingering' that the British unemployment system engendered.[25] The fact that before the Act only one state – Wisconsin, in 1934 – had introduced unemployment insurance demonstrates the strength of opposition to it. American proponents of unemployment insurance had been divided between two possible systems: the Ohio model proposed a pooled state-wide unemployment fund and uniform contribution levels, and the Wisconsin model in which individual firms would build up unemployment insurance funds and firms would be allowed to pay at different contribution levels depending on their circumstances (known as merit-rating). The 1935 Act rejected the single firm fund but did include merit-rating and allowed states to set their own payment scales, gaps of non-payment and maximum claim period. This conceded considerable powers to the vested interests of business and the state political machines. Another serious drawback was the delay in implementation as the first payments under the unemployment insurance system were not made until 1938. Although an advance on the existing situation, it fell well short of British unemployment insurance provision. From a long-term perspective, it was from these flawed foundations that the American welfare state emerged and their limitations (the weak redistributive function, partial coverage, punitive character of relief) are all too apparent today.[26]

The American Experience of Unemployment in the 1930s

There was a degree of uncertainty about the precise level of unemployment in the USA in the 1930s. In Britain, the unemployment insurance system provided unemployment statistics, but on the other side of the Atlantic this was not available until 1935, and even then the treatment of the unemployed varied from state to state. Apart from the 1930 census, there were no reliable national unemployment statistics. President Hoover even argued that the census figures exaggerated the numbers out of work. At the height of unemployment in early 1933, estimates of its scale varied widely. Hopkins quoted the National Research League figure of 17,920,000 for March 1933.[27] The Labour Research Association extrapolated a figure from the 1930 census figure which included estimates for the growth of population, the exclusion from the census of migrants and the homeless, and the numbers of those who were not formerly wage-earners made workless by the depression. It judged unemployment to be 16,774,000 on 13 February 1933. *Business Week* calculated unemployment to be 15,252,000 for November 1932, and the American Federation of Labor believed unemployment to be at its peak in March 1933 with 13,359,000.[28]

In addition to technical problems of measurement, the US's economic and geographical diversity complicated its experience of unemployment. Whilst most of the jobless were drawn from the ranks of the industrial working class, local conditions played a great part in shaping their everyday lives. Many lived in large cities such as New York, Chicago and Minneapolis, which all suffered from high levels of unemployment. Others were 'stranded' in smaller or less industrially diversified areas, sometimes single-industry or company towns. The miners in West Virginia and East Kentucky suffered from isolation, very high levels of unemployment and terrible poverty. The declassed (bankrupted farmers, workless urban professionals and white-collar staff) swelled the ranks of the unemployed. In the economic and financial turmoil, a portion of the middle class lost their savings, possessions and livelihoods. This phenomenon was much more significant in the US than in Britain.

For industrial workers, the first job loss, even when new work was found, usually spelt a future of economic hardship, deskilling and insecurity. A study of the shutdown of three industrial plants in 1929 found that unemployment was 'in most cases a one way journey to work of less skill and lower wages with its consequent blow to the workers' standard of living and status, a blow most severe for the skilled who have most to lose'.[29] This study discovered that whereas in April 1929 30.4 per cent were skilled workers, 44.3 per cent were semi-skilled and 25.3 per cent were unskilled, three years later only

11.4 per cent were in skilled jobs, 17.1 per cent in semi-skilled jobs and 71.5 per cent in unskilled jobs.[30]

Unemployment affected not only the world of work but also the workers' most basic needs, such as shelter. Some moved in with friends, neighbours or relatives as repossessions and evictions left hundreds of thousands of Americans homeless. Others roamed the country looking for work, often jumping aboard freight trains to span the massive distances of the US interior. In 1932, the Southern Pacific Railroad reported 683,457 were ejected from their trains. At its very worst, in the winter of 1932–33, when relief collapsed in many parts of the country, the unemployed were reduced to the level of bare survival. A Philadelphia study revealed that when the relief ran out families resorted to begging, stealing, eating dandelions, selling fruit and scavenging from the docks.[31] Long spells of unemployment sometimes led to absolute destitution. In July 1935, there were 7,500 male transients on relief in New York alone. Their average profile was of a 38-year-old single, white, unskilled worker with elementary education. They hailed from the Eastern towns. They had been unemployed since February 1932, and transient since July 1934.[32] In the country as a whole, in June 1934, there were 465,997 looked after by federal transient bureaux and an estimated 1.25 million transients in American at the height of the depression.[33] The homeless unemployed gravitated to the cities where they had the greatest chance of relief or work. The settlement houses established to provide shelter for them were soon filled to their capacity. Shanty towns ('Hoovervilles') sprang up in the major cities and remained there throughout the 1930s. In Pittsburgh's The Strip district, 300 unemployed sheltered in a Hooverville built of burlap, boxwood and oil paper. Shanty dwellings crowded into an empty reservoir, nicknamed Hoover Valley, in New York City's Central Park. Many others followed the frontier calling of earlier generations and sought a new life in California, New Mexico, Arizona or Florida. As early as November 1930, the Governors of Arizona and California were reporting that local labour markets and relief funds were unable to cope with the growing transient population.[34]

The statistics and generalities of unemployment conceal its individual tragedies and sufferings. 'Mass unemployment is both a statistic and an empty feeling in the stomach', Cabell Phillips observed: 'To fully comprehend it, you have to both see the figures and feel the emptiness.'[35] After five days without food, 17-year-old William Columbo collapsed in a New York street. The same day, August Bauman a 53-year-old passed out in Grand Central Station and was rushed to hospital by police.[36] Only relief stood between the unemployed and starvation. The cause of death registered on death certificates masked the true extent of fatalities from starvation.

Whereas the Bureau of Vital Statistics recorded two deaths resulting from starvation in New York City in 1931, four City hospitals had admitted 95 starvation cases, of whom 20 had died.[37]

Experiencing Relief

At the beginning of the depression, with no federal relief programme, charitable and municipal assistance strove to provide for the needy. In January 1931, New York City, an estimated 85,000 queued in 81 bread-lines. Local businessmen and dignitaries tried to hold the line of private charity by establishing new fund-raising committees to meet the emergency. One cynical observer said that the steel companies which dominated the charities of the steel towns, 'were quite obviously seeking to control relief in order to prevent widespread publicity as to the actual needs and to protect themselves against higher taxes'.[38] These committees went through a cycle of fund-raising, growing demand and exhaustion of reserves as charities received diminishing returns from their public appeals. In New York City, for example, charitable expenditure fell from $21 million in 1932 to $5 million in 1934.[39] Initially, municipal or state authorities try to compensate for the shortfall of the charities, but these in turn succumbed to the rising tide of need. Unlike most places, Ann Arbor, a university town, rode the storm without recourse to turning the relief recipients away, but even here, it was estimated that private and municipal relief would have run out by July 1933 and the settlement house was closed in May 1933.[40] In New Orleans, local sources of relief were completely exhausted in the summer of 1932. The charity committee, chaired by the conservative banker Horatio Lloyd, disbanded. They admitted defeat and recanted their opposition to direct federal aid. Lloyd stated, 'The present need is on a scale that calls not for more charity but for government action to save the health and indeed the lives of a large portion of the citizenry.'[41]

The unemployed suffered hunger and humiliation, and relief carried a host of petty indignities. The bread-line and relief queue meant a public loss of face and the home visit of the social worker a degrading intrusion into family life. The use of food vouchers instead of cash added further insult and sense of grievance because vouchers prevented the unemployed from shopping around and allowed grocers to 'short-weigh' customers on relief.[42] Lorena Hickok, the Chief Investigator of the FERA, reported 'continuous kicks' against food vouchers. One of the unemployed in Pittsburgh told her, 'Does a man's social status change when he becomes unemployed, so that, while he was perfectly able to handle money when he had a job, he can't be trusted when he's out of work?'[43] Without statutory relief, the unemployed were anxious that present relief could be taken away in the future. These personal affronts continued throughout the 1930s even with the 'enlightened reforms' of the New Deal. The WPA, for example, was based on a means test and its participants, only ever a minority of the unemployed, were under constant threat of lay-offs and cutbacks.

Alongside the humiliating experience of relief was the often dispiriting search for work. The sociologist E. Wright Bakke asked a sample of workless men to keep a diary of their attempts to find work. The results revealed that the normal method of finding work was 'pavement pounding', a futile daily routine of walking from one workplace to another. The jobless were generally cynical about the chance of getting work by answering newspaper advertisements or through the employment office. Joseph Turrio recorded a typical day of looking for work. Starting at seven in the morning he visited four industrial establishments with no luck. After this he happened on two friends doing the rounds.

> They said it was useless and they were only looking through force of habit. That's going to be me before long. Even if they hadn't said so, I'm thinking it is useless to run around like this, you just appear ridiculous, and that gets your goat ...[44]

The Hoover government denied that the depression had brought about a deterioration in the nation's health.[45] Other sources were less sanguine. A study of New York City schoolchildren claimed that 20 per cent were malnourished.[46] Department of Health figures for Massachusetts indicated that malnutrition rose from 11 per cent in 1928–29 to 19 per cent in 1932. Pennsylvanian school health inspectors found 18 per cent of the schoolchildren they examined to be undernourished in 1929–30 and 27 per cent three years later. The Philadelphia Community Health Center observed malnutrition amongst 11 per cent in 1929–30 and 23 per cent in 1932 of children under six. In the coal mining region of Western Virginia, the percentage of children under normal height was 23.1 per cent in 1931 and 27.2 per cent in 1932.[47] Lorena Hickok reported on the situation in West Viriginia in autumn 1933:

> From long deprivation the health of the people is beginning to break down. Some of them have been starving for eight years ... I don't suppose anybody really knows how much tuberculosis there is in the state, Tuberculosis and asthma are common among miners, anyway. I heard of whole families having tuberculosis in some of the mining camps. There are the usual epidemics of typhoid – five babies have died of typhoid in Logan County

recently, but the only wonder on the part of the relief workers was that more hadn't died. Dysentery is so common nobody says much about it. 'We begin losing our babies with dysentery in September,' one investigator remarked casually. Diphtheria was beginning to break out in Logan and Mingo counties when I was there.[48]

Part of the problem was the lack of public health provision, cash-strapped private hospitals closed their doors on the poor, and company or private doctors paid scant attention to the unemployed. Hard times also brought an increase in the numbers taking their own lives. In Detroit, where the fortunes of the car industry had dramatically reversed, the town's Bureau of Vital Statistics recorded that whilst there were 113 suicides in 1927, four years later 586 killed themselves.[49] The national suicide figures leapt from 14 per 1,000 in 1929 to 17.4 per 1,000 in 1932.[50]

Unemployment, Race and Gender

The bitter history of racism in the US was reflected in the experience of black and white without work. While studies found discrimination against foreigners and blacks in industrial lay-offs, hiring policies during the depression were even worse.[51] In Philadelphia in 1931, for instance, the unemployment rate amongst native-born whites was 24.3 per cent, but 36.8 per cent amongst blacks.[52] In Boston, local politicians exercised influence over the distribution of jobs, which mirrored the City's rigid ethnic hierarchy of Anglo-Saxon Protestants, Irish, Italians and Jews, with blacks at the bottom of the pile.[53] In a study of the New Haven unemployed, 47 per cent believed that they were overlooked for jobs because of 'lack of pull'; this figure varied considerably between ethnic groups and 30 per cent believed that race or nationality was a principal cause of their ill-fortune. Employers and their foremen could pick and choose. In New Haven, 31 out of 50 firms favoured American citizens over foreigners or 'aliens'; 94 per cent preferred to hire whites; 40 per cent had a policy of not employing blacks at all. Amongst a smaller number there was systematic discrimination on grounds of nationality (8 per cent) and religion (6 per cent).[54] With the lynch mobs still terrorising blacks in the rural South, intimidation deterred some blacks from claiming assistance. A relief official in Georgia demonstrated the attitudes of much of the white South:

> There will be no Negroes pushing wheel-barrows and boys driving trucks getting forty cents an hour when the good white men and

white women, working these fields alongside these roads, can hardly earn forty cents a day.

In Atlanta, the average black relief recipient was paid only three-fifths the amount granted to whites.[55] Others were discriminated against over the receipt of relief jobs or goods.[56] Segregation remained in the Civilian Conservation Corps and on some WPA projects. Blacks were much less likely to get skilled or supervisory jobs. Even after changes forced by the Harlem riot, in New York City, WPA blacks constituted only 5 per cent of 'professional and technical placements' and only 0.5 per cent of supervisory ones.[57] Black wages were therefore considerably lower than whites on work relief projects. A WPA report discovered that the black workers on its books got lower wages in the same occupations despite sometimes working longer hours than whites. Although differences in wages were greater between women and men than black and white in general, in those occupations where both men and women worked, the wage differential was wider on the grounds of race.[58]

Immigration policy became more stringent during the depression. This trend had begun before the Wall Street Crash and was underpinned by eugenic and racist thinking. The 1921 Immigration Act, based on the pseudo-scientific evidence of intelligence testing army recruits, established a quota system for different nationalities. The annual quota system was fixed at 3 per cent of the total of each respective nationality in the 1890 census. This was designed specifically to exclude Jews, Italians and Eastern Europeans, who were deemed to be racially inferior. The 1924 Immigration Act lowered the quota to 2 per cent, established border stations on the US–Mexico frontier and stipulated exclusion on the grounds of mental, physical and moral undesirability. In 1929 a literacy test was introduced to exclude poor Mexicans from entering the US. Between 1930 and 1935, between 300,000 and 500,000 Mexicans were repatriated, many of them American citizens.

The depression also seemed to threaten the progress that American women had made in the previous decades. The American Women's Association (AWA) worried that earlier advances (though these are clearly being exaggerated) were jeopardised:

More women going to work, more women in superior positions, discriminations against women collapsing on all sides ... But now these women who thought that nothing was impossible have learned from the depression that nothing is certain in the present world. Back of them, and in some respects more tragic, is a younger generation that has never had the earlier optimism ...[59]

Women's unemployment was a complex phenomenon with lower than male unemployment rates, and certain typically female occupations fairing better than male-dominated industry. However, the lower unemployment rates were in part a statistical illusion as many women left or did not join the labour market and withdrew into domestic roles. There was no incentive for many women to register as registered unemployed because relief was paid to heads of household only, with the result that married women made up only 4 per cent of all unemployed in New Haven, for example, and only 5 per cent of those eligible for relief.[60] Discriminatory employment practices forced a particularly unfortunate group of married women workers out of work. In a 1930–31 survey of 1,500 cities, it was found that 77 per cent refused employment to married women teachers and over half forced their women teachers to leave work when they married. Some private firms, such as New England Telephone and Telegraph and the Northern Pacific Railway Company, dismissed all their married women employees.[61] Bakke also found that firms preferred employing family rather than single men and single rather than married women, thus reinforcing married women's dependence on the family unit.

Economic conditions increased discrimination against women in business and the professions. The AWA survey found large numbers of women who had lost status and income in the labour market. Of the women in its study 60.5 per cent had seen decreases in their salaries between 1929 and 1933, whilst 97.7 per cent had had to make cuts in their expenditures due to rising prices. While unemployment signalled a blow to the independence a woman could gain through a job as many were forced back into the home and the family for support, there was not a wholesale expulsion of women from the workforce. Women made up a greater portion of total employment at the end of the 1930s than at the beginning because of the growth of clerical work and low-paid jobs. Many male workers believed that they were being displaced by machines and women. 'If you want a job round here,' one of those out of work in New Haven mused, 'you either have to wear wheels or a skirt.'[62]

Representation and Reality of Unemployment

There was a considerable gap between the experience and the representation of unemployment. After temporarily accepting the need for federal relief, business turned against the New Deal. In 1934, business leaders from Du Pont and General Motors founded the American Liberty League an organisation set up to campaign against the New Deal.[63] As well as key industrialists, the League drew into its ranks conservative politicians from both the Republican and Democratic Parties. Given the ownership of the press, the pressure from advertisers and the widespread use of national syndicated columns in local papers, it is no surprise that this antagonism fed through into print. Robert and Helen Lynd commented in their study of Middletown's press:

> a matter-of-fact viewing of the institutions of the culture suggests that in a society in which private business is the dominant institution, and in which the press and radio are themselves private businesses and draw the bulk of their support from private other businesses, rather from listeners or readers, and a political commentator is paid in proportion to his ability to write comment that the owners of newspapers and broadcasting systems and their advertisers like, the coincidence is neither fortuitous nor temporary.[64]

Throughout the 1930s American newspapers were on balance hostile to direct and work relief for the unemployed. As for the Unemployed Councils, they were an un-American red 'menace' or 'poison'. An editorial in a Middletown newspaper demonstrates how harsh such attitudes could be:

> In the meantime the taxpayers go on supporting many that would not work if they had jobs ... Why not have one of these ten or so Federal agencies round here devote itself to an investigation of people who should be on relief but are too proud to ask, and to the kicking-off of a lot of them that never were worth feeding for any purpose? Can't let the utterly worthless starve? Maybe not, but if some plague were to come along ... and wipe them all out, that would not be a tragedy but a big relief.[65]

Many stories confirmed middle-class prejudices about the FERA and WPA. Those on public assistance were deemed 'loafers' or 'chisellers' and those on public works were 'work-shy' or 'shovel-leaners' wasting taxpayers' money on meaningless tasks.

When analysed, the supposed scale of relief abuse withered to nearly nothing, as was the case in Britain. After a series of headlines about relief recipients who would 'rather live on relief', the FERA investigated allegations that certain claimants had refused work. In Washington, a study found that out of 220 allegations only four were confirmed. In Baltimore, a similar inquiry discovered four real cases out of 195 alleged cases. In Memphis, only one in 39 cases was proven.[66]

These beliefs also trickled down to the poor. Letters sent to Roosevelt and Hopkins include some from neighbours alleging abuse and preferential treatment. One relief official testified to a congressional committee that a man had asked the social worker to come to his house to speak to his wife 'because she doesn't believe that a man who walks the street from morning till night, day after day, actually can't get a job in this town. She thinks I don't want to work.'[67] That both work and direct relief were not universal and fell short of reaching all those who suffered from the depression encouraged such sniping. The poor had no statutory right to public assistance and the rancour this produced turned to jealousy and pettiness. This was especially the case when it mixed with the racism of poor whites towards black welfare recipients. A jealous white neighbour sent a letter asking the President to remove a black WPA seamstress from her position.[68]

Images of a loafing, undeserving and dependent poor were countered in several ways. Most importantly, the direct experience of millions contradicted these representations. The high profile of the FERA and WPA projects and the public relations sensitivity of the Roosevelt administration partially undercut these images. Not only was Roosevelt personally adept at playing to his audience through his 'fireside chats' on the wireless, but also certain relief projects had their own influence on American cultural life. New Deal relief produced books, murals, plays, parks, immunisation campaigns and school meals. These projects were woven into the fabric of everyday life. In Boston, for instance, under the aegis of the WPA, subways were extended, airport runways were built, plays were staged and a civic orchestra and a swing band were formed.[69]

A more radical challenge came from an emerging left intelligentsia grouped around the writers' and artists' unions, the *New Masses* journal and the Communist Party's John Reed Clubs. Documentary photographers, travelling journalists and novelists chronicled the plight of the depression's hungry victims.[70] The novels of John Steinbeck and Don Passos are the most enduring examples. For the most part, the film industry dealt with the depression and poverty either through stories of rich and jobless poor falling in love, or comic tramp figures – Chaplin, Laurel and Hardy – or by ignoring it altogether. Yet from the late 1930s, the issue was broached in films such as *How Green Was My Valley*, *The Grapes of Wrath* and *Mr Smith Goes to Washington*.

In Britain, social investigators put the unemployed under the microscope of empirical investigation. Following the research of Booth and Rowntree in the late nineteenth century, their primary concern was the question of the relationship between unemployment and poverty. In the United States, there was much greater emphasis on new approaches (anthropology, psychology and sociology) to the question of unemployment and the American studies provided new insights into the experience of joblessness. Not only is there a wealth of material on the US, an American abroad conducted one of the most thorough and pioneering studies of unemployment of the depression era, Bakke's *Unemployed Man* investigating the Greenwich unemployed.

As in Britain, US social investigation was imbued with the prejudices of its middle-class practitioners. A number of accounts sounded the alarm that unemployment was provoking a moral breakdown in American society. They warned that people were turning away from the Churches, abandoning children, turning to alcohol and indulging in loose sexual morals. More level-headed research contradicted the impressionistic and anecdotal evidence of this moral panic. Some psychologists investigated whether certain individuals were predisposed to unemployment or homelessness. Kaplun, a psychologist for New York's Emergency Relief Bureau, claimed that the non-resident transients in New York were of lower IQ than the general population. To supplement the quantitative picture, four case descriptions were added to highlight their 'feeble-mindedness'. Kaplun's disgust and snobbery is palpable as he describes someone who supposedly 'cannot care for simple personal needs, is unable to dress or to shave without assistance', who 'spends his spare time at movies or burlesque shows' and 'occasionally obliges friends by acting as a passive homosexual'. The other three had deserted their children, had either been arrested for begging, smoked marijuana or were 'neurasthenic', illiterate, delinquent or alcoholic.[71] Shilonsky, Preu and Rose found in a study of 200 homeless unemployed in New Haven that unstable personalities caused vagrancy, 35 per cent were 'chronically maladjusted to their environment before the unemployment situation arose' and 90 per cent reacted to unemployment with 'disturbances of mood having the charcteristics of a mild or moderate reactive depression'.[72]

If 'intelligence', 'emotional instability' or 'feeble-mindedness' caused unemployment or vagrancy then personal flaws rather than a failing economic system condemned the unemployed to their fate. Such results suggested that work-creation and relief were not the solution. Some contemporaries denied such a causal link and proposed that such an approach confused cause with effect.[73] Berlinger found that transients compared favourably in tests of emotional stability to psychoneurotic soldiers and were as neurotic as Columbia University students. He concluded, unsurprisingly given their environment, that the transient, 'is characterised by frequent change of interests, not knowing what he wants to do next, and rest-lessness. There is some evidence that the younger transients are motivated by feelings of insecurity and unhappy home environ-ments.'[74] Despite the subsequent discrediting of intelligence testing, Charles Murray, the doyen of the New Right, has recently reincar-nated this approach in *The Bell Curve*.[75] He concluded that there is a less intelligent underclass, indifferent to work, amongst whom illegitimacy and single parenthood are the norm and who have criminal dispositions.[76] This group – whom he insultingly dubs the 'new rabble' – will be dependent on over-generous and ill-conceived welfare programmes. Policy-makers who accept his analysis of the 'new rabble' have responded with workfare and cuts in benefits for single parents.

Even the most scientifically rigorous social investigator of the 1930s analysed joblessness from the perspective of the typical 'unemployed individual'. The social psychologists, as they themselves acknowledged, studied the unemployed divorced from the context of changing political events and institutional (including relief) settings. As Eisenberg and Lazarfeld in their excellent summary of research findings put it, 'we will deal with no inferences from institutional changes, or general trends through the depression, because we feel they are too complicated by other factors and by broad cultural trends to tell us anything about the effect of unemployment on the individual'.[77] The failure to conceive of the unemployed as part of a historical (i.e. dynamic) process was, despite their important insights, the greatest flaw of the American social investigators. Unemployed struggles and organisations were seen as external factors, viewed without empathy, if considered at all. In particular, it meant that these investigators were incapable of understanding the process of radicalisation. Sometimes historians have been too uncritical of their findings. Verba and Schlozman have examined a study for *Fortune Magazine* in 1939 and adduce that there was little radicalisation or class consciousness amongst the unemployed or American workers during the 1930s. The study with a sample of only 200 unemployed took place after the critical phases of unemployed and industrial agitation, but even this survey revealed that there was a minority of the unemployed and industrial workers who adopted radical positions. According to the *Fortune Magazine* study, 32 per cent of the unemployed wanted relief even if it meant the end of capitalism.[78]

The Struggles of the American Unemployed

The conviction that the pauper had only himself or herself to blame in the land of opportunities was intrinsic to the ideologies of 'the American way' and the Poor Law. The idea of the 'undeserving poor' and the stigma of relief existed on both sides of the Atlantic but the

American dream gave these attitudes a particular sharpness. In circumstances where unemployment had grown to 3.5 million in three months after the Wall Street Crash and remained above that figure until the beginning of the war, these beliefs were shattered. Millions of 'respectable' Americans suffered the degradation of standing in bread-lines and asking for charity or relief, and for some stigma and shame gave way to bitterness and anger. An anonymous letter to President Hoover captured this transformation: 'The people are desperate and this I have written, one typical of the masses of your Subjects. How can we be Law abiding citizens and Educate our children and be Happy Content with nothing to do nothing to Eat [sic]?'[79] A study into the aggressive behaviour of Chicago relief clients found that it was not new workers but higher skilled, native-born Americans from urban origins who were most likely to be aggressive. The study observed the following categories of aggressiveness: demanding, threatening, arrogant, clear cut and concise, wise cracking, loses control, curries favour.[80] Two further studies charted the transformation that had taken place by 1934–35 of the attitudes of those on relief. The first, a study of 100 St Louis relief recipients, found only six were hesitant and felt bad about claiming. Of 147 on relief surveyed by Woolston: 6 per cent 'expressed confidence in the present order', 10 per cent 'admitted depression was very trying, but thought it would pass', 23 per cent 'needed helped to get back on their feet, and were trying to help themselves', 14 per cent 'asked for what they could get without protest or thanks, their courage spent', 27 per cent were 'critics of the social order, felt they were entitled to a job', 8 per cent 'had abandoned all hope' and 12 per cent 'were ready to fight the present order'.[81]

The Communists and the Unemployed Councils

Initially, unemployed protest took the shape of spontaneous looting and rioting by people who chose to break the law rather than see their families starve. In March 1930, 1,100 were waiting outside the Salvation Army in New York City. They seized two lorries delivering food to a nearby hotel and distributed the goods.[82] The communists soon organised marches and formed local Unemployed Councils in a number of cities under the slogans 'Work or wages' and 'Fight – don't starve'. In late January and February 1930, they called demonstrations outside city halls in Buffalo, New York, Chattanooga, Boston and Cleveland.

A long month of agitation culminated on 6 March with the Comintern's international day of unemployed struggle when the Unemployed Councils called demonstrations throughout the country. The scale and militancy varied: some, in Chicago and San Francisco, passed off peacefully; the police dispersed crowds in Washington DC and Seattle with tear gas; but in Detroit, Cleveland, Milwaukee, Boston and New York, police action provoked resistance and rioting. Whilst the New York riot led to the mayor setting up a committee to distribute relief, the Communist Party leaders of the march received six-month jail sentences. These demonstrations, especially the violence in New York suddenly made the Councils front-page news. 6 March seriously dented the optimism of the press, and Congress appointed a house committee to investigate the activities of the communists.[83]

In the course of 1930 and 1931, the Unemployed Councils grew in numbers and popularity principally through the fight against evictions. Initially, communists led small groups to oppose the evictions which were sometimes successful by driving back the landlord's men or by returning the furniture after the bailiffs had gone. The Unemployed Councils even organised squads to restore gas and electricity supplies. The campaign against evictions gathered strength as the numbers of evictions mounted. Vern Smith reported on the work of the Down Town Unemployed Council of New York:

> The Down Town Council for months has held meetings of 1,000 or more in front of the employment agency every day, mobilises a daily march from the agency to its headquarters at 27 East 4 Street, and seldom gets less than a dozen new recruits, nor less than 400 signatures to the Workers' Unemployment Insurance Bill ... The Down Town Council has replaced in their rooms furniture of evicted families almost every day and has become such a terror to landlords that some of them now offer bribes of $5 or so to families they want to evict in order to persuade them not to take their case to the unemployed council. It mobilises such large forces that the police hesitate to attack. It has on various occasions sent committees of 50 or more to pounce on private employment agencies rallying hundreds from the surrounding neighbourhood, and forcing the agencies to return fees that were obtained for jobs the worker refused to take because of scab features or some other swindle.[84]

Opposition to evictions developed into large-scale confrontations with the police. On 3 August, the Chicago police turned their guns on a large crowd of mainly black protesters. Three of their number, Abe Grey, John O'Neill and Frank Armstrong, were shot dead. A week later 100,000 marched at their funerals.[85]

In July 1930, 1,300 delegates attended a national conference of Unemployed Councils. These organisations were now taking up a

range of activities, such as demanding emergency relief, a petition
campaign for a 'Workers' Unemployment Insurance Bill' and hunger
marches. Within months, 1.5 million had signed the petition for
unemployment insurance. In December 1931 and December 1932,
the Unemployed Councils staged two national hunger marches on
Washington. Travelling from various parts of the country, they
descended on Washington. On several occasions they mounted
protest demonstrations in towns on their way to the capital. During
the 1932 march, fighting with the police broke out in Minneapolis,
Detroit and Wilmington. The Federated Press described the police
reception of the marchers in Washington as an

> all-night barrage of insults by the police surrounding the pavement
> 'camp' of the marchers ... of deliberate incitement to riot had been
> attempted. The police taunted and cursed the marchers. They
> manhandled them ... hurled vile epithets ... hitting individuals or
> dragging them from cars.[86]

Unemployed protest entered a new phase when the relief agencies
became the major target of agitation. Relief officials found that
attitudes of their clients were changing rapidly. Previously quiescent,
clients were now becoming increasingly desperate and argumentative.
The charitable or local character of relief meant that there were no
uniform criteria for judging need. These very institutions generated a
sense of injustice, especially for those turned away, and groups of
unemployed began to take issue with the decisions and disrupt the
relief offices. Mrs Willye Jeffries recalled one of these episodes:

> we were going into the relief stations and gettin' arrested two,
> sometimes three times a day. We were fighting for an old lady that
> had died. And the relief wouldn't give 'em that hundred dollars
> towards the burial. They wouldn't give you nothing anyway. We
> got a crowd of about fifty people and went to the station. We gonna
> stay until we get this hundred dollars for this old lady. We finally
> succeeded in getting it.[87]

These sit-ins, pickets and demonstrations often brought
concessions from the relief agencies. This, in turn, added to the
pressures on charitable or municipal relief organisations to find more
funds for the avalanche of the needy unemployed. The poor's sense
of moral economy challenged the right of middle-class social workers
to adjudicate relief, and in some cases, agencies abandoned the hated
home visits. Small victories brought greater numbers into activity
especially in the larger cities where the evictions campaign was
strongest. Mauritz Hallgren reported,

Social workers everywhere told me that without the street demonstrations and hunger marches of the Unemployed Councils no relief whatever would have been provided in some communities, whilst in others even less help than that which had been extended would have been forthcoming. There are on record many instances in which public authorities or charitable agencies, having announced that relief would have to be cut down or suspended, quickly reversed their decision and obtained the necessary funds as a result of mass protests in the form of street demonstrations.[88]

As relief costs grew, so too did the difficulty of balancing the dwindling municipal tax revenues and the pressure from taxpayers to avoid tax increases. The relief bill nationally had increased from $71 million in 1929 to $171 million in 1931. The crucial test came when city authorities decided to cut relief. In Atlanta, in June 1932, city authorities removed 23,000 from relief because of lack of funds. To prevent disorder, the police arrested hundreds of vagrants, but a crowd of 1,000 outside the courthouse forced the authorities to reverse the cuts. In the same year, the Chicago city administration planned to axe relief by 50 per cent and there were proposals to deport all foreign-born unemployed. In response, the socialist-led Chicago Workers' Committee on Unemployment and the Unemployed League organised a demonstration, but city authorities ruled the march illegal, refusing a permit to march and the press predicted bloodshed. Despite this, between 25,000 and 50,000 turned up. William Scot, an Unemployed League member, described the scene,

At one point in the Loop we saw a solid wall of police blocking the road with all the top brass in evidence. The police said that we were defying the law by marching in the Loop without a permit. The march leaders stood solidly on their right to peaceful demonstration and placed all responsibility for the consequences of trying to stop the march on the city administration. At a signal from Joe Weber, the leader of the Unemployed Councils, the leaders started forward, with thousands of marchers behind us. The wall of police fell back and joined others on the sidelines. As we passed them we were roundly cursed and threatened with what would happen the next time they had us at their mercy.[89]

As a result, the city borrowed the money to restore the relief.

This crisis brought a sea change in the outlook of the politicians and businessmen who made up the local city elites. Important sections of the ruling class, big business associations and mayors swung suddenly, but temporarily, in favour of direct federal relief for the unemployed. In June 1932, Mayor Cermak of Chicago told a House Committee that if the federal government did not provide $150 million, they would have to send troops later.[90] The fact that the unemployed would not passively accept starvation precipitated this change in outlook. Harry Hopkins noted that 'there was a great fear of riots and violence in various parts of the country'.[91] This fear materialised on 7 March 1932, in Dearborn, where 50,000 had recently been made redundant from the River Rouge Ford Plant. When communists organised a hunger march, the police turned tear gas, water hoses (in freezing temperatures) and hand guns on the 3,000-strong demonstrators, killing 5 and injuring 18. Dave Moore, a trade unionist activist who was on the march, explained the mood: 'Having no job, no place to stay, no way to provide for your kids, these will have their effect on anybody.'[92]

This context shaped both FDR's electoral landslide and his introduction of federal emergency relief. The actions of the unemployed themselves had played an indispensable part in the securing of the latter. Roosevelt was in no doubt about the gravity of the problems of 1933:

Millions gripped by this greater fear [of starvation], had begun to feel that the machinery of modern American economics and government had broken down so completely under the strain of new demands placed upon it by modern civilisation, that an entirely new type of mechanics for existence should be invented.[93]

Even some in government circles became profoundly pessimistic. Harold Ickes recorded an evening at Secretary of the Treasury Woodin's house,

[Woodin] was worried and frankly said so. He doesn't like the situation. He thinks the dollar ought to be stabilized and he doesn't care much at what point, provided only that it is stabilized. He said that the big financial men in New York are all down in the mouth and think that the NRA campaign will be a failure. As they look at it, it is going to put the country entirely in the hands of labor.[94]

He also noted that Senator Thomas privately believed that Civilian Conservation Corps camps might soon become concentration camps for unemployed marchers. The reports and activities of the FERA testify that the FDR administration was anxious about the activities of the Unemployed Councils. Lorena Hickok's 1933 and 1934 reports repeatedly expressed concern about the growing influence of the communists amongst the unemployed: 'vast numbers of the unemployed in Pennsylvania are "right on the edge" so to speak –

that it wouldn't take much to make communists out of them'. She also voiced her fears about social unrest: 'the unemployment problem together with the labor troubles where jobs are opening up, may result in a good deal of disorder within the next few months'.[95]

The FERA consciously strove to marginalise the Unemployed Councils by various means. In Belle Vernon, West Virginia, a FERA official organised a workshop to make toys for a children's Christmas party to divert unemployed miners from the Unemployed Councils.[96] In general, relief was increased and its administration was improved, but the government also employed repression against the unemployed movement. Its leaders were investigated and awkward questions where put to their landlords. Efforts were made to get a doctor active amongst the unemployed in West Viriginia disbarred. Others faced deportation under the National Origins Act for unemployed agitation. In mining areas, strikers and unemployed council or union activists would be blacklisted and evicted from company housing.

Non-communist Unemployed Protests

As in Britain, the communists were not alone in protesting and organising against unemployment. Indeed, in the US, the non-communist groups were of more significance to unemployed protest than in Britain. A mixture of concern for the unemployed and anti-communism motivated a number of unaffiliated organisations often focusing on self-help and advice work. In January 1932 Father James R. Cox, a Catholic radio priest from Pittsburgh, organised a hunger march from the steel town to Washington. With funding from the Alleghany County Merchants' Association, carrying the stars and stripes and decrying the communists, the 'Mayor of Shantytown' led between 12,000 and 15,000 unemployed to the capital. He explained to a reporter:

> Some weeks ago I read of the invasion of Washington by a communistic group of marchers waving the red flag singing the International and demanding all sorts of fantastic things. This is repugnant to me, and I so stated on the radio. I remarked that while I condemned these demonstrations, I believed a body of real American citizens should go to Washington and protest against unemployment conditions which exist in the US today.[97]

Perhaps the most famous protest was the Bonus Expeditionary Force of unemployed First World War veterans in spring 1932. In 1924 Congress had voted in favour of a bonus for all First World War veterans to be paid in 1945. 2,000 marched to Washington requesting early payment of their bonus. They camped in central Washington or squatted in empty buildings. Hoover was deaf to their pleas and eventually ordered General Eisenhower to evict them. Using tear gas and tanks, the army drove the Bonus March veterans out of Washington.

American trade union officialdom entirely neglected unemployed workers. The American Federation of Labor did not support the call for compulsory unemployment insurance until 1932. Even the Congress of Industrial Organisations (CIO) rebuffed the affiliation of the Workers' Alliance, the national body of the unemployed. The notable exception was the miners' union, United Mine Workers, which organised two hunger marches to Charleston, Virginia.

The American unemployed movement was characterised by distinct phases and an even more pronounced regional unevenness than in the UK. In its early stages, the Communist Party was at the forefront because others parties overlooked the possibility of organising the unemployed. Some of the unemployed turned to self-help groups or spontaneous looting and eviction fights, but from 1932 both the Socialist Party and a second socialist current, identified with Abraham J. Muste (the Musteites), organised amongst the unemployed with some success. Despite their early lead, the communist Unemployed Councils stagnated during these years. In 1936 these three strands were unified in the Workers' Alliance of America.

The most significant non-communist organisations of the jobless were the Unemployed Leagues created by the Socialist Party. The Socialist Party leadership initially shunned the idea of organising the unemployed, a decision that its National Executive reversed only in February 1932. Despite this, some local Socialist Party branches had already set up unemployed organisations.[98] In 1931, socialists launched the Chicago Workers' Committee on Unemployment and it initially pursued a strategy of self-help. Within six months, it numbered 10,000 in its ranks and within a year it claimed 25,000 members in 60 locals (branches). As it grew, it adopted more militant tactics, the eviction fight and relief agency protest and by mid-1932 it was mobilising large numbers to halt Chicago's relief cuts. Before the National Executive decision to sanction unemployed work, Astabula (Ohio), Indianapolis, Terre Haute (Indiana) and Lewiston (Maine) had already acted on Chicago's example. After the ruling, Fairmont (West Virginia), New York City and South Bend (Indiana) quickly followed suit. There was some local variation in the character of the groups. For example, the Baltimore People's Unemployment League restricted itself to self-help and respectability whilst other groups were more militant. In 1933 and 1934, the socialist

Unemployed Leagues profited from the stagnation of the Unemployed Councils and the regional limitations of the Musteites. By the turn of 1935, New York, Pennsylvania, Illinois, Wisconsin, Indiana, New Jersey, Maryland and Oregon constituted the important areas of Unemployed League implantation, claiming 450,000 supporters.[99]

The Musteites also had a significant, though regional, impact among the unemployed. After two years of propaganda on the need for unemployment insurance, the Musteites, at that time the Conference for Progressive Labor Action (CPLA), set up unemployed organisations. In 1931, CPLA member Carl Branin successfully in setting up an Unemployed Citizen's League in Seattle. At first, it worked on the principle of self-help, bartering the labour of its members for goods.[100] CPLA members in other localities followed this example and established groups in Ohio, Pittsburgh, the mining communities of eastern Pennsylvania and West Virginia, and the textile towns of North Carolina. These Unemployed Leagues evolved from self-help to more militant action, especially resistance to evictions. For instance, in the summer of 1933, they succeeded in temporarily halting evictions in Columbus, Ohio. At their height, in 1933, the Unemployed Leagues were sizeable organisations. In Ohio, the Musteite Unemployed Leagues had 100,000 members in 187 locals and in Pennsylvania, they had 40,000–50,000 members, but outside these strongholds their influence was marginal. When the Musteites launched the National Unemployed League in July 1933, it was, and remained, essentially a regional movement. The Musteites themselves were undergoing a political transformation from a loose left-wing forum to an independent Marxist and then a Trotskyist organisation. That same year, they became the American Workers' Party and in 1934 they merged with the Trotskyist Communist League of America to form the Workers' Party.

In 1934, the Musteite Lucas County Unemployed League participated in one of the most militant episodes of the 1930s, the Toledo Auto-Lite strike. Musteites organisers encouraged League members to join the picket of the automotive parts plant resulting in the arrest of two Unemployed League organisers and 44 others. Their release after mass protests at the court raised the stakes of the strike. For six days the police and National Guard attempted to break the picket lines and in the bloody fighting two pickets were killed. After this determined resistance, the company gave in and settled the grievances of the strikers.[101]

From the point at which the Socialist Party recognised unemployed work, leaders of the Leagues sought to create a national organisation. These efforts eventually bore fruit with the founding of the Workers' Alliance in 1935. At its second Conference in April

1936, the WAA had unified the socialist and Musteite Unemployed
Leagues and the communist-led Unemployment Councils. David
Lesser, a Socialist Party member and formerly the head of the New
York Workers' Committee on Unemployment, became its Chairman,
and Herbert Benjamin, the National Secretary of the Unemployed
Councils, became the WAA's Secretary. By December 1936, it
claimed to represent 1,600 locals and 600,000 members. The
Alliance organised many workers in the WPA who struck against lay-
offs and and poor pay rates. Early on the WPA granted a number of
local concessions over these issues.

Paradoxically, the establishment of the Workers' Alliance was the
beginning of the end for the unemployment movement. The difficulties of unemployed organisations have been outlined with the British
case. These combined in a specific manner to undermine the
American movement. Concessions in the form of the FERA and then
the public works schemes subdued the militancy of the unemployed.
Unlike Hoover, Roosevelt was popular amongst the urban poor,
black and white, North and South. He advertised his sympathy for
the plight of the poor and this disseminated through the FERA. The
New Deal meant that relief institutions adopted a new approach to
unemployed organisations with complaints procedures, rights to representation, public relations and appeals offices shifting the focus and
modifying the character of protest. Conflict became institutionalised,
safely channelled and some unemployed activists became enthusias-
tic supporters of the New Deal project as with the two Chicago
Workers' Committee on Unemployment leaders who got FERA
jobs.[102] In one case, an Unemployed Council leader was successfully
encouraged to attend FERA workers' social events.[103] A FERA
report described the transformation in Brooklyn in 1934:

> The precinct with a 15,000 case load includes the Red Hook,
> Puerto Rican, Negro and Italian sections. Formerly it was in
> constant uproar with riots and everything else. The councils found
> it easy to stir up trouble at any time. The situation has changed
> completely in the last six months. The reception room handles a
> thousand persons a day and is as quiet as a library. The reception
> supervisor is accessible to anyone with a complaint. The police
> have all but withdrawn, and the Unemployed Council delegations
> are received in a quiet and orderly manner. This precinct is an
> enlightened example of an administration using its head in
> handling agitation, with the result that the councils have actually
> lost strength and power in this section. The rank and file of clients
> are 100 per cent with the investigators and staff. And this is the sort
> of low-class section one would expect a lot of trouble.[104]

The local roots of protest that had nourished the unemployed movement were withering at the very time that the Workers' Alliance was claiming its greatest influence. Its strategy reinforced these problems. The New Deal ideology turned the WAA's head and the unemployed organisation was drawn to the New Deal's bureaucratic apparatus. The Communist Party adopted the popular front in 1935, a strategy that came to dominate the American Left. The communists, who only a year before had encouraged the unemployed to resist the landlords and police under the slogan 'Don't starve – fight' now advocated an alliance with the New Deal administration. The Works Progress Administration recognised and negotiated with the WAA as the legitimate representative of the relief workers. Roosevelt and Hopkins were able to tantalise the Workers' Alliance with partial reform and bargaining rights. These enticements encouraged the WAA to look to high politics to achieve their goals. They drew up a bill for unemployment insurance, they canvassed support for Congressional amendments, they corresponded with the heads of federal agencies and lobbied sympathetic Senators. The unemployed movement also became less political and mirrored trade union practice of exclusively dealing with 'bread and butter' issues and casework of relief workers.

The more the WAA became drawn to the lobbying approach, the less leverage it had with Congress, the WPA or the President. Their weak response to the abolition of the FERA in July 1936 amply demonstrates the WAA's growing disorientation. There were other reasons for the lack of opposition. Many unemployed, who had had the work ethic instilled in them since birth, welcomed the prospect of work relief instead of public assistance. Work relief did not have the strong associations with task work and the Poor Law that it would have had in Britain. Some radical leaders had been proposing work relief instead of direct relief and the notion of union rates for the job were not as universal as in Britain given the tradition of small America craft unions restricted to certain trades.[105] These factors alone are not sufficient explanation for why the WAA did not make a concerted stand over the abolition of federal assistance for the unemployed. Partly, they were persuaded by Roosevelt's promises. But, the spending and numbers enrolled on the WPA fell far short of FDR's initial projections or the numbers helped by the FERA. The WPA only ever provided work for a fraction, at most a quarter, of the unemployed and the rest were left to the mercies of local and charitable relief. Viewed in this context, the WPA was clearly a retrograde step. Business had quickly reverted to its traditional hostility to federal relief, especially direct relief, and their pressure led Roosevelt to abolish emergency relief. Despite the large sums involved, the WPA was an ideological concession to the conservatives. Even from the early days of the FERA, the attitude of taxpayers to those on relief rolls was that the recipients should at least be 'made work'.[106] The WAA had failed to oppose the most significant attack on those out of work under the FDR presidency and this mistake led the organisation to die at the root and shrivel at the head. One after another, its lobbying projects failed and it was increasingly snubbed by the administration. By 1938, it was in disarray, in 1941 it dissolved itself.

Conclusion

The New Deal was not a coherent single programme but a number of short- and long-term reforms which evolved in accordance with the social and economic environment. From an economic standpoint, the New Deal was not a consistent reflationary project as FDR was anxious about federal deficits and sought to avoid them. The piecemeal implementation of work-creation and public assistance meant that the New Deal was deflationary at one moment, reflationary the next.[107] The administration did not conceive of deficit spending as the road to recovery and it did not enact a consistent reflationary budgetary policy which, according to Keynes, was needed to achieve this. In the short term, the New Deal overcame the acute crisis of the winter 1932–33 when municipal authorities and charities needed bailing out. Financial insolvency and unemployed protests provided a powerful stimulus to this.

After that point, the New Deal failed to live up to its radical rhetoric. Despite the undoubted popularity of wealth redistribution, the FDR administration made key retreats: over the termination of the CWA and FERA, the framing of tax reform and social security legislation. Roosevelt's soul was divided between the traditionalist and the liberal social reformer, perhaps symbolised by his relationship with Douglas and Hopkins respectively. The liberal historian's canvas depicts Roosevelt and Hopkins as the heroic architects of a new America with Hopkins as the unrelenting social worker striving for his vision of progressive welfare reform. There is much more to the social policy of the New Deal than this suggests. It obscures the financial and policy constraints on Hopkins and ignores the role of unemployed unrest in changing attitudes to reform. When, with the FERA's help, the unemployed threat subsided, so too did the willingness of vested interests to accept costly reforms. Liberal historians are too uncritical of Roosevelt's and Hopkins' vision of welfare, which had considerable intellectual continuities with the past, especially over the question of dependency and moral degradation. The New Deal social policy was imposed on the unemployed with strong elements of social engineering and control.

In the US, the uncertainty of unemployment, the withdrawal and feeling of inferiority of its victims, the permanent turnover of its members make the unemployed more difficult to organise than other sections of the working class. The geographical expanse of the US made it more difficult to transform regional protests and organisation into genuinely national ones. Whilst there was clearly a relationship between economic crisis and unemployed protest, misery and hunger did not automatically breed revolt. Lorena Hickok was bemused that there was so little protest in places where relief had entirely been cut off but much greater discontent where the unemployed were in a better state. In Middlesborough, Kentucky, where the unemployed were passive and quiescent, she was told they were 'so starved' they 'couldn't put on a riot', and yet, in Syracuse, New York State, where they 'didn't look undernourished', there was considerable unemployed dissatisfaction.[108] It was a combination of factors that impelled the unemployed to protest. One factor was the politics and strategy of the unemployed activists. The passage from the 'third period' to the popular front clearly accelerated the decline of the movement. From 1936 onwards, despite the advantages of unification and a national organisation, the unemployed movement became little more than the 'conscience' of the New Deal. Ironically, the third period which spelled disaster for the Communist Party's trade union work, was less damaging in activity amongst the unorganised unemployed where the attitude to other trade unionists was not an issue. The communists' ultra-left stance of these days was not so out of step with the elemental rebellion of jobless looters, those fighting evictions or angry crowds outside the relief agencies but efforts to organise the unemployed showed that they were not a new revolutionary vanguard. Their attitudes reflected those of the wider working class. As Verba and Schlozman noted, the unemployed 'were not strikingly different from employed waged workers. In each case, the distinctive groups was the upper-white collar group which was decidedly more conservative.'[109] Their protests could wring concessions from government and relief agencies especially when deepening recession threw the ruling class into turmoil. The paradox was that concessions themselves, in the form of the New Deal, played practical and ideological role in the decline of the movement.

7 Unemployment in Europe between the Wars

When Pinneberg had been sitting for an hour or so in the train, he piled up all his afflictions in his mind, and they flared into quite a pretty little blaze of anger, hatred, and bitterness. But that did not last. When he came to push his way through the Labour Exchange in the grey monotonous stream of his fellows – all kinds of faces and all kinds of clothes, but in all their hearts the same conflict, the same misery, the same bitterness. –

Ah, what's the use? He was in it all, he was one of these six millions shouldering past the pay-desks; why should he get excited?

Hans Fallada, *Little Man – What Now?*[1]

Well we have been given notice! Let us now face the question: after this hard piece of news, is everything still the same as it was before? Frankly, no. After such a scene anyone interested in the psychology of the worker would perceive a miserable sight. When the chief had spoken everything seemed changed: men, machines – everything was different. Although the sun was the same and still shone as before, yet it had somehow altered. The warmth of its heavenly rays was no longer so pleasant, no longer awakened the wish to live and work as it had before, but on the contrary became more and more oppressive. The men were gloomy, and their faces a deathly pale. After a time they broke into groups, making puzzled gestures. As if they were trying to drown that terrible and agonising thought, the machines roared louder and louder, running idle and unfed.

A Polish worker describing losing his job.[2]

When for the first time I held out my hand for my 9 zloty of benefit, I was filled with disgust for the whole of my previous existence ... Why am I here? What was the good of all the time spent on my education and training? What use is all my knowledge? I stand in the ranks of the needy, but I myself want nothing. My whole being revolts and recoils, but I must take these 9 zloty. My father is expecting them.

A young Polish worker recounting his feeling when first drawing unemployment insurance.[3]

A French visitor to Germany in 1932 entered a youth hostel. Young Germans surrounded him and avidly asked: 'Is there any unemployment in France?' Whilst the lack of work dominated their young lives, its effects were evidently different across the border in France. The unevenness of the European experience of unemployment allows us to fill out the picture of the condition of the unemployed, the options for policy-makers and the effects on government during the depression.

Some 10.5 million of the world's estimated 30 million unemployed in 1932 lived in continental Europe. In Germany alone 6 million registered as out of work and this country suffered the most bitter and destabilising effects of unemployment.[4] This chapter focuses on the three themes which have the greatest significance for our general analysis of unemployment: the social policy of unemployment and the experience and protests of the unemployed.

Revisionist historians view the stability of British liberal democracy as an exceptional case. This chapter will describe the character and effects of unemployment in Europe. This same corrosive process was at work across Europe, triggering the nightmare scenario – the Third Reich – and general instability in continental Europe. The parallels with the British experience become apparent, the difference being the greater scale of the depression in some parts of Europe. If the same underlying process existed across Europe and the United Kingdom, then the stability of British society was fragile, its consensus threatened and superficial and social peace was contingent on the avoidance of greater economic misfortune.

Unemployment Insurance in Europe

Between the wars, European governments became concerned about unemployment as never before. The First World War had accelerated both the industrialisation and urbanisation of Europe and, in turn, the development of mass politics. The carnage had ripped Europe apart and strained its political and economic contradictions to breaking point. During wartime, governments had become more sensitive to the popular mood and had promised to incorporate the demands of labour in order to perpetuate its participation in the war effort, creating high expectations of the postwar world. The peace settlement of 1919 replaced the empires of Germany and Austria-Hungary with new, politically unstable nation-states with democratic constitutions. Following demobilisation, the recession of the early 1920s and the greater numbers now relying on industry, unemployment became a visible problem that no government could ignore and at the same time the demographic safety-valve of emigration to the colonies and Americas was largely sealed off. In Germany, average unemployment for the 1900s was 2.6 per cent, whilst for 1919–23 it was 4.2 per cent and for 1924–29, 13.7 per cent.[5] Although European governments responded in a number of ways, there were two principal arms of unemployment policy: unemployment relief (assistance or insurance) and public works.

Rising labour unrest and reconstruction set the scene for the rapid introduction of either emergency unemployment relief or unemployment insurance across much of Europe. Governments worried about the consequences of enforced idleness. Revolution had taken hold in Russia and there was a very real threat of its extension to other parts of Europe. In the years 1918–21, German, Italian, British, Polish and Swiss governments established emergency relief for the unemployed in anticipation unemployment insurance. On 13 November 1918, at the height of the revolution that deposed the Kaiser, a decree was passed in Germany for unemployed assistance (*Erwerbslosenfürsorge*). This could be drawn indefinitely (until an amendment in May 1920 when a 26-week limit was set, with a discretionary extension of up to one year). In these years, the Netherlands, Italy, Czechoslovakia, Belgium and Austria introduced unemployment insurance for the first time, and, in Britain, the unemployment insurance scheme was significantly extended.

Two basic forms of unemployment insurance scheme were being adopted: publicly assisted trade union insurance and compulsory state unemployment insurance. The former scheme was initially conceived in 1900 in Ghent. By the late nineteenth century, some Belgian skilled trade unions had introduced unemployment insurance for their members, but the Ghent unions faced with difficulties financing their unemployment obligations, turned to the town council for help. Aware of the social tensions arising from unemployment, the council reckoned that there would be advantages in granting such aid. As the trade unions were in an ideal position to encourage workers to insure themselves against unemployment, the new scheme could strengthen self-help and tackle the social threat of the unemployed. The council voted unanimously (i.e. Catholic, liberal and socialist factions) on a formula to supplement trade union unemployment funds. This left the burden of administration in the hands of the trade union, so avoiding the need for a new tier of municipal bureaucracy. The Ghent system gradually spread from one municipality to another so that, by 1913, 101 municipalities had adopted the scheme which covered 32 per cent of the total Belgian population.[6] By the outbreak of war, this model had been introduced at local, regional or national level in France, the Netherlands, Switzerland, Germany, Austria-Hungary, Norway, Denmark and Italy. In 1906, Norway established the scheme on a national basis, as did Denmark the following year. Other national voluntary systems were initiated in the Netherlands (1914 and 1917), Finland (1917), Belgium (1920–21), Czechoslovakia (1921), Spain (1923) and Sweden (1934).[7]

The principal flaw of the Ghent system was that coverage depended entirely on the numbers subscribing to voluntary insurance schemes. In France, a quarter of a century after the 1905 national voluntary unemployment insurance scheme, only 200,000 workers were insured against unemployment, because French unions were suspicious of the state scheme and employers were bitterly antagonistic to the extension of the social insurance. The French social insurance laws of 1928 and 1930 likewise failed in the face of workers' strikes and hostility from employers' organisations. The Czechoslovak scheme of 1921 also suffered from a poor take-up rate until further legislation attempted to induce a greater participation.

Another feature of the Ghent system was that new members flocked to the unions during times of high unemployment. Whilst elsewhere unemployment spelled declining membership, in Belgium, Norway, the Netherlands and Denmark, union membership rose during the early 1930s.[8] For union members, however, the Ghent system was a mixed blessing. The more that the time and energies of trade union officialdom were embroiled in unemployment insurance, the less time it had for other matters. Much of the resources of the union were drawn into the administering and financing unemployment insurance. At times of mass unemployment, this left unions with the threat of bankruptcy and with unforeseen bureaucratic responsibilities and therefore undermined the ability to organise solidarity and raise money for strikes. Also, trade union officials could argue against industrial action on the grounds that it would threaten the ability to pay unemployment benefits and create a situation in which the trade unions were dependent upon the state to bail out unemployment funds. By the 1930s, the Left inside the Belgian unions was highly critical of the Ghent system, as were the communist unemployed committees which opposed this form of insurance and called for compulsory unemployment insurance on terms most favourable to the workers.[9]

At the same time, Belgian employers and conservatives lodged their own complaints against the Ghent system. Before the war, the ruling Catholic–Liberal coalition had blocked a national scheme because conservatives believed that unemployment insurance undermined the incentive to find work and that the Ghent system strengthened the unions. They also alleged that left-wing politicians bought trade union support through granting more generous municipal subsidies to unemployment funds.

An alternative to the Ghent model took shape in Britain in 1911 when Lloyd George's Liberal government introduced the first national system of compulsory unemployment insurance. In the long run, most European governments were to follow the compulsory British system. During the interwar period, although Italy (1919), Austria (1920), Ireland (1923), Poland (1924), Bulgaria (1925), Germany (1927) and Norway (1938) all adopted some variant of compulsory unemployment insurance their social function and labour market context produced very different characteristics. In the less developed countries of Eastern and Southern Europe, unemployment insurance covered only a small proportion of the working population. Generally, the value of benefits was much lower and their function was to ease the social and economic strains of industrialisation. In more advanced regions, unemployment insurance generally had a wider coverage and benefits were higher. Here unemployment threatened to force the skilled out of their normal occupations and create skilled shortages once recession had passed. As joblessness persisted, there was greater differentiation in the provision for the unemployed reflecting the complex gradation of skill and occupation in these labour markets.

Coverage varied from country to country. Certain occupational categories might be excluded, such as domestic workers, agricultural workers and sometimes public sector workers. In Poland, a separate scheme existed for white-collar workers, and in Britain those with an income of more than £250 were not covered. In most countries, payments were calculated from the level of earnings (except in Britain and Ireland where benefits were paid as a flat rate).

Whilst the compulsory schemes all worked on the basis that insured workers were authorised benefit if they had paid sufficient contributions within a given period, there was no uniform pattern of eligibility. The 1920 Austrian scheme, the most liberal in Europe, required only 20 weeks' contributions, whereas in the 1919 Italian scheme, 48 weeks' contributions qualified the claimant for benefit. The source of contributions differed from one country to another. In Britain, Ireland and Bulgaria, there was a tripartite division between state, employer and worker. In Austria and Germany, the state was not meant to contribute to unemployment insurance funds, but was ultimately forced to intervene when the unemployment fund deficits deepened. The length of benefit payment also differed from country to country: 12 weeks under the Austrian law of 1920, compared with 26 weeks of the German law of 1927. The generosity of the payments also varied: payments constituted 35 per cent of weekly average earnings in Germany but only 25 per cent in Ireland.

Even from the policy-maker's perspective, the voluntary and compulsory insurance schemes failed to solve the problem of unemployment. Most schemes, though not in Austria and Germany, did not distinguish between workers on the basis of the number dependent upon their income, so neglecting a principal cause of the direst poverty. In the UK and the Netherlands, dependants' allowances were introduced in 1921; in Denmark, 1919; in Italy, 1937; and in France, not until 1967.[10]

Unemployment Insurance in Crisis, 1929–33

States failed to foresee the vast hordes of the jobless over the horizon. In Germany, the calculations of benefits and contributions for the 1927 insurance scheme were based on a projected average of 800,000 unemployed.[11] Mass unemployment threatened state unemployment insurance funds and fostered conservative calls for retrenchment. By 1932, in Austria, the unemployment insurance fund with debts of £3.8 million was losing money at a rate of £1 million pounds a year and the Unemployment Law of 1920 had been amended 28 times in the fight for solvency. In March 1932, the Polish Unemployment Insurance Act was amended to cut benefit from 21 to 10.80 zlotys for a single adult and from 28 to 14.40 zlotys for an adult with 3–5 dependants.[12] In Belgium, a series of royal decrees during the depression limited and centralised unemployment benefits.[13]

The insurance principle was incompatible with mass long-term unemployment. Insurance schemes had been established with guidelines for qualification: workers had to pay a certain number of contributions in a given period and could draw unemployment benefits for a set number of weeks. Problems arose when a large part of the jobless had exhausted their right to benefits. Governments were forced either to extend benefits, and thereby jeopardise the funds of the unemployment insurance scheme, or grant supplementary unemployment allowances.[14] Many governments repeatedly revised their provision for the unemployed, particularly when under political pressure for either increments or retrenchment. Several governments introduced extended benefits or special assistance schemes because unemployment failed to conform to the projections of policy-makers. In Austria, this kind of benefit was brought in as an emergency measure in 1918 and 1922, and then on a permanent basis in 1926. In a number of countries, three tiers of provision (insurance, emergency benefits and poor relief) emerged as an *ad hoc* response to growing unemployment.

Provision for the jobless changed dramatically in the last years of the Weimar Republic. In January 1931, the majority (52.3 per cent) of the jobless were still drawing insurance benefits and roughly equal numbers received no relief (13.8 per cent), welfare relief (17.3 per cent) and emergency relief (16.6 per cent). Twenty-one months into the depression, unemployment insurance was paid to only a small minority of the unemployed (11.4 per cent) because the largest numbers received the miserly means-tested welfare relief and nearly a quarter of the workless could draw no relief whatsoever.[15]

In Poland, a similar pattern occurred in which insurance became subject to narrower eligibility criteria and workers were less likely to have consistent contributions records because of the lack of work opportunities. In 1930, half of the Polish manual workers registered as unemployed received unemployment insurance benefits, but in 1933 only a quarter did so.[16] In both the German and Polish cases, these figures underestimated those without relief as many did not to register at a labour exchange.

As in Britain in autumn 1931, unemployment provision could provoke sharp governmental crises, with Germany providing the most spectacular example. The amendments to unemployment insurance law shattered the Weimar Republic's political centre-ground, which had provided the basis for coalition governments with Reichstag majorities. The development of the unemployment insurance had itself been fraught with political difficulties. In 1924, unemployment relief was linked to the health insurance scheme. Health insurance covered most of the working class and their compulsory contributions would now qualify them for unemployment benefits. Some German employers were already complaining about heavy social costs in the mid-1920s. Paul Silverberg, owner of the leading lignite company, sharply criticised unemployment insurance at a German Industrial Association (*Reichverband der Deutschen Industrie* – RDI) meeting in September 1926. At this point, big business was still relatively reconciled to the compromise of the Weimar Republic which involved co-operation with the unions and reform. After much debate, the German unemployment insurance scheme (*Arbeitslosenversicherung und Arbeitsvermittlung Gesetz* – AVAVG) was finally agreed in July 1927 and signalled, for liberal opinion, the crowning achievement of Weimar reform. The coalition of the Catholic centre and conservative parties (*Bürgerblock*) was responsible for this legislation, which was based on wide agreement spanning both employers' organisations and unions (though not the Nazis, communists and some right nationalists in the *Deutschnationale Volkspartei* – DNVP).

From the first, the AVAVG's troubled finances caused concern. Whilst its first two months provided a surplus, December saw benefit payments outstrip contributions by 11.7 million Reichsmark (RM). In the following year, there was a surplus from May to October, but there was still a 90 million RM shortfall for the year.[17] The situation only worsened. The first year of the Great Depression, 1929, followed the same seasonal pattern, but the balance deteriorated astronomically with the *Reichanstalt* (the unemployment fund) of the AVAVG building up a 376.5 million RM annual deficit.[18]

Whilst registered unemployment rose from 1.6 million in 1929 to 4.6 million in 1931, the costs of unemployment insurance escalated. The pressure to restore the finances of the unemployment insurance fund to good order began to grow. By 1929–30 complaints about the AVAVG, especially from heavy industry and employers' organisations – notably the RDI, *Langnamverein* (Rhineland and Westphalian business association) – increased in volume. On May Day 1929, the Federation of German Employers' Associations (*Vereinigung der Deutschen Arbeitergeberverbände* – VDA) issued a memorandum calling for means testing, for benefits pegged below prevailing local wage levels and for cuts of 400–500 million RM in the annual expenditure of the *Reichanstalt*. In sum, the business agenda sought balanced budgets, tax relief for employers and, at the very least, no increases in their unemployment insurance contributions.[19] In 1930, 731 million RM was added to AVAVG debts and, worryingly, there was not a single month in which contributions were greater than outgoings.[20] Increasingly under the influence of big business, the German People's Party (*Deutsche Volkspartei* – DVP) precipitated a governmental crisis as they pressed insistently for unemployment benefits cuts. In March 1930, Müller, the SPD Chancellor, resigned and the Grand Coalition government fell because his attempt to increase contributions to unemployment insurance had failed. This collapse marked the end of government based on a parliamentary majority, and from this point minority governments rested on the presidential powers of emergency decree. Weimar democracy had begun to dissolve under the corrosive effects of the arguments over reparations and opposition to existing levels of unemployment benefits.

On 26 July 1930, Brüning, the new Chancellor, decreed reforms to the AVAVG with benefits reduced and contributions increased (from 3 to 4.5 per cent of basic wages); in October, contributions increased to 6.5 per cent of wages. One solution to the difficulties of unemployment insurance was to force the jobless onto other means of support. Whilst, in early 1931, 2.5 million people were receiving unemployment insurance benefits, by the summer that figure had more than halved. Despite vicious cuts and the introduction of a means test on all benefits in June 1931, there was still a *Reichanstalt* deficit of 119,533 RM for 1931.[21] By 1932, the succession of emergency decrees (October 1929, July 1930, June 1931, June 1932) restricting the scope of unemployment benefit had finally restored the financial position of the *Reichanstalt* with credit for the year of 199,691 RM.[22] This was achieved by forcing most of the workless off unemployment insurance and onto emergency relief or the local authorities and the price was paid in the hardship and misery of those whose relief had been whittled down by the means test. The AVAVG had promised workers protection from the menace of unemployment and seemed a rational answer to unemployment, but with the remorseless increase in unemployment, the AVAVG proved to be a principal geological faultline of Weimar democracy. The hostility of the employers and the Right grew progressively stronger and the AVAVG was dismantled piece by piece. Unemployment and economic crisis threatened welfare provision for the unemployed at a time when it was most needed.

During the interwar years, unemployment insurance reforms constituted tentative, experimental steps towards the modern welfare state. As such, the British and German examples were keenly debated internationally. Several on the right of the political spectrum maintained that both these examples proved to be disastrous. They insisted that unemployment insurance brought massive financial burdens on taxpayers and encouraged the jobless to remain idle. The National Industrial Conference Board, an American employers' organisation, highlighted the failings of the German scheme which proved to be inadequate with the catastrophic levels of unemployment in the early 1930s.[23] Jacques Rueff, the French economist, blamed the persistently high unemployment in Britain on compulsory unemployment insurance. In his perverse reasoning, unemployment benefits caused unemployment (he failed to notice the much higher unemployment in the US where there were no such benefits).[24] These criticisms of welfare systems failed to appreciate that it was the sheer scale of economic devastation that jeopardised welfare reforms (just as the welfare consensus has been in question since the recessions of the 1970s). Some critics of unemployment insurance favoured labour schemes in which the unemployed would be put to work.

Public Works: Work-Creation and Coercion

The question of work-creation by the state is exceptionally difficult. Both Right and Left proposed various forms of work relief to combat unemployment. Eastern European dictatorships, the French Popular Front government, Mussolini's Italy and Hitler's Germany all developed such schemes. All too often historical discussions of public works attributed them to an incipient Keynesianism in which full employment had become a goal of government through work-creation and deficit spending. This was heavily influenced by hindsight and it ignored strong continuities with the Poor Law and the authoritarian and wage-cutting character of some schemes.

Much of the contemporary and historiographical discussion of public works centres on the German case. The Nazi government claimed to have abolished unemployment through its 'battle for work'. In reality, Hitler benefited from the public works programmes launched by previous governments and the fortuitous timing of the economic upswing that had begun in late 1932. Hitler's three predecessors as Chancellor – Brüning, von Papen and von Schleicher – all instigated labour and public works schemes. The Voluntary Labour Service (*Freiwilliger Arbeitsdienst*, FAD) was the most significant and employed about 250,000 annually between 1932 and 1936. In June 1931, Brüning instigated the Voluntary Labour Service, which had a disciplinary element aimed at stemming the perceived moral decline and radicalisation of jobless youth, but work-creation lost out to the priority of restoring international creditworthiness through reparations payments.

The Ministry of Finance and the Reichsbank (those elements of government closest to business) hampered the public works proposals of successive Ministers of Labour. In June 1932, von Papen increased the numbers on the FAD because of AVAVG debts and the belief that it would offset right-wing criticism of the insurance scheme.[25] It was only in September 1932, that a distinctive change in attitudes came about and Papen formulated a number of emergency decrees to stimulate employment through subsidies to employers (tax credits and a premium paid when new workers were engaged). However, President Hindenburg replaced von Papen with General Kurt von Schleicher as the governmental difficulties continued. The new Chancellor appointed Gunter Gereke to the new post of Commissioner for Work-Creation. The Commissioner drew up an 'immediate programme' worth 500 million RM which was enacted in a series of emergency decrees only days before Hitler's appointment as Chancellor. These programmes and methods set the basic pattern for the Nazi public works.

Elsewhere, a variety of reasons lay behind public work-creation. We must distinguish between the government fanfare of fighting unemployment and the rather mundane realities of each particular scheme. With the exception of the programme of the Swedish Social Democratic government that took office in 1933, none of the schemes followed a Keynesian approach. In the case of Hitler's Germany, during his first three years in office, the government held to the orthodoxy of balanced budgets under the watchful eye of the former head of the Reichsbank and leading conservative Hjalmar Schacht. When this orthodoxy was relaxed in 1936, the primary goal was not full employment but rearmament.

In the case of French Popular Front government of 1936–37, pressure from the liberals (*les radicaux*) and communists ensured that any neo-Keynesian proclivities from sections of the French Socialist Party (SFIO – *Section Française de L'Internationale Ouvrière*) were firmly held in check. Successive French public works schemes of the 1930s (for example, the Laval Plan 1931 and the Marquet Plan 1934) were not Keynesian but stood in the long-standing tradition of counter-cyclical public works to relieve distress. These plans did not seek to increase aggregate demand through government budget deficits as Keynes was suggesting, but sought instead to maintain balanced government finances and provide earnings for the needy. The Marquet Plan was financed out of the surplus of the unemployment insurance funds, the Minister of Labour claimed that this would provide 100,000 jobs, but the actual number of jobs created fell well short of the announced projects.[26] Pierre Saly, the French economic historian, described the French public works of the 1930s as more a trick-of-the-light than a substantial effort to eliminate unemployment.[27]

Some governments conceived of work provision measures as retrenchment, as an alternative to unemployment benefit. These policies clawed back concessions made in the immediate aftermath of war when labour militancy was at its height. Several national governments and municipalities had adopted labour schemes or amended assistance so that the unemployed performed labour in return for unemployment assistance. This continued the traditions of the European Poor Law which required paupers to perform task work in order to discourage malingering. This form of relief appealed to conservative opinion, particularly that voiced by taxpayers' or employers' lobbies. In Austria, 'productive unemployment assistance', a subsidy given to local authorities from the unemployment insurance fund, was thus introduced in October 1922 and provided 70 days' work for 22,000 unemployed working on roads and dykes.[28] Such provision from unemployment insurance funds was also established in Denmark, Italy, Belgium and Germany.[29] In the summer of 1931, the Italian fascist government adopted a public works programme in response to the rise in unemployment. Mussolini himself overrode objections from business leaders and from within his own ranks to pursue public works. Significantly, the regime justified this stance by attacking the British system of unemployment assistance and by reiterating the moral dangers of relief dependency.[30] In 1933, the Polish dictatorship launched a programme of public works under the slogan of 'work instead of relief', so indicating its hostility to relief costs.[31]

Labour schemes often constituted an increasingly authoritarian approach to labour. With the political instability and the collapse of democracies in depression-hit Europe, the complexion of unemployment policy became more authoritarian. In Bulgaria, which had become a dictatorship in 1923, the system of compulsory labour service was extended to the unemployed in November 1934. In this way, from 1935 to 1937, 21,820 workless Bulgarians were compelled to perform six months of labour (usually road construction).[32] These gangs of forced labourers were paid either their unemployment benefits, very low wages, or a combination of the two. If they refused to work, they lost their benefit. In Poland, a labour service scheme was instigated in 1932 under the auspices of the Association for the Assistance of Unemployed Young Persons. This private institution had the support of the Ministry of Social Welfare and was subsidised from the Employment Fund. The young Poles on these schemes lived in barracks, worked long hours (typically rising at 4 o'clock in the morning) and were under the supervision and discipline of former army personnel. Such work was voluntary but most of its participants had little alternative, as they were ineligible for any form of relief.[33] In Austria, the suppression of parliamentary democracy by Dolfuss in 1933 signalled the starting point for the voluntary labour service, an integral part of his 'corporate state'. Paid the price of just ten cigarettes a day, the mainly young labourers were compelled to do the hardest manual labour. The voluntary labour service took on a quasi-military appearance with grey uniforms, pick-and-shovel insignia, barracks and a stringent code of discipline.[34]

This authoritarianism became most apparent in the Third Reich, where the long-term unemployed were increasingly criminalised. The labour service, which from 1931 had some 250,000 annually on its books, became compulsory in June 1935. The unemployed during the depression were visible in the public spaces of the cities: parks, street corners, railway stations. The belief that Hitler had cured unemployment was reinforced by the absence of the homeless and unemployed from the public view. There were several campaigns to clear the so-called 'work-shy' or 'asocials' from the streets. In September 1933, the police rounded up 300,000–500,000 unemployed vagrants and forced them into the labour service or detention camps. Racial hygiene and eugenics 'experts' claimed that the 'asocials' inherited personal failings and therefore required punitive treatment (the regime sterilised up to 400,000, two-thirds of whom were unskilled workers). These notions underpinned the dismantling of welfare provision of the unemployed and its replacement with coercion. Ultimately, some ended up in the extermination camps.[35]

Some job schemes were represssive and authoritarian, while others were a concession to working-class demands. In several cases, partly because of opposition from employers to state intervention, work-creation took the form of government financial support for business, or 'capitalism on the dole' as one critic put it. In late Weimar and Nazi Germany, public works took the form of subsidies and tax-breaks for employers. In France, the decree of 29 January 1935 sought to encourage employers to recruit the unemployed through subsidies from the public unemployment fund surpluses.[36] Workers' organisations were concerned that some schemes simply exploited cheap labour and, in some cases, the unemployed were working for dole payments. This was the case with the so-called productive unemployment assistance in Austria, Germany, Denmark and Poland.[37] In October 1923, the German state provision for the unemployed was amended so that the recipient could be required to perform between eight and 24 hours work a week for their unemployment benefits.[38] The 1927 insurance law allowed those under 21 to be assigned a job, rural work or a scheme. Other schemes were less exploitative as general public works were expanded and those who were recruited were paid the going rate for the job. The Swedish Social Democratic government in 1933 brought existing work relief projects in line with prevailing local pay rates. It also embarked on a new expansive programme of public works to stimulate production. The government spent 250 million crowns in 1933–34 and four times that figure the following year. To increase consumer demand the new jobs created were paid at the going market wage rates.[39]

These differences between public works programmes were reflected in the attitudes and responses of the unemployed to them. The German labour service and productive unemployment assistance were unpopular with the unemployed as they offered low paid, often demeaning, work such as snow-clearing, chopping wood and cleaning schools. The clothing and food provided for workers were inadequate and they often had to live away from home in barracks. The young men on the schemes were paid a miserable sum, sometimes less than dole payments and often in the form of vouchers. The Nazi works programme continued and extended existing work-creation projects. Despite the fact that the fall in unemployment was one of the principal reasons for the popularity of the regime, several reports from SPD members to the exiled party leadership related the sharp dissatisfaction of participants on the work schemes. Subjected to derisory pay, sometimes armed supervision and ill-prepared food, the labour service workers were particularly embittered.[40] According to a Munich police report, the autobahn construction sites were 'hotbeds of communism'.[41] Elsewhere in Europe too, there were strikes and protests from relief and labour service workers. In Austria, there were a number of strikes and protests amongst the 'grey army' of the voluntary labour service.

From the working-class point of view, although work was universally demanded, serious drawbacks often accompanied its provision. Governments and municipalities could use labour schemes to bypass and undermine existing wage norms and thereby boost the rate of exploitation of labour. In the case of Germany, the FAD allowed local authorities to pay less than the legal minimum wage. Schemes were also used to restore order and authority into the structureless and chaotic lives of the unemployed. In this respect, the authorities targeted the young unemployed because they feared the growth of delinquency and radical politics.

The pendulum of government policy towards the unemployed swung between concession, reform, retrenchment and authoritarianism. Whilst the early postwar years provided the greatest impetus for reform, by the early 1930s, the momentum was certainly with retrenchment and greater coercion of the unemployed. Uncertainty reigned as politicians encountered levels of unemployment that did not seem conceivable according to contemporary economic dogma and past experience. Unemployment bewildered policy-makers because it combined the age-old hardship and periodic immiseration encountered by Europe's working poor with the distinctly new poverty of generalised industrial depression. It is to this experience that we now turn.

Europe's Unemployed

National official unemployment data were not comparable, some were collected by trade unions (Belgium, Holland, Norway, Sweden, France), others through compulsory unemployment insurance (United Kingdom, Ireland, Germany) and others still through the operation of employment exchanges (France, Finland, Switzerland). National censuses of population provided detailed snap-shots of unemployment. In some countries, several of these measures coexisted. The reliability of these statistics varied from one system of measurement to another. Particular distortions arise from the partial coverage of trade union returns or the fact that if the unemployed did not have to go to a labour exchange as a condition of benefit many would simply not bother. Grytten's study of the Norwegian trade union figures demonstrates that because joblessness was higher amongst unionised trades, official unemployment rates are exaggerated by the order of 1.5–3 times.[42] In France, the 1931 and 1936 censuses revealed the shortfalls of the official statistics of the jobless supported by the unemployment funds. In 1936, 864,170 were unemployed according to the census, but only 465,127 according to the other measure.[43] Mussolini's dictatorship manipulated its unemployment figures in 1933 when employment exchanges were instructed to revise their statistics downwards to 'correct' the problem of those unemployed who signed on at more than one exchange (despite the fact that many more would not have registered at any); and it simply suppressed this information during the Abyssinian invasion (September 1935 to December 1936).[44]

The large numbers out of work who were not provided for by any relief measure also distorted measurement. Contemporaries were conscious of the unemployed 'invisible' to, or 'hidden' from, the figures and researchers estimated between 1.5 and 2 million invisible jobless in 1932 in Germany, and 600,000 in Poland in 1934. This problem existed elsewhere in Europe.[45] The rural dimension of hidden unemployment was particularly difficult to judge, complicated as it was by the different categories of land ownership and employment status in the European countryside. Many bankrupted smallholding peasants were driven into the ranks of the unemployed. The millions of 'peasant-workers' in Poland (who combined industrial work and smallholding) defy normal labour market classifications. The Polish Institute of Social Economy estimated the rural surplus population of working age which was concentrated in the small farms of the central and Voivodies regions to be 2.4 million.[46] Also, agricultural labourers were typically employed on seasonal or partial basis. The day-labourer of southern Italy (the *braccianti*) normally expected only 200 days of work a year in good times.[47]

Patterns of migration also confuse matters. Perversely, unemployment stimulated emigration just as governments restricted immigration, and even in some cases repatriated immigrant workers. The French government expelled large numbers of Polish coal miners and metal workers, so aggravating the high-point of unemployment in Poland. The USA also reduced its immigration quotas during the depression, particularly for migrants from the poorest parts of Europe. The combined immigration to six traditional receiving countries outside Europe (USA, Argentina, Canada, Australia, Brazil, South Africa) fell from 881,943 in 1927 to 331,094 in 1930–31.[48]

During the interwar years France replaced the US as the world's principal destination for migrants. With an extremely low birth rate and labour shortages aggravated by war losses, France's foreign population doubled from 1.5 million in 1921 to 3 million in 1931. The Italian, Polish and Belgian immigrants performed the dirtiest, hardest and most dangerous work and were treated like 'white negroes'.[49] Foreign labour constituted 34 per cent of those working in mines and quarries and 30 per cent in heavy metal industries but, at times of recession, short-term contracts were terminated and migrants were compelled to return to their country of origin. In 1927, 27,000 more workers left the country than entered and in 1932 the figure was 50,000.

Within national frontiers unemployed migrants roamed from town to town, from countryside to town (or vice versa) in a desperate search for food and work. But again the residency qualifications of municipal relief or repression of internal migration (in the case of Italy) made this more difficult. Franz Schick, a homeless unemployed Austrian in his early twenties, drifted through Yugoslavia. His journal recounted a life of begging and odd jobs: if he was lucky he found a little bread and shelter, if less fortunate, he was turned away hungry by cursing peasants. This was the life of the many 'travellers' and 'vagabonds' he met on his travels.[50]

The demographic structure of labour markets also had a significant bearing on the character of unemployment. Here the contrast between Germany and France is instructive, Germany had a high birth rate immediately before the war which meant that there was a rapid expansion of the population of working age coinciding with the depression. France, by contrast, had a chronically low birth rate (known as the problem of *dénatalité*) which, reinforced by return migration and falling women's activity, produced a contracting labour market in the 1930s.[51] The idea that France was untouched by unemployment or that demographic factors alone explain low unemployment are quite wrong. France's recession was delayed (it began in 1931) and its recovery was weaker and later that other major economies. This produced long-term unemployment, which particularly affected the old and the unskilled in the mid- and late 1930s.

The widespread introduction of short-time working cushioned unemployment and concealed distress. It meant hardship for those workers who were in effect partially unemployed. In Germany, in July 1932, a fifth of male and a third of female industrial workers were working short time.[52] In France, partial unemployment in 1936 accounted for the equivalent of 214,000 fully unemployed workers.[53]

Still more serious, the face of European unemployment in the 1930s had changed; it had developed into the greying and sunken complexion of the long-term unemployed worker. Previously, unemployment had been limited to bouts of distress and large pools of surplus labour were drained by emigration to the US and colonies. In Belgium, for example, 50.4 per cent of unemployed men and 43.5 per cent of unemployed women had been out of work for more than a year.[54] Frieda Wunderlich, a German social researcher, was particularly concerned about the plight of the long-term unemployed who appeared to be permanently unemployed or for whom unemployment had become a profession. She observed that long-term unemployment had a number of very damaging social consequences as people lost income and status. The loss of rank was greatest amongst the large numbers of professional and white collar workers who had not previously known unemployment. Wunderlich noted that the long-term unemployed were excluded from society through prejudice, social policy and employer practices. Despite mass unemployment, some in Germany continue to blame the unemployed for their own plight. In terms of social policy, the provision for the unemployment in Germany was quite literally a downward spiral of greater humiliation and reduced benefit. Wunderlich observed:

> The right to benefits provided in the insurance act is limited to a short time. Then begins the means test, under which all expenses must be justified before strangers and the unemployed is forced to reveal all his sorrow and distress.[55]

Employers were less likely to recruit the long-term jobless because they became shabbier, their skills waned and their strength faded. Long-term unemployment particularly hit older workers, those with skills no longer in demand and in towns and regions of high unemployment.

Unemployed Women in Europe

Governments and social investigators generally deemed women's unemployment not a serious problem. It was hidden from view and, in some respects, governments and employers discriminated against out-of-work women. According to the statistics, women's unemployment was relatively low. In 1934, women made up only 18 per cent of the registered jobless in eight European countries (Austria, Czechoslovakia, France, Great Britain, Italy, Poland and Switzerland) but this was largely the result of the under-recording of women's unemployment. In the census returns, many unemployed married women or mothers would describe themselves as housewives rather than unemployed. With the employment exchanges, many women lacked any incentive to register as unemployed. The voluntary unemployment insurance schemes were based on trade union membership which was disproportionately male. Compulsory unemployment insurance schemes excluded many women through non-coverage of categories that included large numbers of women. In Austria, Bulgaria, the UK, Italy and Poland unemployment insurance excluded all domestic workers; all homeworkers were excluded in Italy and Poland and certain categories of homeworkers in Germany; nurses and teacher were not covered in the UK.[56] With pressures on government resources, women, especially married women, suffered from cuts in relief. Like the Anomalies Act in the UK, the German Unemployment Insurance Act was amended in 1931 so that married women had to prove family hardship to draw unemployment insurance benefits. In the same year, Belgian married women were no longer eligible to extended benefits from the National Emergency Fund.

In some countries, governments attempted to restrict women's employment. In 1935, Henri Fuss, an International Labour Organisation official, noted that,

> in consequence of the economic depression there has been a growing demand during the last few years for restrictions on the employment of women; and although sometimes moral or practical reasons based on woman's duty in the home are alleged, the principal aim is to make room for men in vacancies by the exclusion of women.[57]

Whilst in Britain and Holland the exclusion of married women from public service was already practised before the onset of the depression, elsewhere in Europe the depression occasioned a legislative backlash against women's employment rights.

Nazi Germany took the initiative on 1 June 1933 with the Law for the Reduction of Unemployment which granted marriage loans on condition that a woman gave up employment (unless her husband was particularly low paid, and even this criterion was amended a year later). At the end of the same month, the Nazi-dominated Reichstag curtailed women's employment further in two ways. First, the civil service dismissed all the married women who could be supported by their families; second, no woman could be permanently appointed to a public job until she was 35 years old. The government and the Nazi movement campaigned vigorously against double-earning households where both husband and wife were working. They encouraged regional and local authorities and private enterprises to dismiss or block the recruitment of women who lived in households with 'male breadwinners'. The Nazis took up with renewed gusto the demands for women to return to their traditional role as mothers and housewives. Their slogan '*Kinder, Küche, Kirke*' (children, kitchen, church) epitomised the regime's attitude to women. Ultimately, women workers were needed for Hitler's war economy every bit as much as they had been under the Weimar Republic. The campaign against women's employment rights was of enormous propaganda value as it provided a scapegoat, while at the same time suggesting that the Nazis had a simple and coherent answer to the problem of unemployment.

Other countries followed suit with restrictions on women's employment. In Italy, in late November 1933, a decree either excluded or restricted the number of women applicants for government jobs and this was then extended to private industry. The following October, the Fascist Confederation of Industry and Confederation of Industrial Workers signed an agreement designed to combat unemployment through a reduction in the working week and the replacement of female by male labour. Discrimination was not the exclusive preserve of fascist states as the tendency to reduce women's employment rights spread rapidly across Europe. In Austria, in December 1933, the dismissal of married female public officials was decreed if their husband was also a civil servant earning above a certain amount. In 1934, the Yugoslav, Dutch, Luxembourg and Belgian governments all limited women's employment in the public sector; the latter two also restricted women's work in private industry. Local authorities also imposed restrictions, though there is much less in the way of research on this question.

The distinctive shift in attitude and policy towards working women was not simply the result of the predilections of conservatives and fascists who preferred to see women in the home. (Not that these measures made a significant impact on the levels of women in the European labour force.) The reassertion of the family at the time of the depression reflected the fact that the family unit constituted the cheapest way of housing, feeding and clothing the depression-hit working class. In this light, the household means test and the campaign against married women workers were two sides of the same strategy, which sought to place the upkeep of the unemployed on other members of their family – be that their husbands, their parents, or even their adult children. By this route, the working class were kept alive at the lowest possible cost to the state.

Deprivations of the Unemployed

The social consequences of this family-centred approach were over-crowding, a loss of independence for women and young adults, economic hardships, ill-health and great strain on family relationships.[58] As a result, hundreds of thousands of young unemployed adults left home for the freedom of the streets. In Germany, they were known as migrating birds (*Wandervögel*) and their numbers increased exponentially with the rise in unemployment. Daniel Guérin, a French socialist touring Germany in early 1930s, described their situation:

in Germany in the summer of 1932, those hostelers who wandered by choice were less numerous than the vagabonds who did so out of necessity. At the very least half a million jobless youths wandered the roads. They had no right to social assistance, most often because at least one member of their family was still working. Fed up with twiddling their thumbs in their grim working-class neighbourhoods and being a burden on their families, they set out each spring and knocked about in the world until autumn's end. Some had been drifting like this for several years without any goal, living off charity, taking refuge in shelters and stables.[59]

Housing conditions deteriorated as house-building slumped and the unemployed fell behind on the rent. Some faced eviction and had to move to cheaper or shared accommodation. Guérin described the scene at Kuhle Wampe, a shantytown built on a lake front near Berlin:

> Spread along the lakeshore, under the pines, the tiny dwellings all looked alike: simple wooden posts covered with white or zebra-striped tent canvas. All were well lit, clean and well kept. The builders rivalled each other in the ingenuity and whimsy. Miniature gardens surrounded the most beautiful constructions. At the moment of my arrival an elderly unemployed couple stood in ecstasy, motionless, watering can in hand, before three still-dripping geraniums.[60]

Thousands of unemployed Germans went to live on their allotments. The Czechoslovak Social Institute conducted research into 40 out-of-work families and found that 19 lived in one room and 21 in two-roomed accommodation; only 16 had a bed for each family member. In Poland, 83 per cent of jobless families lived in one room and averaged 4.5 people per room. Amongst unemployed Poles, the practice of selling their beds was very widespread. One study uncovered that in a sample of 91 families, 171 beds had been sold leaving 2.7 people per bed. In 1932, in a deprived district of Berlin, schoolteachers worried for the education of the young as 40 per cent of children did not have a bed to themselves.[61] The unemployed also had great difficulty heating their homes. In Poland, fuel consumption fell by 44 per cent among the unemployed.

As the scarce money of the jobless went on essentials like food, their clothes wore thin and turned to rags and shoes were made to last until they were beyond repair. After months of unemployment, the hero of Hans Fallada's depression novel *Little Man – What Now?* dramatically destroyed his shirt collar, the symbol of his status as a salaried worker:

Pinnberg stopped in front of a dress-shop window, in which there was a large mirror. He looked himself up and down, no not a pleasant sight, his light grey trousers were tar stained from his labours on the hut-roof, his overcoat was worn and faded, his shoes were in their last stages – Puttbrese was right, it was stupid to wear a collar with such clothes. He was just a broken down creature without a job, anyone could see that twenty yards away. Pinnberg grabbed his collar, tore it off, and stuffed his necktie into his coat-pocket.[62]

Over 80 per cent of their children in Lodz and Silesia (Poland) were not attending school mainly because of lack of clothing. The Polish Institute for Social Problems conducted a study of 432 jobless families: three families had no underwear and 131 had only the clothes they were wearing. The Solvay Sociology Institute of Brussels discovered that 58 per cent of unemployed households had given up buying new clothes.[63]

Despite the deprivations of the unemployed, there was no general increase in mortality rates, but public health specialists still had reason to be very worried about the relationship between the depression and health. Mortality figures were aggregated for entire national populations rather than allowing a focused examination of the health of the depression's victims. As contemporary medical experts pointed out, malnutrition did not automatically affect mortality rates. It was the combination of underfeeding and epidemics, as with the influenza of 1919–20, that caused generalised increases in death rates. Whilst government compiled thorough mortality statistics, morbidity (rates of illness) statistics were piecemeal and often misleading. If sickness insurance benefits (from which some morbidity rates were calculated) were higher or lower than unemployment insurance then the unemployed would prefer to be classified as ill rather than unemployed. Morbidity rates based on attendances at the doctor's surgery or hospital were an unreliable guide because, unless they were covered by health insurance, the unemployed could not afford such expenses.

A number of studies into unemployed diets gave much greater cause for concern than the aggregate mortality and morbidity figures. In 1927, the Germany Federal Statistical Office researched the effects of unemployment on the budgets of high- and low-waged workers. It concluded that low-wage earners suffered from actual malnutrition when out of work. Five years later, Dr von Tyszka investigated the nutritional standards of those on municipal welfare relief. He discovered that the nutritional level compared unfavourably with the 1927 study and found that their diet, which consisted largely of margarine and potatoes, was deficient in protein, calorific value and vitamins B and C. In 1932, a German co-operative society with 35,000 members (of whom 18,000 were unemployed) reported that goods consumed had plummeted by 20–30 per cent in a single year. The unemployed were forced to economise on food by cutting out meat and fruit. Their diets became less nutritious and more monotonous. In industrial northern France (Meurthe-et-Moselle), urban households had to cut back on the quantity and quality of food and only 50 per cent were well nourished. Potatoes, rice and pasta replaced green vegetables, fruit, butter and eggs. In the poorest areas of Nancy, investigators were told that some families went without food for days at a time. A study of 30 unemployed families in Nancy observed that eight had cut out meat altogether and only nine had meat more than twice a week. In the countryside, however, the unemployed were able to grow fruit and vegetables in their gardens and provide themselves with a healthier diet.[64]

The depression also threatened the health of the children of the unemployed. According to a report, the health of Prussian school-children noticeably worsened from autumn 1931 onwards with an increase in 'anaemia, scrofula, lice, worms ... caries of the teeth, and nervous conditions leading to rapid fatigue and inattention'.[65] Again in Germany, the Kreuzburg Health Centre (Berlin) recorded a 3–4 kg loss of weight amongst unemployed adults in the space of a few months. Perhaps more worryingly, medical experts in Berlin and Hamburg discovered stunted growth in the children of the unemployed. This problem was not confined to Germany. The Save the Children Fund International found that of 15,295 Polish children whose parents were out of work, 25 per cent went to school without breakfast, 18 per cent had no midday meal and 7.5 per cent had no dinner at home. In some schools as many as 30 per cent of these children relied on school meals as their only respite from starvation.[66] The authorities in various parts of Europe attempted to counter dangerous indices of malnutrition among children through the distri-bution of free milk or school meals but these programmes were not statutory and could themselves fall victim to the depression. In 1932, the distribution of free milk was halved in Berlin and 43 other German towns cut their provision in similar fashion.

The shattering psychological blow of long-term unemployment, like its effects on physical health, were widespread. Contemporary psy-chologists came to the common conclusion that unemployment caused feelings of insecurity, worthlessness, withdrawal and inferiority and they noted an increase in nervous complaints amongst the unemployed. This psychological distress was reflected in the numbers who contemplated or attempted suicide. The year of the greatest unemployment, 1932, also marked a peak year for suicides across most of Europe. In Berlin, ten or eleven youths attempted suicide every day.[67] In Germany as a whole the number of suicides had climbed from 15,974 in 1927 to 18,934 in 1932, but Austria had the highest suicide rate of 440 per million inhabitants in 1932 (followed by Germany with 290 per million).[68] Between 1926 and 1930, in Austria, unemployment accounted for 24 per cent of male suicides and, as recession deepened in the following years, the number of suicides increased.[69] In Hungary, between 1929 and 1933, suicides due to 'misery and lack of earnings' increased almost two and a half times.[70]

Contemporary Social Research into Unemployment

Two particular studies of European unemployment deserve special consideration. First, the Warsaw-based Institute for Social Economy collected 774 unemployed autobiographies and published a representative sample of 57.[71] Second, three Austrian sociologists undertook an in-depth study of a single depressed Austrian industrial village, Marienthal. The researchers combined observation, questionnaires, interviews and diaries and sought to 'immerse themselves' into the life of the village in order to understand the effects of unemployment. These two studies provided extremely valuable insights into the experiences and attitudes of the unemployed.

The Polish study revealed, through written accounts of their own experiences, the condition, attitudes and feelings of the unemployed. This contrasted with the cold scientific language and style of other studies. The unemployed autobiographers give full vent to their emotions. They told of how after 13 weeks on benefit, they had to rely on charity or family and friends, and when these avenues proved inadequate, they had to fend for themselves to earn a few groschen by gathering and selling berries or mushrooms, or taking in washing. A minority turned to begging or stealing, whilst others picked over rubbish dumps. Nearly half had sold or pawned furniture and wedding rings. Over half suffered from prolonged hunger, with their typical diets consisting of potatoes, cabbages and vegetable soups (even bread was not consumed daily). One out-of-work Pole, who lived by hawking picture frames, recalled:

November 8, 1931. Yesterday I earned 1.46 zl. by selling picture frames. For breakfast we had tea and bread. My wife bought half a litre of milk for the children for dinner, and there was potato soup; for supper the rest of the soup from dinner. I sawed five frames the whole day.

November 9, 1931. My wife made flour soup for breakfast. I went away in the morning to sell the frames, which I had sawed on Sunday, and did not come back until evening. I sold two pieces and earned 80 groschen. At night I ate soup left from dinner, cabbage soup with potatoes.

November 12, 1931. For breakfast potato soup. It has become loathsome, but there is nothing else, one has to eat it. My wife is about to finish her work; she has to deliver it tomorrow, but probably she will not be able to do so. I told her I earned 1.50 zl., but I had to pay the policemen a fine of 2 zl. I wish I had never been born! He took my whole earning and I even had to add to them. At night I ate potato noodles with crackling.[72]

Ten out of 57 unemployed autobiographies related episodes of hunger pains, faintness or coughing up blood. An unemployed victim of acute hunger recorded his ordeal (before being rescued by his brother): he had 'fever and pains', then became delirious having nightmares in which he 'saw display windows with bread and other food'. He was so faint he could not move for days and 'red and yellow spots danced before my eyes'.[73]

The unemployed had to contend with the relentless cold of the Polish winter: 22 mention suffering from the cold and 7 out of 57 stayed in bed longer to conserve coal and food. As one recalled:

It is mercilessly cold. My suit is ragged, miserable, my shoes are full of holes, the soles are thin. I have nothing to wear outside to look for work or bread, since for the moment I am outside, frost grips my whole body. The walls are wet, so that the water runs down. The cracks in the window are stopped with rags. If one of the children has something to put on it does so; they bind their feet with rags and sit all day in bed. It is very cold, the four children sleep one on another in the same bed with us.[74]

The psychologists analysing these Polish autobiographies concluded that the unemployed responded to their conditions with apathy, withdrawal and sometimes rage. Whilst only 2 of the sample of 57 had attempted suicide, nearly half had contemplated it and six had considered killing their family as well. The study found that rage was sometimes directed politically (5 were described as having revolutionary attitudes), but more often a nihilism was revealed directed either at everyone or at those in work. One out-of-work essayist warned:

Give us bread and work! Give us our right to live! Let us bring up our children for the good of the State! To-morrow it will be too late: our hands cry out for work; they are not used to lying idle in our pockets. They want to work, to create to build, but if this goes on for an eternity they will also know how to destroy.

By another hand passive resignation was also apparent:

> Life has made me a coward. Sometimes I feel like taking off my hat
> to the world and humbly imploring it: Buy me! Buy me![75]

More than anything else, the Polish autobiographies like their British equivalents *Time to Spare* or *Memoirs of the Unemployed* are valuable because they conveyed how those without work felt. No statistics could give an insight into the emotional suffering of the out-of-work family. One unemployed parent bared his soul in the vain hope of winning a cash prize:

> It is not only we grown-ups, the parents of our children and weighed with responsibilities, who no longer feel the beauty of spring; even our children greet it with indifference. There is much sadness and bitterness in our children's lives. We, their parents, try to hide their misfortunes from them; we want to let them be children, and try to be cheerful ourselves in order to cheer them up. But it is no use; the child who is hungry and cold sees through our pretended cheerfulness which is only intended to cheer him up. It does not deceive him because he has never really been a child. Ever since he can remember he has seen the tears, anxieties and troubles of his parents ... The child of the unemployed parents is a child in appearance only. He is thin, puny, pale and sickly looking. Many sad and painful experiences, much despair, sorrow and suffering are hidden in his brain. He is never thoughtless and gay – a child indeed in outward appearance, but he behaves like an old man. In the early days of our poverty the children used to cry when they wanted something to eat. They dragged themselves about the room, whimpering and jostling each other, which gave rise to still more tears and irritation. To punish them, their mother would hit out at them blindly in the dark, for our big icehouse of a room had seldom any light in the evening. But when they began to cry still louder she cried with them too. She would sit down on the stone floor and put up her arms round the children who crowded up against her, and all four of them would cry and cry and cry. Later they stopped crying. They became silent and gloomy. Their faces looked as though carved out of marble, with wide staring eyes in which there lurked an expression of constant fear. What depths of sadness can be read into these faces out of which all joy has fled before the terrors of hunger and unemployment.[76]

The most thorough investigation of depression-hit Europe was the study of Marienthal, a textile factory village in Austria. Here hard times had preceded the Wall Street Crash. As early as July–December

1926 half of Marienthal's workers had been laid off. Then, in July 1929, the spinning mill closed, followed by the print works in August and the bleaching plant in September. Marienthal's population, numbering nearly 1,500, was devastated; the President of the Theatre Club recalled, 'they all thought they were going to starve'.[77] Three-quarters of its families depended on relief payments.

The investigators stressed that there was no uniform response to unemployment and that the degree of hardship varied between households. Nine per cent of households lived on what they described as the minimal standard of 20 shillings per male adult equivalent. With successive cuts and amendments, the benefit system had become increasingly stringent. The research team recorded three examples of those whose claims had been disallowed: a labourer who cut down some trees in return for firewood, a woman who was given some milk for her children after delivering milk and a man who played his mouth organ for a few coins.

The study distinguished between three unemployed groups, those who were unbroken, apathetic and broken. There was a connection between being 'broken' or 'apathetic' and the direst need. The authors cited these three examples of needy families,

Family 001: husband, wife, 4 children.
Because the former employer of the husband failed to make his social security payments the family lost their right to claim. In spring, the husband had a temporary job as a slater. Apart from that the family had been living by begging and stealing. The children and the home are totally neglected. The husband drinks; the wife is in prison on conviction for slander.
Family 273: mother, one child
The mother had become an alien through marriage and therefore lost her claim to relief. Immediately after the wedding her husband ran away and joined the foreign legion. During the summer she does odd jobs and occasionally receives support from her parents. The woman leads a lonely life and is very apathetic; she continually quarrels with her relatives.
Family 208: husband, wife three children
The husband is an alien, the wife is working and earns 13 shillings a week. Occasionally the husband repairs shoes. They own a garden allotment and admit that they occasionally swipe some coal. The household is tidy but the mood is one of utter despair.

Villagers' diets became impoverished. At the local store, between 1928 and 1930, the consumption of butter, coffee and chocolate fell dramatically (by 62 per cent, 27 per cent and 57 per cent respectively) whilst cheap staples and alternatives such as margarine and flour increased. Horse meat generally replaced pork and beef and only 13 per cent of households ate meat more than twice a week. Diets typically consisted of bread, soup, potatoes and cabbage so that the village wrestling team could simply not find men for the heavier weight categories. Marienthal's unemployed survived by stealing cabbages and potatoes from the fields, pilfering coal, breeding rabbits or keeping allotments. One villager's admission summed up their privations and degradation,

> Cats keep disappearing. Only a few days ago Herr H.'s cat disappeared. Cat meat is very good. Dogs are also eaten. But that began already before unemployment. At S.T.'s, for example, they once roasted a dog. A few days ago a man was given a dog by one of the farmers on condition that the dog be killed painlessly. The man went everywhere to find a basin for the blood and finally got one. But he had to promise a piece of meat in return.[78]

Health also deteriorated. Only 8 per cent of the children had good teeth and nearly a third had three or more teeth that were rotten.

Village life was also transformed by the withering of its vibrant associational culture. Although voting for the Austrian Social Democratic Party (SPÖ) remained stable, its membership fell by a third. Borrowing at the workers' library dropped off sharply, as did participation at the Theatre club. While the gymnastic club and the *Gesangsverein* (glee club) lost over half their members and the football club and wrestling club temporarily closed, the Catholic Happy Childhood nursery, the crematorium club and the cycling club all saw their membership grow.

Time itself had slowed and lost its key points of reference in Marienthal. In a community centred on factory work, the working day set family routines so that when the factory came to a halt so too did the structure of time in the village. For women, the onerous and now increasingly stressful domestic chores still filled the day, but for men, there was nothing but emptiness. Their days now consisted of sitting at home, going for walks, possibly a few household errands like going to the shops and fetching water, or standing on the street corner. A smaller number spent their time at the working men's club playing cards and chess.[79]

The depression affected the most intimate and personal relationships as it clumsily intruded into the private sphere of the home. The researchers stated:

> On the whole it seems, improvements in the relationships between husband and wife as a result of unemployment are definitely exceptions. Generally in happy marriages minor quarrels appear to

occur more frequently than before. In marriages that were already unsettled, difficulties have become more acute.[80]

The investigation concluded that apathy and resignation reigned in Marienthal. They found little evidence of radicalisation:

A casual observer is apt to see only what is the most conspicuous, namely the occasional revolutionary effects of unemployment, or particularly heartrending outbreaks of despair. Our detailed inquiry has led us to see more clearly the paralysing effects of unemployment, an aspect that might easily elude less systematic observation.[81]

The experience of unemployment brought together the hardships of old – hunger, cold, misery – and a new distress, a despairing disorientation that could give rise to apathy or anger, but the researchers in Marienthal could see only apathy. The representativeness of a small village when considering the political demeanour of the unemployed is dubious. Many of the unemployed lived in the cities and it was here that the unemployed struggles took place. Despite the conclusions of the Marienthal study, there is evidence in the Warsaw study to suggest that there was also some political anger among a section of the unemployed. Unemployed protests were the most visible expression of this anger. These protests can be seen as a reaction against the condition of unemployment and also against government confusion and coercion. Social investigators of the day tried to understand the unemployed in a vacuum devoid of politics. Ultimately they ignored the importance of protest because they did not conceive of it as worthy of study in its own right.

European Unemployed Struggles

With the onset of the depression, the Communist International exhorted communists throughout Europe to build unemployed organisations. In the early 1920s, unemployed organisations had developed in several countries. The Comintern had referred to the value of agitation amongst the unemployed in its early years but it was in 1929 when it concentrated its efforts to build unemployed movements in their own right. The basic outlook of the Communist Parties was fixed at the tenth plenum of the Executive Committee of the Communist International (ECCI) which concluded that the capitalist world had entered the 'third period' of crisis characterised by ascending revolutionary struggles. These predictions coincided with the beginnings of the world-wide recession and the spontaneous anger of those suddenly thrown out of work but the prospects for building a movement varied greatly. The depression selected its victims: it singled out Germany yet spared France in comparison.

In late 1929 and early 1930, excited reports filled the pages of internal Comintern bulletins describing demonstrations, hunger marches and the unemployed clashing with police. In the last days of January 1930, the jobless of Kiel, Lübeck, Itzehoe and Flensburg marched on Hamburg. On 1 February they arrived in the streets of Germany's greatest port to find large numbers of police and the massed ranks of sympathetic demonstrators. In the clashes with the police that ensued, one worker was killed and six were injured. On the same day, the unemployed marched through the streets of Berlin, again resulting in pitched battles with the police. German hunger marchers also took to the road in the Ruhr and Worms. Throughout Europe, the communist correspondents related the effect of growing unemployment and inadequate relief. In January 1930, one witnessed a series of unemployed demonstrations in towns across Poland. In Phillipopolis, Bulgaria, a crowd of hungry women surrounded the house of a councillor; they had been refused unemployment relief so they smashed all the windows in his house.[82] In Hungary, despite arrests of communists and raids on printing presses, there had been weeks of street demonstrations against unemployment. In Tamasvar, Romania, the unemployed threw up barricades and occupied the town hall.[83] Even under conditions of fascist Italy there were unemployed protests. In rural areas, where the state was less powerful, unemployed agricultural labourers raided municipal offices. In Milan, the unemployed protested by pulling out their pockets and sarcastically chanting, 'Long live Mussolini!'[84] Reflecting on communist involvement in these outbursts, *Pravda* stated on 10 February:

> everywhere the waves of mass protest are rising ... Everywhere bloody repressive measures are being employed against the growing unemployed movement, and everywhere the movement is spreading and growing by being closer and closer linked up with the strike struggles of the workers of the factories.[85]

The Comintern decided on an 'international day of struggle against unemployment' set for 6 March. Manuilsky, reporting to the ECCI, believed that 'the outstanding feature of the labour movement ... is the further rise of the revolutionary tide in the midst of world crisis and mass unemployment'.[86] Preparations were afoot across the globe for 6 March. Communists were setting up unemployed committees, printing leaflets and newspapers wherever they could to publicise the event. They claimed that the international day of struggle itself was a great success and that well over half a million participated from New York to Berlin, Chicago to Prague.[87] Despite the success of the demonstrations, the ability of the communists to build unemployed organisations was less sure. The Comintern maintained that economic crisis would automatically create 'rising revolutionary struggles' but these failed to materialise. Joblessness had acted as a catalyst for militant protests in many towns and cities in Europe and the USA, and some of these had sparked conflicts with the authorities; however, unemployment also brought apathy and resignation. Whilst at no point did the Comintern argue that the unemployed had displaced the employed in importance in the class struggle, in practice, their isolation from workers in social democratic unions meant that their activity focused largely on the unemployed. This concentration of hopes in the unemployed as a revolutionary force proved ill-founded. The 'third period' attitude to the social democrats reinforced this isolation and limited the impact of unemployed struggles inside the working class. The communists fiercely denounced socialist leaders as social fascists but expected socialist members to flock to communist banners.[88] The communists also tended to raise abstract slogans, like the defence of the Chinese soviets, which must have seemed puzzling to an angry jobless demonstrator on the streets of Berlin.

In August 1931, a special Comintern conference of unemployed delegates was convened to discuss the state of activity amongst the jobless masses. Eleven national movements were represented. Assessing the work of communists across the continent, Walter Ulbricht admitted:

> Although we have succeeded in forming unemployed committees, we have not succeeded in making the vast, unemployed army, an army with a purpose, and only in some cases have we realised the fighting alliance with workers in the shops and factories.[89]

The various national reports revealed the state of the unemployed movements and provided ample confirmation of Ulbricht's view. Unbeknown to the participants, the conference recorded the passing of the high-water mark of the movements. The German movement could boast the most impressive network of unemployed committees. In the summer of 1931, it consisted of 1,513 unemployed committees, with 15 newspapers and a circulation of 485,000. In Czechoslovakia, at their peak, the unemployed newspapers printed 20,000 copies in Czech and 34,000 in German. In France, by comparison, the Parisian unemployed committees had managed to sell only 700 copies.

The delegates recounted their achievements and successes. The 25 February had been fixed as the second international day of struggle against unemployment. The Polish delegate claimed 102 demonstrations had taken place throughout his country involving 120,000 protesters and 198 meetings. In Czechoslovakia, 213,000 demonstrated that day and were accompanied by 50 work stoppages. The conference also revealed a diverse range of activities based on local conditions. In Holland 11,000 relief workers had gone on strike. In Czechoslovakia, protests had forced the authorities to open up heated rooms for the unemployed during the cold winter days. In Bulgaria, the unemployed swelled the picket lines of tobacco and textile strikers. In France, the unemployed took part in protests for longer entitlements to sickness benefit. The German delegate reported a labour exchange strike in which the unemployed refused to sign on until their grievances were met.

Most delegates confessed that their organisations were in retreat (temporary, they insisted). In Czechoslovakia, the number of committees had risen to 1,100 in the winter of 1930–31, but by the time of the conference that figure had slumped to 200–250. In Paris, the number of committees had fallen from 40 to 30. In Germany, sales of the unemployed newspapers had fallen from 485,000 to 200,000 in a matter of months. In Austria and Holland, the unemployed newspaper had ceased to exist.

In the last years of Weimar, the Germany Communist Party highlighted the possibilities for and the limitations of mobilising the unemployed.[90] By 1932, nine out of ten members were out of work and, as early as 1925, the majority were unemployed. The party involved itself in the unemployed movement wherever opportunities presented themselves. The movement first surfaced as part of the workers' and soldiers' councils movement of the revolution of 1918 and 1919 but, up to 1929, unemployed organisations had a staccato existence.[91] Strictly speaking it would be wrong to talk of a national unemployment movement, instead, there was a series of regional and local organisations, often short-lived. Up to 1924, inflationary polices brought virtually full employment. From 1929, however, the dramatic increase in unemployment was accompanied by jobless protests, anti-eviction fights, campaigns for special provisions of coal and food, protests against benefit cuts and strikes by municipal relief workers. The unemployed activists scored some notable victories in these battles.[92] The unemployed councils had an estimated 80,000 members but their influence reached much wider numbers of the unemployed over special demands and campaigns.[93] Viewed through the Communist Party looking-glass, the unemployed movement was an elusive phenomenon. In practice, the boundaries blurred between the party, its affiliated trade union movement (RGO), the unemployed committees and the anti-fascist organisations (*Kampfbund gegen Fascismus, Antifa*). The unemployed activity brought a degree of party success, between 1929 and 1932 the organisation trebled in size, and its vote climbed to 6 million.

These gains concealed serious drawbacks and a strategic dilemma for the communists. The KPD, based on an unemployed membership, subject to a rapid turnover and instability was hardly the stable cadre that Lenin envisaged. Success at the polls was something very different from the kind of political mobilisation, as had taken place in 1920, needed to prevent the establishment of a dictatorship. Partly these problems were of the KPD leadership's own making, its intense sectarianism towards the SPD not only reinforced the organisational and ideological divisions within the labour movement, but also compounded the cleavages inside working-class communities: between those in and out of work, between young and old, between workplace and neighbourhood and between 'respectable' and 'rough'.[94] It trapped the KPD in a ghetto, out of which, despite its goal of recruiting factory workers, it could not escape as its orientation fell by default onto the neighbourhood and not the workplace. This marginalised the undoubted radicalisation of a section of the working class at the end of Weimar and it confounded attempts to build united opposition to the Nazis. The German case does demonstrate that the unemployed were not simply inundated by a wave of political apathy. Radicalism amongst the unemployed was both transitory and contradictory. Without political organisation and leadership, it is unlikely to live beyond the shortest spontaneous outburst. Also without avenues for that radicalism to generalise (as almost certainly happened in the British case) it could achieve little of lasting significance. Ultimately the scale of retrenchment massively outweighed the victories of the movement and a 'demonstration-weariness' set in amongst the unemployed.[95] By the end of 1932 the German unemployed movement had in effect collapsed.[96]

Hitler's appointment as Chancellor on 30 January 1933 not only marked the end of the unemployed movement in Germany but it signalled a new, less turbulent, phase in unemployed protest internationally.[97] Hunger marches and unemployed activity took place elsewhere after that date. In France, the workless miners of Nord and Pas-de-Calais marched from Dunkirk to Paris in December 1933.[98] In the Netherlands, the Unemployed Agitation Committees played an important role in the campaign that secured the Plan for Work of 1935. Also the NUWM was engaged in some of its most significant activities between 1934 and 1936. However, the largest Communist Party and unemployed movement in continental Europe had been extinguished in Gestapo and Brownshirt raids. This must have chilled the blood of the Comintern officials and Stalin: the third

period strategy was in tatters and new allies were to sought from old
enemies. The popular front policy was formally adopted in 1935.
Rather than expecting the dispossessed to bring about revolution,
this strategy sought alliances with the middle class, progressive
capitalists and their political representatives. In practice, the
Comintern relegated the importance of unemployed protests. This
coincided with the gradual recovery from the depths of the international recession and a rising tide of anti-fascist and industrial
struggles in various parts of Europe. The political and economic
conjuncture effectively marked the end of the episode of sharp
unemployed struggles which touched to greater or less extent much
of continental Europe.

Conclusion

The study of unemployment in Europe reinforces some of the
conclusions drawn about unemployment in Britain and the US. First,
it is clear that the workless were not a new revolutionary force in their
own right, but Europe's unemployed did not apathetically withdraw
into their shells and Europe's rulers did feel sufficiently threatened to
introduce a series of quite costly reforms that were obviously
unpopular with parts of their own natural constituency. The protest
of the unemployed had both material and ideological dimensions.
Not only were concessions won, though they were also at times
overturned, but also unemployed agitation raised the question of the
recognition, rights and self-worth of the unemployed. Not only were
the unemployed faced with material hardships, but also the
accusation of dole abuse and the threat of a more authoritarian social
policy harking back to the Poor Law with means testing and labour
service. It must also be said that the British unemployed movement
was more persistent and important than its European counterparts.
Not even the German movement could match the six national hunger
marches and the dramatic victory against the UAB of early 1935. The
German movement at its height rivalled the British in terms of size
and militancy, but its life was brief and it ultimately fell victim to the
brown plague of Nazism.

Surveying the experience of the jobless in depressed Europe two
things become clear in comparison with Britain and the USA. First,
the unemployed essentially shared the experience, albeit with
differing social provision and varying degrees of intensity. Second, as
unemployment stemmed from the international phenomenon of
depression, one should counsel against the belief that, in say Britain
or France, things were not really that bad after all. Ultimately, the

world economic crisis demonstrated that it was capable of inflicting not only suffering in Germany, Austria or Poland, but also the political consequences of fascism and war. Britain was spared the worst excesses of economic crisis domestically but it was certainly not immune from its horrifying international repercussions.

Conclusions

The total loss of the world economic system between 1930 and 1934 as a result of the depression (as far as production, commerce and transport are concerned) amounted in round figures to between 149,000 and 176,000 million '1913 dollars' – a fateful figure, equal to the total cost of the Great War. The immediate cause of all calamities of the depression was the shrinkage in industrial production: the poverty of the unemployed, the difficulties of the farmers, the decline of the volume of international exchanges, the disorganisation of public finance, the various political and social disturbances and all the other outward signs of the great depression may be attributed to the fact that the wheels of the gigantic machinery of capitalist industry were turning more slowly or had ceased to turn altogether.

> W. Woytinsky, *The Social Consequences of the Economic Depression*, 1936[1]

The superior strength of true, practical class consciousness lies in the ability to look beyond the divisive symptoms of the economic process to the unity of the total social system underlying it. In the age of capitalism it is not possible for the total system to become directly visible in external phenomena. For instance, the economic basis of a world crisis is undoubtedly unified and its coherence can be understood. But its actual appearance in time and space will take the form of a disparate succession of events in different countries at different times even in different branches of industry in a number of countries.

> G. Lukács, *History and Class Consciousness*, 1971[2]

The years between the two world wars witnessed a profound change. The economy underwent a shift towards new industries, women's economic activity rates increased, and the economic geography of the industrial world was reshaped. Consumption too experienced fundamental developments with the rise of commodified leisure (cinemas, radio, sport) and the growth of consumer goods. Road transport and electricity spun modernising webs across entire countries. Against this background and partly as a consequence, unemployment took on a more persistent and mass character. This cannot be explained away either by the argument that it was a statistical mirage brought about by more sensitive statistical indicators or by the argument that unemployment benefits encouraged joblessness. Instead, the dole queues were a consequence of severe dislocations in the world economy that seemed to abate by the mid-1920s only to be followed by the great disruptions of the 1930s. As such those without work were indeed part of a common socio-economic phenomenon and not different categories grouped in some spurious rhetorical aggregation. Certainly, the characteristics of the unemployed were disparate according to all sorts of criteria (gender, age, geographical concentration, duration, etc.), but all these aspects sprung from a common source. For instance, it has been asked whether casual labourers should be included amongst the ranks of the jobless. This example makes the point very well: labour market conditions for casual labourers were radically altered by mass joblessness. Unemployment, then, can be likened to a hammer shattering a window pane. Just because every fragment is unique does not mean that they were not the result of a single blow. This common cause was the character of the modern capitalist economy and its particularly intractable vicissitudes of those years.

At the social and political level, the First World War and the threat of revolution posed new problems to the ruling classes of Europe. Their initial delaying strategy widened franchises and granted social reforms. These new circumstances demanded new institutional forms and in general government decision-making was increasingly negotiated with organised groups, notably with trade unions and employers' associations. The new conditions of universal suffrage and state expansion precipitated the need for a more formal, organised and public representation of capitalist interests. In Britain, heavy industry found its collective voice in the shape of the National Confederation of Employers' Organisations and the Federation of British Industries. As far as the Ministry of Labour and the government were concerned the NCEO spoke for industrialists and it articulated a consistent and clear programme that occupied a central position in the formation of a conservative ideological response to mass unemployment and social insurance. Corporatism in Europe, after stabilising bourgeois rule, began to break down. In parts of Europe harder hit by depression, social reforms and democratic institutions were dismantled. In the US, the US Chamber of Commerce, the National Industrial Conference Board, the National Association of Manufacturers and the American Liberty League articulated business opposition to the development of welfare reform.

The contours of both government policy and unemployed struggles are related to the broader undulations of class relations. In the USA, the 1920s were years of capitalist optimism and unemployment was a neglected problem. In the 1930s that optimism shattered and the unemployed, and then labour more generally, grew in militancy. Europe in the 1930s witnessed a complex pattern of unemployed protest, labour unrest, dictatorial repression and anti-fascism. In Sweden and France reforming governments seemed to offer hope to the unemployed. Whilst in 1936 in France and Spain the possibility of workers' revolution briefly rekindled, in Germany, Austria and Poland dictatorships presided over the dismantling of welfare reforms. In Britain, the immediate postwar militancy spurred the unemployed to action and the government to give concessions. After that point, retrenchment and pacification became the order of the day but universal suffrage and the threat of unemployed disorder set important limits on retrenchment. Unemployment ranked highly on the political agenda in one guise or another in all the interwar elections. When these limits were breached the tinder of unemployed protest was relit by the NUWM. By the late 1930s a recovery of working-class political and industrial confidence was underway. Although not unambiguously reflected in Labour electoral performance, the recovery was more subtle and was demonstrated by anti-fascism (both domestic and sympathy for the Spanish Left), a slow rise in industrial conflict, growing union, Labour Party and Communist Party membership and the re-emergence of rank-and-file organisation in the aircraft industry and on the London buses. Unfortunately, a fuller description of the recovery is not within the remit of this account but others have given it more serious consideration, although more work needs to be done on the subject.[3]

This recovery, partial and faltering though it may have been, had a profound significance when working class co-operation was sought during the Second World War. Important elements of their political agenda had to be incorporated into the new establishment ideology of the people's war that significantly included welfarism and anti-fascism. That is why 'middle opinion', those within the establishment that had broken with Baldwinism in the 1930s (such as Macmillan, Boothby, the Political and Economic Planning Group, etc.) or the great liberals, Beveridge and Keynes, should not exclusively take the credit for the postwar welfarist consensus. After Dunkirk, there was a rapid shift to the left in popular attitudes which underpinned the 1945 landslide victory for Labour. Although workers did not foresee or demand a welfare state, they did demand better wages, and more regular 'work or maintenance' when out of work. In effect, what they were offered was a capitalist and technocratic version of work and maintenance. Indeed, as regards maintenance, the groundwork had already been prepared. When first introduced in 1911, unemployment insurance was intended only to supplement working-class savings. Over the course of the 1920s and 1930s government acknowledgement of its responsibility for the maintenance of the unemployed increasingly replaced the ideology of self-help and thrift. On one level, the nutrition debate signalled the extent to which political pressure had pushed the government towards the ideology of maintenance.

The political limits of interwar unemployment policy, as has already been hinted, were set by a combination of factors. Electoral pressure both in national and local elections could affect relief. At general elections pressure could be exerted in favour of cuts or concessions. In the case of retrenchment, the ruling class wheeled out its ideological apparatus to proclaim the need for economy or the danger of dole abuse. Local authorities were susceptible to electoral and popular pressure to grant more liberal relief, particularly to those authorities more sympathetically disposed to the unemployed, hence Poplarism. The European experience pointed to the inability of democracies to dismantle existing rights and social benefits past a certain point. The Nazi regime set about the systematic unravelling of unemployed welfare and the establishment of compulsory cheap labour schemes, Nazi charity (Winter Help) and conscription in their stead. It could only do so after abolishing elections. Pressure from below defined the limits that democratic governments transgressed at the risk of widespread unrest. Perhaps the most significant factor in this pressure was the organisational focus provided by the unemployed movements. In Britain, these boundaries themselves are easily recognised: the transfer of the unemployed to the Poor Law or general cuts in benefits. When these were attempted in 1921, 1931–32 and 1935 it provoked unemployed resistance. Piecemeal retrenchment through individualised reassessment and disallowances, such as the GSW or the anomaly regulations, however, was a different matter.

This interpretation of the NUWM is at odds with the orthodoxy which claims it to be of little or no significance and its success and attractiveness to the unemployed being purely in terms of its advice work. This disagreement is linked to assessment of the 'unemployed condition'.

Mistakenly, much of the literature on the unemployed condition approaches it from the perspective of the psychology of the typical jobless person. While this does provide useful information and some insights, the individual is ripped from his or her context of changing political events. It assumes implicitly and inadvertently that the unemployed are not participants in political questions and that their attitudes are relatively inert and unchanging in different circumstances. It rules out from the outset the possibility of sudden, momentary and dramatic changes in unemployed consciousness: precisely what was observable in the brief but significant episodes of unemployed struggle. The most common description of the unemployed is one of apathy and demoralisation, and this was the case for the most part, but many studies remarked upon the co-existence of apathy and bitterness without considering the contradiction between these states of mind at times of unrest. Apathy clearly reigned given the dulling routine of joblessness, but the moments of mass protest must not be forgotten. This is not to exaggerate the potential for an unemployed movement or to overstate the numbers involved. But it is sociologically naive to argue, as some do, that the unemployment movement was not a success because it did not involve the majority of the unemployed and that the mass membership did not fully accept the ideas of the leading activists. This is a pattern that is repeated in many social movements whose success is not questioned.

Whilst the 'Baldwin consensus' dominated high politics in the interwar period, the attitudes of the unemployed, where they can be identified, were more complex, fluid and contradictory. In the immediate postwar period, both strike and unionisation figures demonstrate considerable evidence of militancy and surging working-class confidence. The early unemployed movement took place in this context. Cole and Postgate were right, therefore, to talk of dole and revolution. In January 1920 a Cabinet report from the Director of Intelligence, Sir Basil Thomson, stated: 'The most serious factor of the moment is unemployment, which is driving many of the more moderate ex-servicemen into the revolutionary camp.'[4] However, despair and the experience of defeat were crucial in shaping working-class attitudes: the defeats of the miners, engineers, textile workers and the débâcle of the general strike crushed the militancy that emerged from the war.

It is too simplistic, therefore, to contrast the instability of Europe with the inherent stability of British political culture between the wars. The stability was a product of the working-class experience of defeat, the relative economic fortune of the British ruling class and a propitious turn of events. From the evidence available for unemployed attitudes, it seems that bitterness, radicalism and despair freely mixed. Events bear this out, sudden surges in membership and activity of the NUWM indicated hope and radicalisation but this subsided equally rapidly. During these periods, governments worried, the police spied but eventually concession and repression allowed the authorities to regain the initiative. To explain why unemployed struggles did not threaten revolution, we have to look at the limited response inside the workplace which was conditioned by defeat and the threat of the dole.

Britain was much more stable that the rest of Europe, but in order to understand that stability, it is the threat to stability that needs investigation. Instead, British historians have tended to focus on the converse: the apathy of the working class and its receptiveness to mass capitalist culture, the strength of parliamentary institutions, the containment by the police of small 'extremist' opposition. Across Europe there was an obvious and observable connection between economic turmoil and political instability. Without the great inflation of 1923 and the collapse of German banking system in 1931, Hitler would have gone to his grave an anonymous ex-corporal. The Great Depression made a lesser impact on Britain than on parts of continental Europe or the US. There was no generalised collapse of middle-class savings, no catastrophic banking collapses, no decimation of small and medium business, millions of farmers and peasants did not face ruin; all this was witnessed elsewhere. These factors precipitated continental instability, their absence in Britain is surely the principal explanation of the 'failure of extremes'. After all, Britain was still the world's largest empire – a fact that proved to be a key advantage at a time when the world economy was breaking up into rival protectionist blocs. Britain also benefited from the collapse in price of raw materials and agricultural imports, allowing the expansion of new consumer markets such as the motor car. To attribute the political stability to institutional or cultural factors is comforting from a national point of view, but it seems entirely speculative in character.

As the material conditions for revolution in Britain were lacking, certainly after 1920, it is unrealistic to expect the NUWM to have been able to rally larger numbers to the banner of communism. Having said that, considering the world economy, it might have seemed reasonable to expect, in say 1932 or 1937, a further deterioration in the economic situation.

The fundamental importance of the slump in Britain is its connection in popular (especially working-class) memory and imagination with the formation of the welfare state. There has been a very strong and persistent attachment to these principles throughout the 1980s and 1990s at a time when politicians and political scientists have questioned its future. Much of what is offered by way of reform and innovation is clearly a regression to the situation pre-1945. The means testing of benefits, the rhetoric of the impossible growth in cost of social services, the scare stories of dole abuse, the virtues of the market are repeated now as then. We are now in a situation where ministers talk in admiring terms of Samuel Smiles whose nineteenth-century injunctions to thrift and self-help were the ideological opposite of the demand for work or maintenance. Unemployment, though largely avoided by politicians and ignored by inflation-obsessed Chancellors, is still high in the political priorities of the British public. The danger, then, in attacking the 'myth' of the 1930s, as revisionist historians do, is that, wittingly or unwittingly, they attack the popular attachment to welfarism. The objection to this last statement is obvious: historians should be dispelling not perpetuating myths. However, thanks to historical fashion, the term 'myth' is bandied around without rigour and in this case, the 1930s remain in popular memory as an icon – a selective reminiscence rooted in the real experience of the means test, the panel doctor, TB, rickets and the dole queues. These experiences were not fictional. Despite qualified improvements for some, the 1930s were hard times for the working class and after the prosperity experienced by many in the 1950s and 1960s, the idea of the 1930s ever returning is something to dread.

Tables

1. British unemployment figures

	Total unemployed	Unemployed rate (%)
1921	2,212	12.2
1922	1,909	10.8
1923	1,5867	8.9
1924	1,404	7.9
1925	1,559	8.6
1926	1,759	9.6
1927	1,373	7.4
1928	1,536	8.2
1929	1,503	8.0
1930	2,379	12.3
1931	3,252	16.4
1932	3,400	17.0
1933	3,087	15.4
1934	2,609	12.9
1935	2,437	12.0
1936	2,100	10.2
1937	1,776	8.5
1938	2,164	10.1

Source: Minstry of Labour Gazettes.

2. Scales of benefit under Unemployment Acts, 1919–39 (in shillings)

	Single man	Single woman	Wife	Child	Family of four
December 1919	11	11	0	0	11
December 1920	15	12	0	0	15
March 1921	20	16	0	0	16
June 1921	15	12	0	0	15
November 1921	15	12	5	1	22
August 1924	18	15	5	2	27
April 1928	17	15	7	2	28
March 1930	17	17	9	2	30
October 1931	15	13	8	2	27
April 1934	17	17	9	2	30
May 1934	17	17	9	3	32

Out of work donation: man 29, woman 25, first child 6, other children 3.

Source: Ministry of Labour Reports.

3. Comparison of wages and UAB scales

Ages	Average wage (1)	Average UAB allowance (2)	(2) as % of (1)
18–24	33s 7d	22s 4d	66
25–34	45s 0d	29s 3d	65
35–44	50s 1d	32s 5d	65
45–54	51s 0d	26s 8d	52
55–64	49s 9d	22s 6d	45

Source: Pilgrim Trust, *Men without Work*, 1938, p. 119.

4. Comparison of unemployed income and need

Family: Man and wife and	Food (BMA)	Fuel, clothing, lighting, cleaning, light	Total	Unemployment Assistance Allowance (without rent)	Unemployment Insurance Benefit (including rent)
No dependants	11s 11d	5s 4d	17s 3d	16s 6d	26s 0d
1 child (2yrs)	15s 4d	6s 6d	21s 10d	20s 6d	28s 8d
3 children (3, 5, 7 yrs)	23s 4d	8s 9d	32s 1d	25s 6d	32s 0d
4 children (5, 7, 9, 11 yrs)	25s 3s	9s 11d	35s 2d	29s 6d	34s 0d
1 unemployed son 18 yrs	18s 9d	6s 8d	25s 5d	24s 0d	40s 0d

Source: *Manchester Guardian*, 14 December 1934.

5. British coal exports (000s/tons)

	British Empire countries	Foreign countries
1913	2,300	71,000
1920	1,900	23,000
1921	1,900	22,800
1922	3,800	60,400
1923	3,500	75,900
1924	4,600	57,100
1925	4,500	46,300
1926	1,800	18,800
1927	5,000	46,200
1928	4,600	45,400
1929	5,300	55,000
1930	4,800	50,000
1931	4,200	38,600
1932	4,700	34,200
1933	4,200	34,900

6. Average number of persons employed in and about the coal mines in Great Britain

	Wage-earners below ground	Wage earners above ground	Clerks and salaried persons
1930	739,056	175,272	17,048
1931	685,980	165,643	16,241
1932	645,539	158,076	15,709
1933	618,786	154,854	15,451

Source: Parliamentary Debates, House of Commons, Fifth Series, vol. 295, col. 660, 27 November 1934.

7. Maternal mortality in Wales, per 1,000 live births

	1924–28	1929–33
'Industrial' Wales	5.33	5.94
'Non-industrial' Wales	5.37	5.56
All Wales	5.34	5.85
Special Areas	5.40	6.54
Non-Special Areas	5.95	5.32

Source: Report on Maternal Mortality in Wales, 1936.

8. Infant mortality rate: social class and inequalities by region, 1930–32

class:	I	II	III	IV	V
Greater London	29.6	39.8	49.7	62.3	71.2
Rest of S-E	33.1	38.4	41.6	46.8	54.0
North 1[1]	37.8	50.3	71.9	86.8	100.6
North 2	39.2	52.6	61.7	73.1	82.3
North 3	34.4	46.9	67.8	74.7	84.6
North 4	31.3	51.2	66.8	78.9	93.9
Midland 1	32.7	44.5	58.9	63.8	77.7
Midland 2	35.6	45.0	61.2	64.5	76.0
East	29.9	41.7	46.7	55.9	61.5
South West	35.0	43.7	45.4	54.4	58.6
Wales 1	43.1	52.2	70.0	73.0	77.4
Wales 2	38.6	54.5	61.7	69.6	70.3

Source: Registrar General's Reports for England and Wales.

9. Suicide rates during the depression in Great Britain

	England	Scotland	Northern Ireland	Wales	Total
1929	4,684	474	71	273	5,502
1930	4,760	495	61	268	5,584
1931	4,891	493	63	256	5,703
1932	5,457	500	71	286	6,314
1933	5,373	523	70	281	6,247

Source: Parliamentary Debates, House of Commons, Fifth Series, vol. 297, col. 816, 4 February 1935.

10. General Election results, 1918–35

General Election	Labour (seats, votes, %)	Conservatives (seats, votes, %)	Liberals (seats, votes, %)
	57	382[2]	163[3]
14 December 1918	2,245,777	4,144,192	2,785,374
	20.8%	38.6%	33.4%
	142	344	115[4]
15 November 1922	4,237,349	5,502,298	4,139,460
	29.7%	38.5%	28.8%
	191	258	158
6 December 1923	4,439,780	5,514,541	4,301,481
	30.7%	38.0%	29.7%
	151	412	40
29 October 1924	5,489,087	7,854,523	2,928,737
	33.3%	46.8%	17.8%
	287	260	59
30 May 1929	8,370,41	8,656,225	5,308,738
	37.1%	38.1%	23.6%
	46	470	36[5]
27 October 1931	6,324,737	11,905,925	1,472,788
	29.3%	55.0%	7.0%
	154	387	54[6]
14 November 1935	8,325,491	10,496,300	2,309,447
	38.0%	47.8%	10.4%

Source: F.W.S. Craig, *British Electoral Facts 1832–1980*, 1981.

11. Unemployment rates and figures, selected countries (000s, %)

	Austria (trade union returns)	Belgium (insurance figures)	France (labour exchange)	Germany	Hungary (labour exchange)	Netherlands (insurance figures)	Poland (labour exchange)	Czechoslovakia (trade union)	Great Britain*	USA
1929	47,4 11.1%	13.0 1.9%	10.1	1,898.6 9.2%	15.2	24.3 7.1%	129.5 4.9%	23.8 2.2%	1,215.5 10.4%	1.0%
1930	84.8 19.3%	36.0 5.4%	13.9	3,075.6 15.2%	43.6	37.8 9.7%	226.7 8.8%	51.4 4.5%	1,917.3 16.1%	7.9%
1931	117.9 27.4%	110.0 14.5%	75.2	4,519.7 23.3%	52.3	82.8 18.1%	299.5 12.6%	102.2 8.3%	2,629.6 21.3%	16.4%
1932	120.5 29.0%	211.0 23.5%	308.1	5,575.5 30.1%	66.2	153.5 29.5%	255.6 11.8%	184.6 13.5%	2,744.8 22.1%	24.9%
1933	104.0 25.1%	210.0 20.5%	307.8	4,804.4 26.3%	60.61	63.0 31.0%	249.6 11.9%	247.6 16.9%	2,520.6 19.9%	25.1%
1934	86.9 20.5%	235.0 23.4%	376.3	2,718.3 14.9%	52.2	160.4 32.1%	342.2 16.3%	246.0 17.4%	2,159.3 16.7%	20.5%
1935	71.8 16.5%	210.9 21.7%	465.9	2,151.0 11.6%	52.0	173.7 36.3%	381.9 16.7%	235.6 15.9%	2,036.4 15.5%	7,449.8 18.9%
1936	54.0 12.2%	154.0 16.2%	475.3	1,592.7 8.3%	52.1	169.4 36.3%	367.3 15.6%	208.1 13.1%	1,755.0 13.1%	7,705.3 15.5%
1937	41.8 9.3%	125.9 13.1%	379.1	912,3 4.6%	48.4	137.7 29.2%	375.1 14.6%	151.2 8.8%	1,484.4 10.5%	5,154.7 13.2%
1938	40.5 8.7%	173.9 17.6%	408.0	429.5 2.1%	47.4	134.3 27.2%	347.5 12.7%	161.4 9.1%	1,790.7 12.6%	7,404.2 19.5%
1939	47.1 9.9%	195.2				114.0 22.1%			1,513.6 10.3%	17.3%

*Percentages from insurance, absolute figures from labour exchanges.
Source: International Labour Office.

12. Bankruptcies in selected countries (monthly averages)

	1927	1928	1929	1930	1931	1932	1933	1934
Britain	381	365	345	369	389	415	367	326
Germany	475	665	821	945	1,133	717	321	226
France	689	684	726	756	906	1,170	1,147	1,250
USA	1,929	1,987	1,992	2,196	2,652	1,692	1,015	

Source: W. Woytinsky, *The Social Consequences of the Economic Depression*, 1936.

Number of bankruptcies index (monthly averages)

	1927	1928	1929	1930	1931	1932	1933	1934
Britain	100	96	91	97	102	109	96	86
Germany	100	140	173	199	239	151	68	48
France	100	99	105	110	131	170	166	181
USA	100	103	103	114	122	137	88	53

Source: W. Woytinsky, *The Social Consequences of the Economic Depression*, 1936.

13. Various indicators of the economic effects of the depression, selected countries

	% change in exports 1929–33	% change in industrial production	% change in steel output 1929–33	Unemployment peak 1929–33 000s (year) %
Austria	−64.6	−37.2	−64.3	406 (1933) 29.0
Belgium	−55.2	−33.9	−33.5	72 (1934) 23.4
Czechoslovakia	−71.1	−39.4	−66.5	738 (1933) 16.9
France	−63.1	−19.5	−30.3	470 (1936)
Germany	−53.7	−34.0	−53.1	5,575 (1932) 30.1
Italy	−59.4	−8.9	−16.5	1,019 (1933)
Netherlands	−60.2	−9.2	—	414 (1936) 32.7
Poland	−65.9	−31.5	−35.9	342 (1933) 16.3
Spain	−68.1	−16.0	−49.5	697 (1935)
Sweden	−39.5	−9.1	−9.2	126 (1933) 23.7
UK	−49.5	−3.8	−27.0	2,745 (1932) 22.5
USA	−69.5	−36.0	−58.9	11,904 (1933) 24.9

Source: B. Mitchell, *Historical Statistics*, 1976 and *International Labour Review*, vol. 31, 1935.

14. Origins of social insurance and welfare provision, selected countries

	Unemployment Insurance	Employment exchanges	Accident insurance	Sickness insurance	Pension insurance
Germany	1927	1910 & 14	1880	1883	1911
France	1958	c1900	1946	1928	1910
UK	1911 & 20	1908	1880	1911	1908
Austria	1920	c1900	1887	1918	1906
Switzerland	1924	c1900	1911	1911	1931
Denmark	1921	1913		1922	1891
Netherlands	1919		1901	1892	1920
Belgium	1920	c1900	1903	1919	1927
Sweden	1935	1906	1901		1913
Japan	1947	1921 & 25	1916	1926	1926
USA	1935	1933	1917		1935

15. Suicide rates per 10,000 in Europe

	1925	1926	1927	1928	1929	1930	1931	1932	1933	1934
Germany			2.5	2.5	2.6	2.8	2.9	2.9	2.9	
Belgium	1.4	1.5	1.6	1.6	1.6	1.7	1.8	1.8		
Denmark		1.6	1.6	1.8	1.6	1.7	1.7	1.9	1.8	1.8
Estonia		2.4	2.5	2.5	2.6	2.9	2.9	2.9	2.8	
Finland	1.5	1.5	1.7	1.7	1.9	2.2		2.0		
France		1.9	2.0	1.9	1.9	1.9	1.9	2.1		
Greece			0.4	0.5	0.5	0.5	0.5	0.5	0.6	
England & Wales	0.4	0.3	1.2	1.2	1.3	1.3	1.3	1.4	1.3	
Ireland	0.3	0.3	0.3	0.4	0.3	0.4	0.4	0.3		
Italy		1.0	1.0	1.0	0.9	1.0	1.0	1.0	0.9	0.9
Lithuania		0.6	0.5	0.9	0.9	0.9	1.0	1.0	0.9	0.9
Luxembourg		1.2	1.5	1.6	1.5	1.7	2.0	1.7	2.1	1.7
Netherlands			0.7	0.7	0.7	0.8		0.9	0.8	0.8
Norway	0.5	0.6	0.6	0.7	0.7	0.7	0.7	0.7		0.6
Austria		3.4	3.3	3.7	3.6	3.9	4.1	4.4		
Portugal					0.7	0.8	1.1	1.1	1.2	
Sweden	1.4	1.5	1.5	1.4	1.5	1.6	1.6	1.8		
Switzerland			2.4	2.5	2.4	2.6	2.5	2.7	2.6	
Spain			0.4	0.4	0.4	0.4	0.4	0.3	0.4	
Czechoslovakia			2.6	2.8	2.8	3.0	3.0	3.0	2.7	
Hungary			2.9	3.1	2.9	3.1	3.4	3.5	3.2	

Source: *Statistisches Jahrbuch für das Deutsche Reich.*

Notes

Introduction

1. W.H. Beveridge, *Full Employment in a Free Society: Misery Breeds Hate*, 1944, p. 248.
2. M. Kalecki, 'Political aspects of full employment' in E. Hunt and J. Schwartz (eds), *A Critique of Economic Theory*, 1972, p. 430.
3. Quoted in Beveridge, *Full Employment in a Free Society*, p. 248.
4. A. Keyssar, *Out of Work: The First Century of Unemployment in Massachusetts*, 1986; J.A. Garraty, *Unemployment in History: Economic Thought and Public Policy*, 1978; P. Baskerville and E. Sager, *Unwilling Idlers: The Urban Unemployed and their Families in Late Victorian Canada*, 1998; R. Salais, N. Baverez and B. Reynaud, *L'Invention du Chômage: Histoire et Transformations d'une Catégorie en France des Années 1890 aux Années 1980*, 1986; M.J. Poire, 'Historical perspectives and the interpretation of unemployment' *Journal of Economic Literature*, vol. 25, December 1987; J. Burnett, *Idle Hands: The Experience of Unemployment 1790–1990*, 1994.
5. Salais, Baverez and Reynaud, *L'Invention du Chômage*, 1986.
6. K. Matthews and D. Benjamin, *US and UK Unemployment between the Wars: A Doleful Story*, 1992.
7. For fuller discussion of revisionism, see 'Unemployment in Britain between the wars: revisionism and its critics' in Chapter 1 of this volume. For revisionist case, see in particular, J. Stephenson and C. Cook, *The Slump*, 1977.
8. E. Cannan, *An Economist's Protest*, 1927, p. 398.
9. C. Cameron, A. Lush and G. Meara, *Disinherited Youth: Report on the 18+ Age Group Enquiry Prepared for the Carnegie Trust*, 1943, pp. 78–9.

1 Unemployment: History and Perspectives

1. R. Price (ed.), *Documents of the French Revolution of 1848*, 1996, pp. 48–9.
2. Ibid., p. 122.
3. J.-F. Bergier, 'The industrial bourgeoisie and the rise of the working class', in C. Cipolla (ed.), *The Fontana Economic History of Europe*, 6 vols, vol. 3: *Industrial Revolution*, 1980, p. 421.

4. W. Minchinton, 'Patterns of demand', in C. Cipolla (ed.), *The Fontana Economic History of Europe*, 6 vols, vol. 3: *Industrial Revolution*, 1980, p. 88.

5. R. Easterlain, 'Regional income trends 1840–1950', in R. Fogel and S. Engerman (eds), *Reinterpretations of American Economic History*, 1972, p. 48.

6. E.K. Hunt and J.G. Schwartz, *A Critique of Economic Theory*, 1972, p. 8.

7. E.P. Thompson, 'Time, work-discipline, and industrial capitalism', *Past and Present*, no. 38, December 1967; K. Thomas, 'Work and leisure in pre-industrial society', *Past and Present*, no. 29, 1964, p. 52.

8. S. Pollard, 'Factory discipline in the industrial revolution', *Economic History Review*, vol. 16, no. 2, 1963.

9. J. Zeitlin and C. Sabel, 'Historical alternatives to mass production', *Past and Present*, no. 108, August 1985.

10. D. Levine, 'Industrialization and the proletarian family in England', *Past and Present*, no. 107, 1985.

11. M.J. Poire, 'Historical perspectives and the interpretation of unemployment', *Journal of Economic Literature*, vol. 25, December 1987, p. 1836.

12. E.J. Hobsbawm, *Labouring Men*, 1968, pp. 34–63.

13. J. Benson, *Penny Capitalists: A Study of Nineteenth Century Working Class Entrepreneurs*, 1983, p. 130.

14. P. Richards, 'The state and early industrial capitalism: the case of the handloom weavers', *Past and Present*, no. 83, May 1979; E.P. Thompson, *Making of the English Working Class*, 1963.

15. E. Hobsbawm and G. Rudé, *Captain Swing*, 1973.

16. A. Maddison, *Phases of Capitalist Development*, 1982, p. 64.

17. I. Wallerstein, *The Modern World Systems 1: Capitalist Agriculture and the European-World Economy in the Sixteenth Century*, 1974, p. 274.

18. R. Salais, N. Baverez, and B. Reynaud, *L'Invention du Chômage: Histoire et Transformations d'une Catégorie en France des Années 1890 aux Années 1980*, 1986.

19. A. Beier, *The Problem of the Poor in Tudor and Early Stuart England*, 1983; A. Beier, *Masterless Men: the Vagrancy Problem in England 1560–1640*, 1985; C. Lis and H. Soly, *Poverty and Capitalism in Pre-Industrial Europe*, 1979.

20. A. Digby, *British Welfare Policy*, 1989, pp. 35–6.

21. D. Fraser, 'The English Poor Law and the origins of the British welfare state', in W.J. Mommsen (ed.), *The Emergence of the Welfare in Britain and Germany*, 1981.

22. M.E. Rose, 'The crisis of Poor Law relief in England 1860–1890', in W.J. Mommsen (ed.), *The Emergence of the Welfare in Britain and Germany*, 1981, pp. 61–2.

23. A. Maddison, 'Origins and impact of the welfare state, 1883–1983', *Banca Nazionale del Lavoro*, March 1984.

24. J.A. Garraty, *Unemployment in History: Economic Thought and Public Policy*, 1978, p. 131.

25. M. Blaug, *Economic Theory in Retrospect*, 1978, pp. 15, 175–6 and 192; E. Roll, *A History of Economic Thought*, 1973, p. 485; I. Rubin, *A History of Economic Thought*, 1979.

26. M. Casson, *Economics of Unemployment: an Historical Perspective*, 1983, pp. 37–9.

27. S. Smiles, *Self-Help*, 1997, quoted from Preface to 1866 edition, p. xii; S. Smiles, *Thrift*, 1876.

28. J.A. Garraty, *History of Unemployment: Economic Thought and Public Policy*, 1978, pp. 17–18.

29. B.S. Rowntree, *Poverty: A Study of Town Life*, 1899; B.S. Rowntree, *Poverty and Progress: A Second Social Survey of York*, 1941.

30. R. Williams, *Keywords*, 1983, p. 326.

31. Garraty, *History of Unemployment*; Salais, Baverez and Reynaud, *L'Invention du Chômage*.

32. A. Keyssar, *Out of Work: The First Century of Unemployment in Massachusetts*, 1986, p. 3.

33. Salais, Baverez and Reynaud, *L'Invention du Chômage*, p. 28 [my translation].

34. *Census of England and Wales 1881*, vol. 4, General Report, cmd. 3739, 1883, p. 49.

35. *Thirteenth Census of the United States 1910*, volume IV: Population-Occupation Statistics, Bureau of Census, 1914.

36. Thompson, *Making of the English Working Class*, pp. 853–4.

37. W. Sewell, *Work and Revolution in France: Languages of Labour from Old Regime to 1848*, 1980, p. 207.

38. J. Beecher, *Charles Fourier: The Visionary and his World*, 1986, pp. 213–14.

39. F. Eyck, *The Revolutions of 1848–9*, 1972.

40. R. Price, *The Revolutions of 1848*, 1988.

41. A. Keyssar, *Out of Work: the First Century of Unemployment in Massachusetts*, 1986, pp. 246–51.

42. M. Langan, 'Reorganising the labour market: unemployment, the state and the labour movement 1880–914', in M. Langan and B. Schwarz, *Crises in the British State*, 1985; R. Flanagan, *'Parish-Fed Bastards': A History of the Politics of the Unemployed in Britain 1884–1939*, 1991.

43. J. Harris, *Unemployment and Politics: A Study of English Social Policy 1886–1914*, 1972, p. 365.

44. K. Marx, *Capital: a Critique of Political Economy*, 3 vols: vol. 1, 1887, p. 607.

45. Garraty, *Unemployment in History*, p. 106.

46. Langan, 'Reorganising the labour market: unemployment, the state and the labour movement 1880–1914', p. 109.

47. J. Stevenson and C. Cook, *Britain in the Depression, Society and Politics 1929–39*, 1994 [as it is called in its latest edition]; C. Mowat, *Britain between the Wars, 1918–48*, 1955.

48. M. Beloff, 'Introduction' in G. Peele and C. Cook (eds), *The Politics of Re-appraisal*, 1975, pp. 1–2.

49. D. Aldcroft, *The Inter-War Economy: Britain 1919–39*, 1970. D. Benjamin and L. Kochin, 'Searching for an explanation of interwar unemployment in Britain', *Journal of Political Economy*, vol. 87, 1979.

50. R. McKibbin, 'The economic policy of the second Labour Government 1929–31', *Past and Present*, no. 68, 1975; R. Skidelsky, *Politicians and the Slump: The Labour Government 1929–31*, 1970.

51. R. Middleton, *Towards the Managed Economy*, 1985. J. Tomlinson, *Problems of British Economic Policy 1870–45*, 1981.

52. M. Mitchell, 'The effects of unemployment on the social condition of women and children in the 1930s', *History Workshop Journal*, no. 19, 1985; C. Webster, 'Health, welfare and unemployment during the Depression', *Past and Present*, no. 109, 1985; C. Webster, 'Healthy or hungry thirties', *History Workshop Journal*, no. 13, 1982; J. Winter, 'Infant mortality, maternal mortality, and public health in Britain in the 1930s', *Journal of European Economic History*, vol. 8, 1979; J. Winter, 'Unemployment, nutrition and infant mortality in Britain 1920–50', in J. Winter (ed.), *The Working Class in Modern British History: Essays in Honour of Henry Pelling*, 1983; R. Croucher, *We Refuse to Starve in Silence: A History of the National Unemployed Workers' Movement 1921–46*, 1987; P. Kingsford, *The Hunger Marchers in Britain 1920–39*, 1982; Flanagan, 'Parish-Fed Bastards'.

53. J.E. Cronin, *Labour and Society in Britain 1918–1970*, 1984; N. Kirk, *Labour and Society in Britain and the USA*, 2 vols: vol.2: *Challenge and Accommodation 1850–1939*, 1994.

54. A. Howkins and J. Saville, 'The nineteen-thirties: a revisionist history', in R. Miliband and J. Saville (eds), *Socialist Register*, 1979, p. 93.

55. E. Zimmerman, 'The 1930s world economic crisis in six European countries: a first report on the causes of political instability and reaction to crisis', in P. Johnson and W. Thompson (eds), *Rhythms in Politics and Economics*, 1985.

56. For a summary of the literature, see G. Therborn, 'Classes and states, welfare state development 1881–1981', *Studies in Political Economy: A Socialist Review*, vol. 13, 1984. For the German case, see G. Steinmetz, 'The local welfare state: two strategies for social domination in urban Imperial Germany', *American Sociological Review*, vol. 55, December 1990. For early reactions to unemployment, Langan, 'Reorganising the labour market: unemployment, the state and the labour movement 1880–1914'.

57. J. Goldthorpe, 'The development of social policy in England, 1880–1914', *Transactions of the 5th World Congress of Sociology*, 1962.

58. F. Greene (ed.), *Time to Spare, What Unemployment Means by Eleven Unemployed*, 1935, p. 83.

59. Parliamentary Papers (PP): *Report on the Effects of Existing Economic Circumstances on the Health in the Community in the County Borough of Sunderland and Certain Districts of Durham*, cmd. 4886, 1935.

60. Public Record Office (PRO): AST 12/26 UAB circular to District UAB officers, 6 March 1936; letter, W. Eady (Ministry of Labour) to all district officers, letter, 20 December 1936.

61. *Dictionary of National Biography*, 1941–50 and 1951–60. For example, the Blanesburgh Committee, which proposed the 'not genuinely

seeking work' clause, was staffed by three industrialists, three trade union officials, one City accountant, a knighted solicitor, a peer and top judge (Blanesburgh himself), a Vicountess, a (soon to be knighted) insurance company managing director, a top Ministry of Labour civil servant and a shipping magnate.

62. D. Colledge and J. Field, "'To recondition human material ...'" an account of a British labour camp in the 1930s an interview with William Heard', *History Workshop Journal*, no. 15, Spring 1983, p. 160.

63. R. Harrison, 'New light on the police and the hunger marchers', *Society for the Study of Labour History*, no. 37, Autumn 1978; J. Saville, 'The hunger marches of the nineteen thirties: some random comments', *North-West Labour History*, August 1988; L. Flynn, 'Hiding the history of the hunger marches', *New Statesman*, 1 September 1978.

64. G. Orwell, *Road to Wigan Pier*, 1989, p. 69.

65. Rowntree, *Poverty and Progress*; H. Llewellyn Smith (ed.), *The New Survey of London Life and Labour*, 1934; H. Tout, *The Standard of Living in Bristol*, 1938; H.A. Mess, *Tyneside Papers*, 1926–1933; D.M. Goodfellow, *Tyneside: the Social Facts*, 1942; D. Caradog Jones (ed.), *The Social Survey of Merseyside*, 1934; H. Jennings, *Brynmawr: A Study of a Depressed Area*, 1934; A. Owen, *A Survey of Juvenile Unemployment and Welfare in Sheffield*, Sheffield Social Survey Pamphlet, no. 6, April 1933.

66. Pilgrim Trust, *Men Without Work*, 1938, p. 71.

67. A. Calder and D. Sheridan (eds), *Speak for Yourself: A Mass Observation Anthology 1937–49*, 1985, p. 159.

68. F. Brockway, *Hungry England*, 1932; J.B. Priestley, *English Journey*, 1934; G. Orwell, *Road to Wigan Pier*, 1937.

69. Orwell, *Road to Wigan Pier*; G. Orwell, *Collected Essays, Journalism and Letters*, 4 vols: vol.1, 1920–40, 1968.

70. W. Greenwood, *There Was a Time*, 1968.

71. Greene, *Time to Spare*.

72. P. Scannell, 'Broadcasting and the politics of unemployment 1930–35', *Media, Culture and Society*, no. 2, 1980.

73. H. Harmer, 'The National Unemployed Worker's Movement in Britain 1921–39: Failure and Success', unpublished PhD, London School of Economics, 1987, pp. 52, 57, 59, 305–6 and 317.

2 Government, Employers and Unemployment

1. PRO: CAB 24/116: Reports on Revolutionary Organisations in the UK, quoted in W.R. Garside, *British Unemployment 1919–39: A Study in Public Policy*, 1990, p. 37.

2. PP: *Commission of the Enquiry into Industrial Unrest: Summary of the Reports of the Commission*, cmd. 8696, 1917, pp. 5–8.

3. J.E. Cronin, *Labour and Society in Britain 1918–1979*, 1984, p. 19.

4. *Ministry of Labour Gazette*, January 1934.

5. PP: Provisional Joint Committee (Munroe Report), *Industrial Conference, Report to the Meeting of April 4th*, 1919, cmd. 501, 1919.

6. W. Hannington, *Unemployed Struggles 1919–36*, 1979, p. 2.

7. *The Economist*, 1921 (various dates).

8. Hannington, *Unemployed Struggles 1919–36*. Victimisation was exacerbated by unemployment and defeat with the greatest wave of victimisations following the General Strike in mining.

9. *The Economist*, 2 July 1921, p. 5.

10. Quoted in R. Martin, *Communism and the British Trade Unions 1924–33*, 1969, p. 23.

11. S. Webb, 'British labour in the depression', *International Labour Review*, no. 2, 1923, p. 213.

12. J. Tomlinson, *Problems of British Economic Policy 1870–1945*, 1981. Ministry of Labour, Departmental Committee (Blanesburgh Report), *Unemployment Insurance*, Report, 1927. Unemployment Insurance Statutory Committee, *Financial Condition of the Unemployment Fund on 31st December, 1935*, Report, 1936.

13. PP: *Scheme of the Out-of-Work Donation*, Interim report, cmd. 196, 1919; Final Report, cmd. 305, 1919.

14. PP: Royal Commission, *Unemployment Insurance*, First Report, cmd. 3872, 1931, pp. 66–7.

15. PP: *Scheme of the Out-of-Work Donation*, Interim report, cmd. 196, 1919; Final Report, cmd. 305, 1919.

16. PRO: CAB 24/127, CP 3295 and PRO: CAB 24/128, CP 3317 quoted in A. Deacon, 'Concession and coercion: the politics of unemployment insurance in the twenties', in A. Briggs and J. Saville (eds), *Essays in Labour History 1918–39*, vol. 3, 1977, p. 13.

17. PP: *Committee on National Expenditure*, First Report, cmd. 1581, 1921.

18. R. Davison, *The Unemployed: New Policies and Old*, 1929, p. 128.

19. Ministry of Labour, Departmental Committee (Blanesburgh Report). *Unemployment Insurance*, Report, 1927.

20. The GSW was originally introduced in March 1921 just for the uncovenanted; it was extended by Labour in 1924 for all unemployed.

21. A. Deacon, *In Search of the Scrounger: The Administration of Unemployment Insurance in Britain 1920–31*, 1976, p. 9.

22. W. Brierley, *Means Test Man*, 1935, p. 80.

23. For positive reactions to individual clerks, see Pilgrim Trust, *Men Without Work*, 1938, p. 187 and M. Cohen, *I Was One of the Unemployed*, 1945, p. 100. For negative reactions, see K. Armstrong and H. Beynon, *Hello Are You Working? Memories of the 1930s in the North-East of England*, 1977, and N. Gray, *The Worst of Times: An Oral History of the Great Depression in Britain*, 1985.

24. F. Miller, 'The British unemployment assistance crisis of 1935', *Journal of Contemporary History*, vol. 14, 1979, p. 332.

25. F. Miller, 'National assistance or unemployment assistance? The British Cabinet and relief policy, 1932–3', *Journal of Contemporary History*, vol. 9, 1974.

26. *The Prevention of Unemployment after the War*, 1917, reproduced in Labour Party, *Unemployment: a Labour Policy*, 1921.

27. *Unemployment Grants Committee*, Report to 31 December 1931, cmd. 4029, 1932.

28. *Unemployment Grants Committee*, Final Report, cmd. 4354, 1933.

29. D. Colledge, *Labour Camps: The British Experience*, 1989.

30. The long-term unemployment rate is the proportion of the unemployed who have been out of work for more than a year. PP: *First Report of the Commissioner for the Special Areas (England and Wales)*, cmd. 4957, 1935, pp. 10 and 97.

31. W. Hannington, *The Problems of the Distressed Areas*, 1937, p. 27.

32. F. Miller, 'The unemployment policy of the National Government, 1931–6', *Historical Journal*, vol. 19, 1976, p. 467.

33. *Manchester Guardian*, 15 November 1934.

34. Hannington, *The Problems of the Distressed Areas*, p. 218.

35. W.R. Garside, *British Unemployment 1919–39: A Study in Public Policy*, 1990, p. 258.

36. PP: Committee of Ministry of Reconstruction. Joint Industrial Councils. *Relations between Employers and Employed. Interim Report.* cmd. 8606, 1917–8. *Final Report*, cmd. 9153, 1918.

37. A. Vinson, 'Poor relief, public assistance and the maintenance of the unemployed in Southamption between the wars', *Southern History*, no. 2, 1980.

38. *Recommendations of the Joint Committee of the National Industrial Conference*, 4 April 1919, in Labour Party, *Unemployment: a Labour Policy*, 1921.

39. T. Rodgers, 'Sir Allan Smith, the Industrial Group and the Politics of Unemployment', *Business History*, no. 28, 1986.

40. A. McIvor, '"A crusade for capitalism": the Economic League, 1919–39', *Journal of Contemporary History*, vol. 23, 1988; A. McIvor and H. Paterson, 'Combating the left: victimisation and anti-labour activities on Clydeside 1900–1939', in R. Duncan and A. McIvor (eds), *Militant Workers: Labour and Class Conflict on the Clyde 1900–1950*, 1992.

41. PP: *Scheme of the Out-of-Work Donation*, Interim report, cmd. 196, 1919. Final Report, cmd. 305, 1919.

42. Appended in Ministry of Labour, Departmental Committee (Blanesburgh Report). *Unemployment Insurance*, vol. 2: Minutes of Evidence, 1927, pp. 85–92.

43. Ministry of Labour, Departmental Committee (Blanesburgh Report). *Unemployment Insurance*, vol. 2: Minutes of Evidence, 1927, pp. 71–94.

44. Quoted the NCEO contribution to the Beveridge Report: PP: *Social Insurance and Allied Services* (Beveridge Report) Appendix G: Memoranda from Organisations, cmd. 6405, 1942.

45. NCEO, The Industrial Situation, 1931 quoted in PP: *Social Insurance and Allied Services* (Beveridge Report), Appendix G: Memorandum from Organisations, cmd. 6405, 1942.

46. *The Economist*, 21 February 1931, p. 384.

47. Quoted in *The Economist*, 9 May 1931, p. 983.

48. PP: *Social Insurance and Allied Services* (Beveridge Report), Appendix G: Memorandum from Organisations, cmd. 6405, 1942.

49. A. Slaven, 'Self-liquidation: the NSS Ltd. and the British Shipbuilders in the 1930s', in S. Palmer and G. William (eds), *Chartered and Uncharted Waters*, 1982, pp. 125–47.

50. H. Gospel, 'Employer's labour policy: a study of the Mond–Turner talks', *Business History*, vol. 21, 1979; G. McDonald and H. Douglas, 'The Mond–Turner talks, 1927–33: a study in industrial co-operation', *Historical Journal*, vol. 16, 1973.

51. S. Pollard, 'TUC reactions to the economic crisis', in S. Pollard (ed.), *The Gold Standard and Employment Policies Between the Wars*, 1970, p. 151.

52. A. Marwick, 'Middle opinion in the 1930s: planning, progress and political agreement', *English Historical Review*, vol. 79, 1964.

53. Recently, philanthropy has been the subject of lively debate and increasing research interest. F. Prochaska, *The Voluntary Impulse: Philanthropy in Modern Britain*, 1988; 'Philanthropy' in F.M.L. Thompson (ed.), *Cambridge Social History of Britain*, vol. 3, 1992; J. Lewis, 'The boundary between the voluntary and statutory social service in the late nineteenth and early twentieth centuries', *Historical Journal*, vol. 39, no. 1, 1996, pp. 155–77; B. Harris, 'Responding to adversity: government-charity relations and the relief of unemployment in interwar Britain', *Contemporary Record*, vol. 9, no. 3, 1995, pp. 529–61; G. Finlayson, 'The moving frontier: voluntarism and the state in British social welfare, 1911–49', *Twentieth Century British History*, vol. 1, 1990, pp. 183–206.

54. Harris, 'Responding to adversity: government–charity relations and the relief of unemployment in interwar Britain'.

55. A. MacAdam, *New Philanthropy*, 1934.

56. Birmingham Central Library: MS 396/1–12 *National Council of Social Services, Newspaper Cuttings*.

57. C. Mowat, *Britain between the Wars, 1918–39*, 1955, p. 488.

58. A. Thorpe (ed.), *The Failure of Political Extremism in Interwar Britain*, 1988; J. Stevenson and C. Cook, *Britain in Depression: Society and Politics 1929–39*, 1994; G. Peele and C. Cook (eds), *The Politics of Reappraisal 1918–39*, 1975.

3 The Experience of Unemployment

1. F. Unwin, *Reflections on the Mersey: Memoirs of the Twenties and Thirties*, 1983, p. 104.

2. J.B. Priestley, *English Journey*, 1934, p. 409.

3. N. Whiteside and J. Gillespie, 'Deconstructing unemployment: developments in Britain in the interwar years', *Economic History Review*, 2nd series, vol. 44, no. 4, 1991.

4. C. Seymour-Ure, 'The press and the party system between the wars', in G. Peele and C. Cook (eds), *The Politics of Reappraisal, 1918–39*, 1975.

5. The *Daily Mail* described the hunger marchers as 'Moscow dupes' in 1932. E. Trory, *Between the Wars: Recollections of a Communist Organiser*, 1974.

6. M. Turnbull, 'Attitude of government and administration towards the Hunger Marches of the 1920s and 30s', *Journal of Social Policy*, vol. 2, no. 2, 1973, p. 133.

7. *The Times*, 7 December 1932.

8. PRO: CAB 24/264, CP. 256.

9. *Sunderland Echo*, 11 September 1931.

10. *Daily Mail*, 24 August 1931.

11. W. Hannington, *Chamberlain: Face the Facts*, 1939. *The Times*, 29 January 1938.

12. F. Greene (ed.), *Time to Spare: What Unemployment Means by Eleven Unemployed*, 1935, p. 84. Pilgrim Trust, *Men Without Work*, 1938, p. 183.

13. W. Brierley, *Means Test Man*, 1935, p. 98.

14. *Sunderland Echo*, 11 September 1931.

15. *Birmingham Mail*, 7 May 1936.

16. *Birmingham Gazette*, 13 May 1935.

17. Birmingham Central Library (BCL): MS 396/1–12 National Council of Social Services, Newspaper Cuttings.

18. Tyne-and-Wear Archive Service (TWAS): G/EMP2/1: *Daily Express*, 24 October 1934 and letter, R.J. Pitchers to Mayor Dodds, 15 November 1934.

19. H.E. Browning and A.A. Sorrell, 'Cinemas and cinema-going in Great Britain', *Journal of the Royal Statistical Society*, vol. 117, 1954.

20. PRO: MEPO 2/3091.

21. J. Richards, 'BBFC and content control in the 1930s', *Historical Journal of Film, Radio and Television*, vol. 1, no. 2, 1981.

22. Ibid.

23. E.W. Bakke, *The Unemployed Man: A Social Study*, 1933, p. 182.

24. M. Jahoda, *Employment and Unemployment: a Social Psychological Analysis*, 1982, p. 22.

25. E.P. Thompson, 'Time, work-discipline and industrial capitalism', *Past and Present*, no. 38, 1967; K. Thomas, 'Work, leisure in pre-industrial society', *Past and Present*, no. 29, 1964; S. Pollard, 'Factory discipline and the industrial revolution', *Economic History Review*, vol. 16, no. 2, 1963.

26. J.B. Priestley, *English Journey*, 1934, p. 407.

27. Greene, *Time to Spare*, p. 89.

28. BCL: NCSS press cuttings: *Birmingham Gazette*, 26 October 1935.

29. Pilgrim Trust, *Men Without Work*, 1938, p. 151.

30. Bakke, *The Unemployed Man*, p. 128.

31. P. Eisenberg and P. Lazarfeld, 'The psychological effects of unemployment', *Psychological Bulletin*, 1938.

32. J. Ennis, *Jarrow Reminiscences*, 1982; S. Davis, P. Gill, L. Grant, M. Nightingale, R. Noon and A. Shallice, *Genuinely Seeking Work*, 1992.

33. M. Krafchik, 'Unemployment and vagrancy in the 1930s: deterrence, rehabilitation and the depression', *Journal of Social Policy*, vol. 12, no. 2, 1983; K. Armstrong and H. Beynon, *Hello Are You Working? Memories of the 1930s in the North-East of England*, 1977, p. 65.

34. *Ministry of Labour Gazette*, June 1940.

35. W.R. Garside, *British Unemployment 1919–1939: A Study in Public Policy*, 1990, p. 5.

36. N.F.R. Crafts, 'Long-term unemployment in the 1930s', *Economic History Review*, 2nd Series, vol. 40, no. 3, 1987.

37. *Census of England and Wales, 1931, Industry Tables*, 1934, pp. 182–309.

38. A. McInnes, 'Surviving the slump: an oral history of Stoke-on-Trent between the wars', *Midland History*, vol. 18, 1993.

39. E. Hopkins, 'Working class life in Birmingham between the wars, 1918–39', *Midland History*, vol. 15, 1990.

40. Pilgrim Trust, *Men Without Work*, 1938, p. 64.

41. Greene, *Time to Spare*, p. 94.

42. Armstrong and Beynon, *Hello Are You Working?*, pp. 86–7.

43. J. Hurstfield, 'Women's unemployment in the 1930s: some comparisons with the 1980s', in S. Allen, A. Watson, K. Purcell and S. Wood (eds), *The Experience of Unemployment*, 1989, p. 37.

44. In 1931 there were 1,262,000 private domestic servants. R. McKibbin, *Classes and Cultures in England 1918–1951*, 1998, p. 109.

45. Greene, *Time to Spare*, p. 39.

46. Ibid., p. 36.

47. M. Rice, *Working Class Wives*, 1939.

48. PP: *Royal Commission on Unemployment Insurance*, cmd. 4185, 1932, p. 71.

49. Greene, *Time to Spare*, p. 40.

50. H. Francis, 'Welsh miners and the Spanish Civil War', *Journal of Contemporary History*, vol. 5, no. 3, 1970, p. 191.

51. N. Gray, *The Worst of Times: An Oral History of the Great Depression in Britain*, 1985, p. 10.

52. TWAS: Transport and General Worker's Union, *Area Secretary's Report*, 19 April 1932.

53. J. Stevenson and C. Cook, *Britain in the Depression: Society and Politics 1929–39*, 1996, p. 96.

54. *Registrar General's Statistical Review of England and Wales*, 1930 and 1940; F. Brockway, *Hungry England*, 1932.

55. Parliamentary Debates, House of Commons, Fifth Series, vol. 295, col. 680, 27 November 1934; vol. 297, col. 816, 4 February, 1935; vol. 298, col. 1283, 28 February 1935; vol. 328, col. 1881, 11 November 1937.

56. Quoted in S. Kelly, *Idle Hands, Clenched Fists: The Depression in a Shipyard Town*, 1987.

57. P. Sainsbury, *Suicide in London: an Ecological Study*, 1955, p. 55; J. Hayes and P. Nutman, *Understanding the Unemployed: the Psychological Effects of Unemployment*, 1981.

58. Armstrong and Beynon, *Hello Are You Working?*, p. 25.

59. *Newcastle Chronicle*, 21 January 1938.

60. Ministry of Labour and National Service, *Weekly Expenditure of Working Class Households 1937–8*, 1949.

61. M. Chamberlain, *Growing up in Lambeth*, 1989, p. 23.

62. NUWM, *Jubilee Chimp: Her Birth, Food and Drink*, 1935.

63. H. Jennings, *Brynmawr: a Study of a Depressed Area*, 1934, pp. 92–3.

64. G. Orwell, *Collected Essays, Journalism and Letters of George Orwell*, 4 vols, vol. 1: 1920–1940, 1968, p. 202.

65. *Census of England and Wales, 1931, Housing Report and Tables*, 1935, pp. 35–41.

66. Quoted in J. Burnett, *Plenty and Want: A Social History of Diet in England from 1815 to the Present*, 1979.

67. G.C.M. M'Gonigle and J. Kirby, *Poverty and Public Health*, 1936.

68. *On the State of Public Health, Annual Report of the Cheif Medical Officer to the Ministry of Health, 1932*, 1933, p. 16.

69. A.M. Carr-Saunders, D. Caradog Jones and C.A. Moser, *A Social Survey of Social Conditions of England and Wales*, 1958, p. 11.

70. J. Boyd Orr, *Food, Income, Health*, 1936; M'Gonigle Kirby, *Poverty and Public Health*; J.C. Spence, *Investigation into the Health and Nutrition of Certain Children of Newcastle between the Ages of 1 and 5*, 1934.

71. J.B. Priestley, *English Journey*, 1934; Orwell, *Road to Wigan Pier*; W. Hannington, *The Problem of the Distressed Areas*, 1937.

72. M'Gonigle and Kirby, *Poverty and Public Health*, p. 268.

73. PP: Ministry of Health, *Report on an Investigation into Maternal Mortality*, cmd. 5422, 1937.

74. Lady Williams, 'Malnutrition as a cause of maternal mortality', *Public Health*, October 1936.

75. Ibid and PP: Ministry of Health, *Report on Maternal Mortality in Wales*, cmd. 5423, 1937.

76. Ibid.

77. PP: Ministry of Health, *Report on Maternal Mortality in England and Wales*, cmd. 5422, 1937.

78. M. Mitchell, 'Effects of unemployment on the social conditions of women and children in the 1930s', *History Workshop Journal*, no. 19, 1985, p. 107.

79. Ibid., p. 110, i.e. for the Registrar General's groups I and V.

80. *Ministry of Health Circular*, 1290, 1932.

81. Board of Education Committee on Adenoids and Enlarged Tonsils report, 1927, quoted in M'Gonigle and Kirby, *Poverty and Public Health*, pp. 64–74.

82. Save the Children Fund, *Unemployment and the Child*, 1933, p. 124.

83. Spence, *Investigation into the Health and Nutrition of Certain Children of Newcastle between the ages of 1 and 5*.

84. B. Harris, 'The height of school children in Britain 1900–50', in J. Komlos (ed.), *Stature, Living Standards and Economic Development*, 1994.

85. J. Boyd Orr, *Food, Health, Income*, 1936, p. 80.

86. Lord Boyd Orr, *As I Recall*, 1966, pp. 115–17.

87. E. Percy, *Some Memories*, 1958, p. 116.

88. Letter to *The Times* quoted in Hannington, *The Problem of the Distressed Areas*, p. 61.

89. Greene, *Time to Spare*, p. 32.

90. Dr J. Halliday, 'Psychoneurosis as a cause of incapacity among insured persons', *British Medical Journal* supplement, 16 March 1935.

91. Quoted in G. Barnsby, *A History of Wolverhampton, Bilston and District Trades Council, 1865–1900*, 1994, p. 19.

92. M. Cohen, *I Was One of the Unemployed*, 1945, p. 6.

93. C. Cameron, A. Lush and G. Meara, *Disinherited Youth: a Report on the 18+ Age Group Enquiry prepared for the Carnegie Trust*, 1943, p. 82.

94. A. Calder and D. Sheridan (eds), *Speak for Yourself: A Mass Observation Anthology 1937–49*, 1985, pp. 27–8.

95. *Ministry of Labour Gazette*, January 1933.

96. Armstrong and Beynon, *Hello Are You Working?*, p. 29.

97. H.L. Beales and R.S. Lambert, *Memoirs of the Unemployed*, 1934, p. 105.

98. E. Warburton and C. Butler, *Disallowed: The Tragedy of the Means Test*, 1935, p. 24.

99. Ibid., p. 36.

100. Ibid., pp. 55–6.

101. Cohen, *I Was One of the Unemployed*, p. 97.

102. A. Deacon and J. Bradshaw, *Reserved for the Poor: The Means Test in British Social Policy*, 1983, pp. 27–8.

103. *Report of the 1923 Trades Union Congress in Plymouth*, 1923.

104. J. Sarsby, *Missuses and Mouldrunners: An Oral History of Women Pottery Workers at Work and at Home*, 1988, quoted in A. McInnes, 'Surviving the slump: an oral history of Stoke-on-Trent between the wars', *Midland History*, vol. 18, 1993.

105. PP: Royal Commission. *Unemployment Insurance*. Final report, cmd. 4185, 1932, p. 470.

106. Parliamentary Debates, House of Commons, 5th Series, vol. 295, col. 675, 27 November 1934.

107. J. Newsom, *Out of the Pit*, 1936, p. xii.

108. R. McKibbin, '"Social psychology" of unemployment in interwar Britain', in R. McKibbin, *Ideologies of Class: Social Relations in Britain 1880–1950*, 1990.

109. John Rankin in Greene, *Time to Spare*, p. 46.

110. H.L. Beales and R.S. Lambert, *Memoirs of the Unemployed*, 1934, p. 76.

111. Newsom, *Out of the Pit*, p. 20.

112. BCL:MS 396/1: *National Council of Social Services Press Cuttings*: *Birmingham Post*, 16 September 1936.

113. P. Eisenberg and P. Lazarsfeld, 'The psychological effects of unemployment', *Psychological Bulletin*, vol. 35, no. 6, June 1938. p. 372.

114. W. Hannington, *Unemployed Struggles 1919–36*, 1936, p. 323.

115. H.N. Brailsford, *Peace or Prosperity*, 1934, p. 96.

116. Bakke, *Unemployed Man*, p. 251; P. Snowden, *An Autobiography*, 2 vols, vol. 2: 1919–34, 1934, p. 847.

117. Cato, *Guilty Men*, 1941, p. 18.

4 The Labour Party and Unemployment

1. P. Addison, *The Road to 1945*, 1975.

2. J.H. Thomas, *When Labour Rules*, 1920, p. 11.

3. Labour Party, *Unemployment: A Labour Policy*, 1921, p. 11, quoting the presentation of War Aims to the Inter-Allied Conference, August 1917.

4. Labour Party, *Unemployment*, p. 6.

5. Quoted in E. Percy, *Some Memories*, 1958, p. 138.

6. J.R. MacDonald, *Labour's Policy versus Protection*, 1923.

7. A. Booth and M. Pack, *Employment, Capital and Economic Policy: Great Britain 1918–39*, 1985, p. 18.

8. Labour Party, *How to Conquer Unemployment*, 1929, p. 26.

9. H.N. Brailsford, J.A. Hobson, A.C. Jones and E.F. Wise, *The Living Wage: A Report Submitted to the National Administrative Council of the ILP*, 1926, p. 8.

10. J.A. Hobson, *Economics of Unemployment*, 1922, p. 7.

11. H.N. Brailsford, *Property or Peace*, 1934, p. 99.

12. N. Thompson, *Political Economy and the Labour Party*, 1996, p. 45.

13. F. Williams, *Nothing so Strange: An Autobiography*, 1970, p. 102.

14. J.R. MacDonald letter to the King, 10 October 1924, in M. Cowling, *The Impact of Labour 1920–24*, 1971, p. 359.

15. Parliamenary Debates, House of Commons, Fifth series, vol. 169, col. 760, 12 February 1924.

16. Quoted in R.W. Lyman, *The First Labour Government 1924*, 1957, p. 136; Parliamentary Debates, House of Commons, Fifth Series, vol. 170, col. 2083, 10 March 1924.

17. A. Deacon, *In Search of the Scrounger: The Administration of Unemployment Insurance 1920–31*, 1976, p. 33.

18. Ibid., p. 34.

19. Parliamentary Debates, House of Commons, Fifth Series, vol. 169, col. 987, 24 March 1924 and col. 2134, 2 April 1924; vol. 172, col. 797, 11 April 1924; vol. 173, col. 440, 7 May 1924 and col. 1973, 13 May 1924.

20. S. Webb, *War against Poverty: How the Government Can Prevent Unemployment*, ILP, 1912; S. Webb, *The War and the Workers: Handbook of Some Immediate Measures to Prevent Unemployment and Relieve Distress*, Fabian Society Tract, no. 176, 1914; S. Webb, *When Peace Comes: The Way of Industrial Reconstruction*, Fabian Society Tract, no. 189, 1916.

21. K. Middlemas (ed.), *Thomas Jones: Whitehall Diary*, 3 vols, vol. 1: 1916–25, 1969, p. 273.

22. Parliamentary Debates, House of Commons, Fifth Series, vol. 169, col. 1973, 21 February 1924; vol. 170, col. 1974, 10 March 1924; vol. 173, col. 2550, 22 May 1924.

23. Quoted in Liberal Party, *We Can Conquer Unemployment*, 1929.

24. K. Middlemas (ed.), *Thomas Jones*, vol. 1: 1916–25, 1969, p. 283.

25. C. Cook, *A Short History of the Liberal Party 1900–92*, 1993, pp. 98–100.

26. ILP Information Centre, *Six Months of Labour Government*, 1924.

27. R. Lyman, *The First Labour Government 1924*, 1957, p. 142.

28. Labour Party, *Work for the Workless*, 1924, p. 4.

29. Labour Party, *How to Conquer Unemployment*, 1929, p. 26.

30. Ibid.

31. PP: *Procedure and Evidence for the Determination of Claims for Unemployment Insurance Benefit*. cmd. 3415, 1929.
32. A. Deacon, 'Concession and coercion: the politics of unemployment insurance in the twenties', in A. Briggs and J. Saville (eds), *Essays in Labour History 1918–39*, vol. 3, 1977.
33. PP: *Procedure and Evidence for the Determination of Claims for Unemployment Insurance Benefit*. cmd. 3415, 1929.
34. P. Snowden, *An Autobiography*, 2 vols, vol. 2: *1919–34*, 1934, p. 847.
35. M. Cole, 'The Labour movement between the wars', in D. Martin and D. Rubinstein (eds), *Ideology and the Labour Movement*, 1979, p. 215.
36. R. Skidelsky, *Politicians and the Slump: The Labour Government of 1929–31*, 1970, p. 336.
37. A.J.P. Taylor, *English History 1914–45*, 1965, p. 286.
38. W. Hannington, *Ten Lean Years*, 1940, p. 24.
39. *The Times*, 27 January 1931.
40. F. Williams, *Nothing So Strange: An Autobiography*, 1970, p. 96.
41. P. Williamson, *National Crisis and National Government: British Politics, Economy and Empire, 1926–32*, 1992, p. 199.
42. Labour Party, *How to Conquer Unemployment*, 1929, p. 29.
43. Snowden, *An Autobiography*, vol. 2: *1919–34*, p. 891.
44. *The Economist*, 2 May 1931, p. 928 (reporting on House of Commons debate of 11 February 1931).
45. *The Economist*, 14 February 1931, p. 331.
46. M. Cole (ed.), *Beatrice Webb Diaries 1924–32*, 1956, p. 277.
47. Snowden, *An Autobiography, vol. 2*, p. 904.
48. PP: Royal Commission, *Unemployment Insurance*. First Report, Cmd. 3872, 1931.
49. J.D. Tomlinson, 'Women as anomalies', *Public Administration*, vol. 62, no. 4, 1984.
50. K. Middlemas (ed.), *Thomas Jones: Whitehall Diary*, vol. 1: *1916–25*, 1969, p. 265.
51. M. Cole (ed.), *Beatrice Webb Diaries 1924–32*, 1956, p. 277.
52. H. Dalton, *Call Back Yesterday: Memoirs 1882–1931*, 1953, p. 290.
53. F.W. Pethick-Lawrence, *This Gold Crisis*, 1931, p. 170.
54. PRO: T175/51 Hopkins to Snowden 'very secret' memo, 24 July 1931.
55. S. Pollard, *The Development of the British Economy, 1914–1990*, 1992, p. 104.
56. The Cabinet economy committee was comprised of MacDonald, Snowden, Thomas, Henderson and Graham.
57. Lord Citrine, *Men and Work: An Autobiography*, 1964, p. 284.
58. Cole, *Beatrice Webb Diaries 1924–32*, p. 282, emphasis in the original.
59. Quoted in L. MacNeill Weir, *The Tragedy of Ramsay MacDonald*, 1938, p. 407.
60. H. Dalton, *Call Back Yesterday: Memoirs 1887–1931*, 1953, p. 298.
61. K. Laybourn, *The Labour Party 1881–1951*, 1988, p. 92.
62. S. Pollard, 'Trade union reactions to the economic crisis', in S. Pollard (ed.), *Gold Standard and Employment Policies Between the Wars*, 1970, p. 146.

63. R.H. Tawney, 'The choice before the Labour Party', *Political Quarterly*, Summer 1932, p. 330.

64. PRO: MEPO 2/3050: letter W. Citrine (TUC GC) to HM Office of Works, 3 December 1932.

65. For example, TUC Circular 16 1934 banning members of the CP, NUWM, etc. from trades councils. In 1935 eleven trades councils were stripped of recognition. Opposition to the CP and NUWM was also spelled out in National Council of Labour, *British Labour and Communism*, 1936.

66. W. Hannington, *A Short History of the Unemployed*, 1940.

67. M. Cole, *Growing up into Revolution*, 1949, p. 98.

68. R. Croucher, 'Divisions in the movement: the NUWM and its rivals in comparative perspective', in G. Andrews, N. Fishman and K. Morgan (eds), *Opening the Books: Essays on the Social and Cultural History of the British Communist Party*, 1995.

69. R. Hayburn, 'Response to Unemployment in South-East Lancashire', unpublished PhD, University of Hull, 1970.

70. Labour Party, *Labour's Immediate Programme*, 1937.

71. J. Jupp, *The Radical Left in Britain 1931–41*, 1982, p. 170.

5 Unemployed Struggles

1. I. MacDougall (ed.), *Voices from the Hunger Marches: Personal Recollections by Scottish Hunger Marchers of the 1920s and 1930s*, 2 vols, vol. 2, 1991, p. 327.

2. W. Hannington, *Problem of the Depressed Areas*, 1937, p. 43.

3. *The Road to Jarrow*, BBC, 1996. Alan Travis, '175 years of protest from Peterloo to the Poll Tax', *Guardian: Society Supplement*, 8 May 1995, p. 5.

4. For a general account, see R. Croucher, *We Refuse to Starve in Silence: A History of the National Unemployed Workers' Movement 1920–46*, 1987.

5. North Tyneside Community Development Project, *North Shields: Working Class Politics and Housing 1900–27*, 1978, p. 27.

6. For example, the NUWM legal and research department wrote a *Guide to the Unemployment Assistance Board Scales and Regulations*, at 1d, which carefully steered the unemployed man or woman through the considerable intricacies of eligibility, the means test and their rights.

7. H. McShane, *No Mean Fighter*, 1978, p. 128.

8. J. Marriott, *The Culture of Labourism: The East End between the Wars*, 1991, p. 123.

9. PRO: CAB 24/129, cp. 4308, Director of Intelligence Report, 14 October 1921.

10. G. Garrett, *Unemployed Struggles: Liverpool 1921–2*, n.d.

11. W. Hannington, 'Who scrapped the gap?', *Out of Work*, vol. 1, no. 37, 1922.

12. W. Gray, M. Jenkins and R. Frow, *Unemployed Demonstrations: Salford and Manchester, October 1931*, 1982; E. and R. Frow, *The Battle of*

Bexley Square: Salford Unemployed Workers Demonstration 1st October 1931, 1994; G. Rawlinson, 'Mobilising the unemployed: the National Unemployed Worker's Movement in the west of Scotland', in R. Duncan and A. McIvor (eds), *Militant Workers: Labour and Class Conflict on the Clyde 1900–50*, 1992, pp. 188–90.

13. S.W. Davies, 'The membership of the National Unemployed Workers' Movement, 1923–1938', *Labour History Review*, vol. 57, no. 1, 1992.

14. S. Kelly, *Idle Hands, Clenched Fists: The Depression in a Shipyard Town*, 1987, p. 70.

15. Mrs Davin, wife of an invalided ex-serviceman quoted by W. Hannington, *Unemployed Struggles 1919–36*, 1979, p. 237.

16. Kelly, *Idle Hands, Clenched Fists*, p. 80.

17. Davis, 'The membership of the NUWM 1923–38', p. 34.

18. North Tyneside Community Development Project, *North Shields: Working Class Politics and Housing 1900–27*, 1978, pp. 30–3.

19. W. Hannington, *Unemployed Struggles 1919–1936*, 1979, p. 241.

20. Ibid., p. 250.

21. PRO: MEPO 2/3065, 3c.

22. R. Croucher, *We Refuse to Starve in Silence: a History of the National Unemployed Workers' Movement 1920–46*, 1987, p. 161.

23. *Royal Commission on Unemployment Insurance*, Final Report, cmd. 4185, 1932.

24. F. Miller, 'The British unemployment assistance crisis 1935', *Journal of Contemporary History*, vol. 14, 1979.

25. B. Moore, *All Out: The Dramatic Story of the Sheffield Demonstration on February 6, 1935*, 1985.

26. Ibid., pp. 29–30.

27. NMLH:CP/IND/HANN/01/02: National Administrative Council, circular d.39, 6 February 1935.

28. PRO: CAB 23/85 1 July 1936.

29. Labour Research Department, *Standards of Starvation*, 1936.

30. PRO: CAB 24/264 cp. 256, March of the Unemployed, appendix II, 12 October 1936.

31. Croucher, *We Refuse to Starve in Silence*, p. 181.

32. G. Orwell, *Collected Essays, Journalism and Letters of George Orwell*, 4 vols, vol. 1: *An Age Like This 1920–40*, 1970, p. 201.

33. *Birkenhead News*, 29 October 1932, quoted in Kelly, *Idle Hands, Clenched Fists*, p. 84.

34. E.W. Bakke, *Unemployed Man*, 1933, p. 151.

35. J. Stevenson and C. Cook, *Britain in the Depression: Society and Politics 1929–39*, 1994, p. 216.

36. Davies, 'The membership of the National Unemployed Workers' Movement, 1923–1938'.

37. E. Wilkinson, *The Town That Was Murdered*, 1939, p. 202.

38. W. Hannington, *Never on our Knees*, 1969, pp. 314–16; McShane, *No Mean Fighter*, pp. 217–18.

39. Reports on German unemployed movement in *International Press Correspondence*, for particularly interesting examples: no. 4, 1930; no. 5, 1930; no. 6, 1930.

40. Pilgrim Trust, *Men Without Work*, 1938, p. 162.

41. McShane, *No Mean Fighter*, p. 171.

42. M. Cohen, *I Was One of the Unemployed*, 1945, pp. 20–1.

43. H. Harmer, 'Failure of the communists: the NUWM, 1921–39, a dis-appointing success', in A.J. Thorpe, *The Failure of Extremism in Inter-War Britain*, 1989.

44. N. Fishman, *The British Communist Party and the Trade Unions, 1933–45*, 1995, p. 33; K. McDermott and J. Agnew, *The Communist International: A History of International Communism from Lenin to Stalin*, 1996.

45. H. Harmer, 'Failure of the communists', p. 38.

46. 'Experiences of the Unemployed Movement in the Capitalist Countries: Reports of the Representatives of the Communist Parties at the Prague conference', *International Press Correspondence*, vol. 11, no. 56, 30 October 1931. Zorgiebiel was the Berlin Police chief under SPD municipal control whose men fired on communist protesters in 1930.

47. NMLH: CPGB, CC minutes, 5 January 1936.

48. McShane, *No Mean Fighter*, p. 215.

49. J. Degras (ed.), *Communist International 1919–43: Selected Documents*, 3 vols, vol. 3:*1929–43*, 1972, p. 187.

50. W. Paynter, *My Generation*, 1972, pp. 84–5.

51. R.Croucher, *Engineers at War 1939–45*, 1982, pp. 33–9.

52. Croucher, *We Refuse to Starve in Silence*.

53. 'Experiences of the Unemployed Movement in the Capitalist Countries: Reports of the Representatives of the Communist Parties at the Prague conference', *International Press Correspondence*, vol. 11, no. 56, 30 October 1931.

54. S. MacIntyre, *Little Moscows*, 1980.

55. TWAS: 673/42: *TGWU: Unemployment benefit claims and other financial matters, 1932–6*, letter from Frank Stillwell to J. White, 7 April 1932.

56. M. Turnbull, 'Attitude of government and administration towards the Hunger Marches of the 1920s and 1930s', *Journal of Social Policy*, vol. 2, no. 2, 1973.

57. R. Hayburn, 'Police and the hunger marchers', *International Review of Social History*, vol. 17, 1972; J. Stevenson, 'Police and the 1932 Hunger March', *Society for the Study of Labour History Bulletin*, no. 38, spring 1979.

58. E. Trory, *Between the Wars: Recollections of a Communist Organiser*, 1974; H. McShane, *No Mean Fighter*, 1978.

59. McShane, *No Mean Fighter*.

60. *Report of the 1923 TUC Conference in Plymouth*, 1923, p. 343.

61. M. Turnbull, 'Attitude of government and administration towards the Hunger Marches of the 1920s and 1930s', *Journal of Social Policy*, vol. 2, no. 2, 1973, p. 142.

62. MacIntyre, *Little Moscows*; P. Bagguley, *From Protest to Acquiescence? Political Movements of the Unemployed*, 1991.

63. R. Luxemburg, *Reform or Revolution*, 1989, p. 67.

64. For example, Dr G.C.M. M'Gonigle and J. Kirby, *Poverty and Public Health*, 1936.

65. A. Horner, *Incorrigible Rebel*, 1960, p. 57.

66.   J. Stevenson and C. Cook, *Britain in the Depression: Society and Politics 1929–39*, 1994, pp. 215–6; S. Constantine, *Unemployment Between the Wars*, 1980, pp. 42–3; J. Stevenson, *British Society 1914–45*, 1984, pp. 290–1; Harmer, 'Failure of the communists'.

67.   Stevenson and Cook, *Britain in Depression*, p. 205.

6 The Unemployed in the United States

1.   S. Terkel, *Hard Times: an Oral History of the Great Depression*, 1970, p. 20.

2.   H. Hopkins, *Spending to Save*, 1937, p. 74.

3.   IEA Health and Welfare Unit (ed.), *Charles Murray and the Underclass: The Developing Debate*, 1996; C. Murray and R. Herrnstein, *The Bell Curve: Intelligence and Class Structure in American Life*, 1994.

4.   K. Matthews and B. Benjamin, *US and UK Unemployment between the Wars: a Doleful Story*, 1992.

5.   D. Ashton, *Unemployment under Capitalism: The Sociology of British and American Labour Markets*, 1986; D. King, *Actively Seeking Work: The Politics of Unemployment and Welfare Policy in the United States and Great Britain*, 1995.

6.   C. Emsley (ed.), *Essays in Comparative History: Economics, Politics and Society in Britian and America*, 1984; D. Englander (ed.), *Britain and America: Studies in Comparative History, 1760–1970*, 1997.

7.   W. Woytinsky, *The Social Consequences of the Economic Depression*, 1936, pp. 38, 138, 205, and 348.

8.   D. Brody, *Workers in Industrial America: Essays on the 20th Century Struggle*, 1980, p. 60.

9.   National Industrial Conference Board, *Unemployment Benefit and Insurance*, New York, 1931, quoted in R. Lubove, *The Struggle for Social Security 1900–35*, 1968, p. 167.

10.   H. Ford, *Moving Forward*, 1931, p. 67.

11.   Lubove, *The Struggle for Social Security 1900–35*, pp. 161–2.

12.   F. Piven and R. Cloward, *Regulating the Poor: The Functions of Public Welfare*, 1974, pp. 46–8.

13.   Hopkins, *Spending to Save*, p. 37.

14.   Ibid., pp. 45–6.

15.   Ford, *Moving Forward*, p. 70.

16.   D. Nelson, *Unemployment Insurance: The American Experience 1915–35*, 1969, pp. 141–5.

17.   E. Huntington, *Unemployment Relief and the Unemployed in the San Francisco Bay Region 1929–34*, 1939, p. 9.

18.   J. Harris, 'County finances in the state of Washington with particular reference to the finacial problems of county welfare activities and unemployment relief', *University of Washington Publications in the Social Sciences*, vol. 5, no. 4, February 1935, pp. 323 and 377.

19.   Hopkins, *Spending to Save*, pp. 75–7.

20.   New Deal Network: '*http://newdeal.feri.org*' Hopkins Papers, *Louisa Wilson to Harry Hopkins, FERA report*, Flint, Michigan, 17 November 1934. '*http://newdeal.feri.org/hopkins/hop13.htm*', 6/4/98.

21.   R. Lowitt and M. Beasley, *One Third of a Nation: Lorena Hickok Reports on the Great Depression*, 1981, p. 37.

22. White House Statement on a Plan for Relief, 28 February 1934, in *The Public Papers and Addresses of Franklin D. Roosevelt*, vol. 3, 1934, 1938, p. 102.

23. A. Badger, *The New Deal: The Depression Years, 1933–1940*, 1989, pp. 190–2.

24. Department of Commerce (Bureau of Census), *Statistical Abstract of the United States 1939*, 1940, p. 360.

25. Lubove, *The Struggle for Social Security 1900–35*, p. 167.

26. For statistics on the redistribution of income, see R. McElvaine, *The Great Depression: America 1929–41*, 1984, p. 331.

27. Hopkins, *Spending to Save*, p. 14.

28. 'Some recent censuses or estimates of unemployment', *International Labour Review*, vol. 28, 1933, pp. 58–61.

29. E. Clague, W. Couper and E.W. Bakke, *After the Shutdown*, 1934, p. 111.

30. Ibid., p. 92.

31. E. Clague, 'When relief stops what do they eat?', *The Survey*, vol. 68, November 1932, quoted in B. Schwartz, 'Unemployment relief in Philadelphia, 1930–1932: A study in voluntarism', B. Sternsher (ed.), *Hitting Home: The Great Depression in Town and Country*, 1970, p. 78.

32. D. Kaplun, 'Feeblemindedness as a factor in transiency', *Mental Hygiene*, vol. 21, 1937, p. 97.

33. H. Shilonsky, P. Preu and M. Rose, 'Clinical observations on the reactions of a group of transients to unemployment', *Journal of Social Psychology*, pt. 8, 1937, p. 74; L. Chandler, *America's Greatest Depression*, 1970, p. 46.

34. Hopkins, *Spending to Save*, p. 18.

35. C. Phillips, *From Crash to Blitz, 1929–1939*, 1969, p. xii.

36. B. Blumberg, *The New Deal and the Unemployed: The View from New York City*, 1979, p. 17.

37. M. Hallgren, *Seeds of Revolt*, 1934, p. 4.

38. Ibid., p. 85.

39. B. Blumberg, *The New Deal and the Unemployed: The View from New York City*, 1979, p. 21.

40. D. Katzman, 'Ann Arbor: Depression City', in B. Sternsher (ed.), *Hitting Home: The Great Depression in Town and Country*, 1970.

41. G. Springer, 'Getting the most from federal relief', *The Survey*, vol. 68, November 1932, quoted in B. Schwartz, 'Unemployment relief in Philadelphia, 1930–1932: A study in voluntarism', in B. Sternsher (ed.), *Hitting Home: The Great Depression in Town and Country*, 1970, p. 80.

42. Lowitt and Beasley, *One Third of a Nation: Lorena Hickok Reports on the Great Depression*, p. 4.

43. Ibid., p. 13.

44. E.W. Bakke, *The Unemployed Worker: A Study of Making a Living without a Job*, 1940, pp. 170–1.

45. Hopkins, *Spending to Save*, p. 79.

46. Blumberg, *The New Deal and the Unemployed*, p. 28.

47. R. Lopes, 'The economic depression and public health', *International Labour Review*, no. 29, 1934, pp. 799–800.

48. Lowitt and Beasley, *One Third of a Nation: Lorena Hickok Reports on the Great Depression*, p. 20.

49. M. Sugar, *The Ford Hunger March*, 1986, p. 26.

50. Badger, *The New Deal*, p. 11.

51. P. Eisenberg and P. Lazarfeld, 'The psychological effects of unemployment', *Psychological Bulletin*, vol. 35, no. 6, June 1938, p. 362.

52. E. Clague and W. Powell, *Ten Thousand Out of Work*, 1933, p. 50.

53. C. Trout, *Boston: The Great Depression and the New Deal*, 1977, p. 191.

54. Bakke, *The Unemployed Worker*, pp. 236–48.

55. R. McElvaine, *The Great Depression: America 1929–41*, 1984, p. 190.

56. R. McElvaine(ed.), *Down and Out in the Great Depression: Letters from the 'Forgotten Man'*, 1983, pp. 83–94.

57. Blumberg, *The New Deal and the Unemployed*, p. 291.

58. G. Palmer and K. Wood, *Urban Workers on Relief: Part One: the Occupational Characteristcs of Workers on Relief in Urban Areas, May 1934*, 1936, p. xxvi.

59. L. Pruette (ed.), *Women Workers through the Depression: a Study of White Collar Employment made by the American Women's Association*, 1934, p. 5.

60. Bakke, *The Unemployed Worker*, p. 297.

61. Pruette, *Women Workers through the Depression*, pp. 147–8.

62. Bakke, *The Unemployed Worker*, p. 70.

63. G. Wolfskill, *The Revolt of the Conservatives: A History of the American Liberty League 1934–1940*, 1962.

64. R. Lynd and H. Lynd, *Middletown in Transition: A Study in Cultural Conflicts*, 1937, pp. 377–8. Middletown was an assumed name for Muncie, Indiana.

65. Ibid., pp. 142–3.

66. New Deal Network: *'http://newdeal.feri.org'* 'They don't want to work', *The Nation*, vol. 141, no. 3660, 28 August 1935, p. 229. *'http://newdeal.feri.org/nation/na36186.htm'*, 6/4/98.

67. Hopkins, *Spending to Save*, p. 84.

68. McElvaine, *Down and Out in the Great Depression*, pp. 93–4.

69. Trout, *Boston*, pp. 183–4.

70. D. Peeler, *Hope Among Us Yet: Social Criticism and Social Solace in Depression America*, 1987.

71. D. Kaplun, 'Feeblemindedness as a factor in transiency', *Mental Hygiene*, vol. 21, 1937, pp. 99–100.

72. H. Shilonsky, P. Preu and M. Rose, 'Clinical observations on the reactions of a group of transients to unemployment', *Journal of Social Psychology*, pt. 8, 1937, p. 85.

73. Eisenberg and Lazarfeld, 'The psychological effects of unemployment', p. 363.

74. W. Berlinger, 'The emotional stabilty of the transient', *Journal of Applied Psychology*, vol. 20, 1936, p. 207.

75. S. Gould, *The Mismeasure of Man: Revised and Updated*, 1996.

76. C. Murray and R. Herrnstein, *The Bell Curve: Intelligence and Class Structure in American Life*, 1994.

77. Eisenberg and Lazarfeld, 'The psychological effects of unemployment', p. 358.

78. S. Verba and K. Schlozman, 'Unemployment class consciouness and radical politics: what didn't happen in the 1930s', *Journal of Politics*, vol. 39, 1977, p. 302.

79. McElvaine, *Down and Out in the Great Depression*, p. 43.

80. A. Gabriel and H. Lasswell, 'Aggressive behaviour by clients towards public relief administrators', *American Political Science Review*, vol. 28, 1934.

81. Quoted in Eisenberg and Lazarfeld, 'The psychological effects of unemployment', p. 373.

82. F. Piven and R. Cloward, *Poor People's Movements: Why They Succeed, Why They Fail*, 1977, p. 49.

83. D. Leah, '"United we don't eat": the creation of the Unemployed Councils in 1930', *Labor History*, vol. 8, 1967, p. 308.

84. *International Press Correspondence*, no. 7, 1931, p. 143.

85. *International Press Correspondence*, no. 46, 1931, p. 858.

86. *International Press Correspondence*, no. 1, 1933, p. 6.

87. S. Terkel, *Hard Times: an Oral History of the Great Depression*, 1970, p. 397.

88. M. Hallgren, *Seeds of Revolt*, 1934, quoted in A. Fried, *Communism in America: A History in Documents*, 1997, p. 132.

89. R. Rosenzweig, '"Socialism in our time": the Socialist Party and the unemployed', *Labor History*, vol. 20, 1979, p. 492; A. Fried, *Communism in America: A History in Documents*, 1997, p. 135.

90. Piven and Cloward, *Poor People's Movements*, p. 61.

91. Hopkins, *Spending to Save*, p. 86.

92. Quoted in *Detriot News*, 14 January 1998. For fullest account of the march, see M. Sugar, *Ford Hunger March*, 1986.

93. *The Public Papers and Addresses of Franklin D. Roosevelt*, 5 vols, vol. 2: *The Year of Crisis 1933*, 1938, p. 3 (introduction).

94. *The Secret Diary of Harold L. Ickes*, 3 vols, vol. 1: *1933–5*, 1954, pp. 99–100, and 21.

95. R. Lowitt and M. Beasley, *One Third of a Nation: Lorena Hickok Reports on the Great Depression*, 1981, pp. 5, 8, 11, 12–13 and 17.

96. New Deal Network: '*http://newdeal.feri.org*', Hopkins papers, *Report on Morgantown, West Virginia*, H. Francis to H. Hopkins, 18 November 1934, '*http://newdeal.feri.org/texts/155.htm*', 6/4/98.

97. Quoted in F. Folsom, *America before Welfare*, 1991, p. 299.

98. R. Rosenzweig, '"Socialism in our time": the Socialist Party and the unemployed', *Labor History*, vol. 20, 1979, p. 494.

99. Ibid., p. 499.

100. A. Hillman, 'Unemployed Citizen's League of Seattle', *University of Washington Publications in the Social Sciences*, vol. 5, no. 3, February 1934.

101. R. Rosenzweig, 'Radicals and the jobless: the Museteites and the Unemployed Leagues 1932–6', *Labor History*, vol. 16, 1975.

102. Piven and Cloward, *Poor People's Movements*, p. 79.

103. New Deal Network: '*http://newdeal.feri.org*' Hopkins Papers, *Louisa Wilson to Harry Hopkins, FERA report*, Flint, Michigan, 17 November 1934. '*http://newdeal.feri.org/hopkins/hop13.htm*', 6/4/98.

104. New Deal Network: '*http://newdeal.feri.org*' Hopkins Papers, *Wayne W. Parrish to Harry Hopkins, FERA report*, New York, 24 November 1934.'*http://newdeal.feri.org/hopkins/hop11.htm*', 6/4/98.

105. Although the AFL did attempted to enforce the rate for the job in New York: Blumberg, *The New Deal and the Unemployed*, pp. 52–7.

106. Lowitt and Beasley, *One Third of a Nation*, p. 36.

107. R. McKibbin, 'The economic policy of the second Labour government', in R. McKibbin, *Ideologies of Class: Social Relations in Britain 1880–1950*, 1990; E. Brown, 'Fiscal policy in the 1930s: a re-appraisal', *American Economic Review*, vol. 46, 1956.

108. Lowitt and Beasley, *One Third of a Nation*, pp. 28 and 31.

109. Verba and Schlozman, 'Unemployment class consciouness and radical politics: what didn't happen in the 1930s', p. 303.

7 *Unemployment in Europe between the Wars*

1. H. Fallada, *Little Man – What Now?* 1933, p. 415.

2. J. Rosner, 'An enquiry into the life of unemployed workers in Poland', *International Labour Review*, vol. 27, no. 3, March 1933, pp. 382–3.

3. Ibid., p. 385.

4. W. Woytinsky, *The Social Consequences of the Economic Depression*, 1936, pp. 143 and 333.

5. B. Mitchell, *European Historical Statistics 1750–1970*, 1981.

6. G. Vanthemsche, 'Unemployment insurance in interwar Belgium', *International Review of Social History*, vol. 35, no. 3, 1990, pp. 335–6.

7. 'Unemployment Insurance: tabular analysis of the legislation in force', *International Labour Review*, vol. 23, January 1931.

8. Vanthemsche, 'Unemployment insurance in interwar Belgium', p. 361.

9. Vanthemsche, 'Unemployment insurance in interwar Belgium'.

10. J. Alber, 'Government responses to the challenge of unemployment: the development of unemployment insurance in Western Europe', in P. Flora and A. Heidenheimer (eds), *The Development of Welfare States in Europe and America*, 1984, p. 156.

11. P. Stachura (ed.), *Unemployment and the Great Depression in Weimar Germany*, 1986, p. 12.

12. *Ministry of Labour Gazette*, September 1932, p. 327.

13. *Ministry of Labour Gazette*, February 1935, p. 52; and *Ministry of Labour Gazette*, November 1935, p. 416.

14. International Labour Organisation, *Unemployment Insurance: A Study of Comparative Legislation*, Studies and Reports, Series C (Employment and Unemployment), no. 10, 1925, pp. 83–5.

15. National Industrial Conference Board, *Unemployment Insurance and Relief in Germany*, 1932, p. vi.

16. J. Rosner, 'Measures to combat the depression and unemployment in Poland', *International Labour Review*, vol. 30, no. 2, August 1934, p. 170.

17. *Statistisches Jahrbuch für das Deutsche Reich*, 1929, p. 375.

18. *Statistisches Jahrbuch für das Deutsche Reich*, 1930, p. 417.

19. B. Weisbrod, 'The crisis of German unemployment insurance in 1928/9 and its political repercutions', in W. Mommsen (ed.), *The Emergence of the Welfare State in Britain and Germany 1850–1950*, 1981.

20. *Statistisches Jahrbuch für das Deutsche Reich*, 1931, p. 397.

21. *Statistisches Jahrbuch für das Deutsche Reich*, 1932, p. 395.

22. *Statistisches Jahrbuch für das Deutsche Reich*, 1933, p. 405.

23. National Industrial Conference Board, *Unemployment Insurance and Relief in Germany*, 1932.

24. J. Rueff, 'Assurance-chômage, cause du chômage permanent', *Revue D'Économie Politique*, March–April 1931.

25. M. Schneider, 'The development of state work creation policy in Germany, 1930–33', in P. Stachura (ed.), *Unemployment and the Great Depression in Weimar Germany*, 1986.

26. *Ministry of Labour Gazette*, July 1934, p. 236.

27. P. Saly, 'La politique française des grands travaux (1929–39): fut-elle Keynesienne?' *Revue Économique*, vol. 31, no. 4, 1980, p. 742.

28. *Ministry of Labour Gazette*, March 1924, p. 83.

29. International Labour Organisation, *Unemployment Insurance: A Study of Comparative Legislation*, Studies and Reports, Series C (Employment and Unemployment), no. 10, 1925, pp. 61–3.

30. G. Toniolo and F. Piva, 'Unemployment in the 1930s: the case of Italy', in B. Eichengreen and T. Hatton (eds), *Interwar Unemployment in International Perspective*, 1988, p. 233.

31. Rosner, 'Measures to combat the depression and unemployment in Poland'.

32. 'Results of compulsory labour service in Bulgaria from 1933 to 1936–7', *International Labour Review*, vol. 38, no. 4, October 1938, pp. 510–21.

33. J. Rosner, 'Productive occupation for the unemployed young workers in Poland', *International Labour Review*, vol. 31, no. 4, April 1935.

34. V. Pawlowsky, 'Werksoldaten, graue Mandeln, 50-Groschen-Dragoner: der Freiwillige Arbeitsdienst in Österreich', *Zeitgeschichte*, vol. 17, no. 5, 1990.

35. J. Noakes, 'Social outcasts in the Third Reich', in R. Bessel (ed.), *Life in the Third Reich*, 1987, p. 92.

36. *Ministry of Labour Gazette*, February, 1935, p. 53.

37. International Labour Organisation, *Unemployment and Public Works*, Studies and Reports, Series C (Employment and Unemployment), no. 15, 1931, pp. 100–3.

38. K. Hasen, 'Unemployment also hits women: the new and old woman on the dark side of the golden twenties', in P. Stachura (ed.), *Unemployment and the Great Depression in Weimar Germany*, 1986, p. 101.

39. 'Swedish unemployment policy', *International Labour Review*, vol. 39, no. 2, February 1939, pp. 228–9; B. Ohlin, 'Economic recovery and labour market problems in Sweden', *International Labour Review*, vol. 31, nos 4 and 5, April and May 1935; *Monthly Summary of the ILO*, no. 1, January 1935, p. 6.

40. *Deutschlands Berichte So-Pa-De*, 7 vols, vol. 1, 1980, pp. 221–4.

41. I. Kershaw, *Public Opinion and Political Dissent in the Third Reich: Bavaria 1933–1945*, 1983, p. 82.

42. O. Grytten, 'The scale of Norwegian labour unemployment in international perspective', *Scandinavian Economic History Review*, vol. 42, no. 2, 1995, pp. 226–50.

43. N. Baverez, 'Chômage des années 1930, chômage des années 1980', *Mouvement Social*, no. 154, 1991.

44. G. Toniolo and F. Piva, 'Unemployment in the 1930s: the case of Italy', in B. Eichengreen and T. Hatton (eds), *Interwar Unemployment in International Perspective*, 1988. pp. 227–8.

45. R. Hachtman, 'Arbeitsmarkt und Arbeitszeit in der Deutschen Industrie, 1929 bis 1939', *Archiv für Sozialgeschichte*, 1987, p. 179; W. Hemmer, *Die Unsichtbaren Arbeitlosen. Statistische Methoden – Soziale Tatschen*, 1935, p. 114; Rosner, 'Measures to combat the depression and unemployment in Poland'.

46. L. Landau, J. Panski and E. Strzelecki, *Chômage des Paysans*, 1939, p. 258.

47. Toniolo and Piva, 'Unemployment in the 1930s: the case of Italy', p. 224.

48. *Statistisches Jahrbuch für das Deutsche Reich*, 1929, p. 21*; *Statistisches Jahrbuch für das Deutsche Reich*, 1933, p. 25*.

49. G. Mauco, 'Immigration in France', *International Labour Review*, vol. 27, no. 6, June 1933, p. 772.

50. K. Kaser, 'Als Vagabund durch Jugoslawien: die Wanderung des arbeitslosen Österreiches Franz Schick im Jahr 1933', *Österreiche Osthefte*, vol. 34, no. 1, 1992.

51. R. Salais, 'Why was French unemployment so low?', in B. Eichengreen and T. Hatton (eds), *Interwar Unemployment in International Perspective*, 1988.

52. K. Hasen, 'Unemployment also hits women: the new and old woman on the dark side of the golden twenties', in P. Stachura (ed.), *Unemployment and the Great Depression in Weimar Germany*, 1986, p. 108.

53. N. Baverez, 'Chômage des années 1930, chômage des années 1980', *Mouvement Social*, no. 154, 1991, p. 106; 'Le chômage, l'emploi et la production industrielle depuis 1928', *Bulletin de la Statistique Générale*, vol. 24, January–March 1935.

54. B. Eichengreen and T. Hatton, 'Interwar unemployment: an overview', in B. Eichengreen and T. Hatton (eds), *Interwar Unemployment in International Perspective*, 1988, p. 40.

55. F. Wunderlich, 'New aspects of unemployment in Germany', *Social Research*, vol. 1, 1934, p. 102.

56. M. Thibert, 'Economic depression and the employment of women', *International Labour Review*, vol. 27, nos 4 and 5, April and May 1933, p. 457.

57. H. Fuss, 'Unemployment and employment among women', *International Labour Review*, vol. 31, no. 4, April 1935, p. 466.

58. F. Wunderlich, 'New aspects of unemployment in Germany', *Social Research*, vol. 1, 1934, pp. 105–7.

59. D. Guérin, *The Brown Plague: Travels in Late Weimar and Early Nazi Germany*, 1994, p. 52.

60. Ibid., p. 68.
61. R. Lopes, 'The economic depression and public health', *International Labour Review*, vol. 29, no. 6, June 1934, pp. 787–9.
62. Fallada, *Little Man – What Now?*, p. 432.
63. Lopes, 'The economic depression and public health', *International Labour Review*, p. 785.
64. C. Thovenot and A. Minot, 'Incidence de la crise de 1929 sur les consommations en Meurthe-et-Moselle', *Annales de L'Est*, vol. 22, no. 3, 1970.
65. 'Economic depression and public health', *International Labour Review*, vol. 16, no. 6, December 1932, pp. 843–5.
66. Lopes, 'The economic depression and public health', p. 800.
67. P. Stachura, 'The social and welfare implications of youth unemployment in Weimar democracy 1929–33', in P. Stachura (ed.), *Unemployment and the Great Depression in Weimar Germany*, 1986, p. 136.
68. *Statisches Jahrbuch für das Deutsche Reich*, 1936.
69. 'Die Selbstmorde in Österreich in den Jahren 1913 bis 1931', *Statistische Nachrichten*, no. 8, August 1932, p. 163.
70. M. Incze, 'Conditions of the masses in Hungary', *Acta Historica*, no. 3, 1954, p. 32.
71. Instytut Gospodarstwa Spolecznego, *Pamietniki Bezrobotnych*, 1933.
72. B. Zawadzki and P. Lazarfeld, 'The psychological effects of unemployment', *Journal of Social Psychology*, vol. 6, 1935, p. 229.
73. Ibid., pp. 230–1.
74. Ibid., p. 231.
75. Rosner, 'An enquiry into the life of unemployed workers in Poland', p. 390.
76. Ibid., p. 388.
77. M. Jahoda, P. Lazarfeld and H. Zeisel, *Marienthal: the Sociography of an Unemployed Community*, 1972.
78. Ibid., p. 26.
79. Ibid., p. 76.
80. Ibid., p. 86.
81. Ibid., p. 3.
82. *International Press Correspondence*, no. 6, 1930, p. 101.
83. *International Press Correspondence*, no. 9, 1930, p. 162.
84. *International Press Correspondence*, no. 11, 1930, p. 189.
85. *Pravda*, 10 February 1930, quoted in *International Press Correspondence*, p. 163, 1930.
86. *International Press Correspondence*, no. 13, 1930, p. 231.
87. F. Folsom, *America before Welfare*, 1991, p. 355.
88. O. Piatniksky, *Unemployment and the Tasks of Communists*, 1931, p. 41.
89. *International Press Correspondence*, no. 56, 1931, p. 1016.
90. R.-M. Huber-Koller, 'Die kommunistische Erwerbslosenbewegung in der Endphase der Weimarer Republik', *Gesellschaft: Beiträge zur Marxschen Theorie*, no. 10, 1977.
91. K.-C. Führer, 'Solidarität und Magenfrage – Arbeitslosenproteste und Arbeitlosenräte in Hamburg 1918–23', *1999: Zeitschrift für Sozialgeschichte des 20 und 21 Jahrhunderts*, vol. 6, no. 2, 1991.
92. C. Fischer, *German Communists and the Rise of the Nazis*, 1991, p. 142.

93. A. McElligot, 'Mobilising the unemployed: the KPD and the unemployed workers' movement in Hamburg-Altona during the Weimar Republic', in R. Evans and D. Geary (eds), *The German Unemployed: Experiences and Consequences of Mass Unemployment from the Weimar Republic to the Third Reich*, 1987.

94. D. Geary, 'Unemployment and working-class solidarity: the German experience 1929–33', in R. Evans and D. Geary (eds), *The German Unemployed: Experiences and Consequences of Mass Unemployment from the Weimar Republic to the Third Reich*, 1987.

95. W. Fuss, 'Zwischen Protest und Resignation: Arbeitslose und Arbeitslosenbewegung in der Zeit der Weltwirtschaftkrise', *Österreichische Zeitschrift für Geschichtswissenschaft*, vol. 1, no. 2, 1990, p. 30.

96. R. Croucher, 'Communist unemployed organisations between the wars', *Archiv für Sozialgeschichte*, vol. 30, 1990, p. 595.

97. See *International Press Correspondence*; *Tidsskrift for Arbeiderbewegelsens Historie*, no. 1, 1983; A. Oord, *Voor Arbeid en Brood*, 1990.

98. C. Tillon, *On Chantait Rouge*, 1977, pp. 165–77.

Conclusions

1. W. Woytinsky, *The Social Consequences of the Economic Depression*, 1936, p. 300.

2. G. Lukács, *History and Class Consciousness*, 1971, p. 74.

3. J. Saville, 'May Day, 1937', in A. Briggs and J. Saville (eds), *Essays in Labour History 1918–39*, vol. 3, 1977; J.E. Cronin, *Labour and Society in Britain 1918–1979*, 1984; N. Kirk, *Labour and Society in Britain and the USA*, 2 vols, vol. 2: *Challenge and Accommodation 1850–1939*, 1994, p. 353.

4. PRO: CAB 24/96, CP. 429, 9 January 1920.

Tables

1. North 1: Durham and Northumberland; 2: Cumberland, Westmoreland, Yorks. (East & North Riding); 3: Yorks. (West Riding), York, 4: Cheshire and Lancs.; Wales 1: Brecknockshire, Carmarthenshire, Glamorganshire, Monmouthshire; 2: Rest of Wales; Midlands 1: Gloucestershire, Hereford, Shropshire, Staffordshire, Warwickshire, and Worcestershire; 2: Derbyshire, Leicestershire, Nottinghamshire, Northamptonshire, Peterborough; East: Cambridgeshire, Isle of Ely, Huntingdonshire, Lincolnshire, Norfolk, Rutlandshire, Suffolk; South-West: Cornwall, Devon, Dorset, Somerset, Wiltshire.

2. Coalition Unionist and Conservative.

3. Coalition Liberal and Liberal.

4. National Liberal and Liberal.

5. National Liberal and Liberal.

6. National Liberal and Liberal.

Select Bibliography

Britain

Addison, P., *The Road to 1945*, 1975.

Aldcroft, D., *The Inter-War Economy: Britian 1919–39*, 1970.

Armstrong, K. and Beynon, H., *Hello Are You Working? Memories of the 1930s in the North-East of England*, 1977.

Bakke, E.W., *The Unemployed Man: A Social Study*, 1933.

Beales, H.L., and Lambert, R.S., *Memoirs of the Unemployed*, 1934.

Benjamin, D. and Kochin, L., 'Searching for an explanation of interwar unemployment in Britain', *Journal of Political Economy*, vol. 87, 1979.

Beveridge, W.H., *Full Employment in a Free Society: Misery Breeds Hate*, 1944.

Booth, A. and Pack, M., *Employment, Capital and Economic Policy: Great Britain 1918–39*, 1985.

Burnett, J., *Plenty and Want: a Social History of Diet in England from 1815 to the Present*, 1979.

Burnett, J., *Idle Hands: the Experience of Unemployment 1790–1990*, 1994.

Calder, A. and Sheridan, D. (eds), *Speak for Yourself: a Mass Observation Anthology 1937–49*, 1985.

Chinn, C., *They Worked All Their Lives: Women of the Urban Poor in England, 1880–1939*, 1988.

Cohen, M., *I Was One of the Unemployed*, 1945.

Cole, M., 'The labour movement between the wars', in D. Martin and D. Rubinstein (eds), *Ideology and the Labour Movement*, 1979.

Colledge, D., *Labour Camps: the British Experience*, 1989.

Cowling, M., *The Impact of Labour 1920–24*, 1971.

Crafts, N.F.R., 'Long-term unemployment in the 1930s', *Economic History Review*, Series 2, vol. 40, no. 3, 1987.

Cronin, J.E., *Labour and Society in Britain 1918–1979*, 1984.

Croucher, R., *We Refuse to Starve in Silence: a History of the National Unemployed Workers Movement 1920–46*, 1987.

Davis, S.W., 'The membership of the National Unemployed Workers' Movement, 1923–1938', *Labour History Review*, vol. 57, no. 1, 1992.

Davis, S., Gill, P., Grant, L., Nightingale, M., Noon, R. and Shallice, A., *Genuinely Seeking Work*, 1992.

Deacon, A., *In Search of the Scrounger: The Administration of Unemployment Insurance in Britain 1920–31*, 1976.

Deacon, A., 'Concession and coercion: the politics of unemployment insurance in the twenties', in Briggs, A. and Saville, J. (eds), *Essays in Labour History 1918–39*, vol. 3, 1977.

Digby, A., *British Welfare Policy*, 1989.

Fishman, N., *The British Communist Party and the Trade Unions, 1933–45*, 1995.

Flanagan, R., *'Parish-Fed Bastards': a History of the Politics of the Unemployed in Britain, 1884–1939*, 1991.

Garraty, J.A., *Unemployment in History: Economic Thought and Public Policy*, 1978.

Garside, W.R., *British Unemployment 1919–39: a Study in Public Policy*, 1990.

Gospel, H., 'Employer's labour policy: a study of the Mond–Turner talks', *Business History*, vol. 21, 1979.

Gray, N., *The Worst of Times: an Oral History of the Great Depression in Britain*, 1985.

Greene, F. (ed.), *Time to Spare: What Unemployment Means by Eleven Unemployed*, 1935.

Hannington, W., *The Problems of the Distressed Areas*, 1937.

Hannington, W., *Unemployed Struggles 1919–36*, 1979.

Harris, J., *Unemployment and Politics: a Study of English Social Policy 1886–1914*, 1972.

Harrison, R., 'New light on the police and the hunger marchers', *Society for the Study of Labour History*, no. 37, Autumn 1978.

Hayburn, R., 'Police and the hunger marchers', *International Review of Social History*, vol. 17, 1972.

Hopkins, E., 'Working class life in Birmingham between the wars, 1918–39', *Midland History*, vol. 15, 1990.

Howkins, A. and Saville, J., 'The nineteen-thirties: a revisionist history', in R. Miliband and J. Saville (eds), *Socialist Register*, 1979.

Hurstfield, J., 'Women's unemployment in the 1930s: some comparisons with the 1980s', in Allen, S., Watson, A., Purcell, K. and Wood, S. (eds), *The Experience of Unemployment*, 1989.

Jahoda, M., *Employment and Unemployment: a Social Psychological Analysis*, 1982.

Jennings, H., *Brynmawr: a Study of a Depressed Area*, 1934.

Jupp, J., *The Radical Left in Britain 1931–41*, 1982.

Kelly, S., *Idle Hands, Clenched Fists: The Depression in a Shipyard Town*, 1987.

Kingsford, P., *The Hunger Marchers in Britain 1920–39*, 1982.

Kirk, N., *Labour and Society in Britain and the USA*, 2 vols, vol. 2: *Challenge and Accommodation 1850–1939*, 1994.

Krafchik, M., 'Unemployment and vagrancy in the 1930s: deterrence, rehabilitation and the depression', *Journal of Social Policy*, vol. 12, no. 2, 1983.

Langan, M., 'Reorganising the labour market: unemployment, the state and the labour movement 1880–1914', in Langan, M. and Schwarz, B., *Crises in the British State*, 1985.

Laybourn, K., *The Labour Party 1881–1951*, 1988.

Laybourn, K., *Britain on the Breadline: a Social and Political History of Britain between the Wars*, 1990.

Lowe, R., *Adjusting to Democracy: the Role of the Ministry of Labour in British Politics 1916–39*, 1986.

Lyman, R.W., *The First Labour Government 1924*, 1957.

McDonald, G. and Douglas, H., 'The Mond–Turner talks, 1927–33: a study in industrial co-operation', *Historical Journal*, vol. 16, 1973.

MacDougall, I. (ed.), *Voices from the Hunger Marches: Personal Recollections by Scottish Hunger Marchers of the 1920s and 1930s*, 2 volumes, 1991.

McInnes, A., 'Surviving the slump: an oral history of Stoke-on-Trent between the wars', *Midland History*, vol. 18, 1993.

MacIntyre, S., *Little Moscows: Communism and Working-Class Militancy in Inter-War Britain*, 1980.

McIvor, A., ''A crusade for capitalism': the Economic League, 1919–39', *Journal of Contemporary History*, vol. 23, 1988.

McKibbin, R., 'The economic policy of the second Labour Government 1929–31', *Past and Present*, no. 68, 1975.

McKibbin, R., *Ideologies of Class: Social Relations in Britain 1880–1950*, 1990.

McKibbin, R., *Classes and Cultures in England 1918–1951*, 1998.

McShane, H., *No Mean Fighter*, 1978.

Marriot, J., *The Culture of Labourism: The East End between the Wars*, 1991.

Marwick, A., 'Middle opinion in the 1930s: planning, progress and political agreement', *English Historical Review*, 79, 1964.

Matthews, K. and Benjamin, D., *US and UK Unemployment between the Wars: a Doleful Story*, 1992.

M'Gonigle, G.C.M. and Kirby, J., *Poverty and Public Health*, 1936.

Miller, F., 'The British unemployment assistance crisis of 1935', *Journal of Contemporary History*, vol. 14, 1979.

Miller, F., 'National assistance or unemployment assistance? The British Cabinet and relief policy, 1932–3', *Journal of Contemporary History*, vol. 9, 1974.

Miller, F., 'The unemployment policy of the National Government, 1931–6', *Historical Journal*, no. 19, 1976.

Mitchell, M., 'Effects of unemployment on the social conditions of women and children in the 1930s', *History Workshop Journal*, no. 19, 1985.

Mommsen, W.J. (ed.), *The Emergence of the Welfare State in Britain and Germany*, 1981.

Orr, J. Boyd, *Food, Income, Health*, 1936.

Orwell, G., *Road to Wigan Pier*, 1937.

Orwell, G., *Collected Essays, Journalism and Letters of George Orwell*, 4 vols, vol. 1: *An Age Like This 1920–40*, 1970.

Peele, G. and Cook, C. (eds), *The Politics of Reappraisal, 1918–39*, 1975.

Pilgrim Trust, *Men Without Work*, 1938.

Poire, M.J., 'Historical perspectives and the interpretation of unemployment', *Journal of Economic Literature*, vol. 25, December 1987.

Pollard, S., 'Trade union reactions to the economic crisis', in Pollard, S. (ed.), *Gold Standard and Employment Policies Between the Wars*, 1970.

Pollard, S., *The Development of the British Economy, 1914–1990*, 1992.

Priestley, J.B., *English Journey*, 1934.

Rice, M.S., *Working Class Wives*, 1939.

Richards, J., 'BBFC and content control in the 1930s', *Historical Journal of Film, Radio and Television*. vol. 1, no. 2, 1981.

Roberts, E., *A Woman's Place: an Oral History of Working-Class Women 1890–1940*, 1984.

Rodgers, T., 'Sir Allan Smith, the Industrial Group and the Politics of Unemployment', *Business History*, no. 28, 1986.

PP: Royal Commission, *Unemployment Insurance*, First Report, cmd. 3872, 1931.

PP: Royal Commission, *Unemployment Insurance*, Final report, cmd. 4185, 1932.

Sarsby, J., *Missuses and Mouldrunners: an Oral History of Women Pottery Workers at Home and Work*, 1988.

Saville, J., 'The hunger marches of the nineteen thirties: some random comments', *North-West Labour History*, August 1988.

Scannell, P., 'Broadcasting and the politics of unemployment 1930–35', *Media, Culture and Society*, no. 2, 1980.

Skidelsky, R., *Politicians and the Slump: the Labour Government of 1929–31*, 1970.

Stevenson, J., 'Police and the 1932 Hunger March', *Society for the Study of Labour History Bulletin*, Spring, no. 38, 1979.

Stevenson, J. and Cook, C., *Britain in Depression: Society and Politics 1929–39*, 1994.

Taylor, A.J.P., *English History 1914–45*, 1965.

Thorpe, A.J. (ed.), *The Failure of Extremism in Inter-War Britain*, 1989.

Tomlinson, J., *Problems of British Economic Policy 1870–1945*, 1981.

Tomlinson, J., 'Women as anomalies', *Public Administration*, vol. 62, no. 4, 1984.

Thompson, E.P., *Making of the English Working Class*, 1963.

Thompson, N., *Political Economy and the Labour Party*, 1996.

Turnbull, M., `Attitude of government and administration towards the Hunger Marches of the 1920s and 30s', *Journal of Social Policy*, vol. 2, no. 2, 1973.

Webster, C., 'Healthy or hungry thirties', *History Workshop Journal*, no. 13, 1982.

Webster, C., 'Health, welfare and unemployment during the Depression', *Past and Present*, no. 109, 1985.

Whiteside, N. and Gillespie, J., 'Deconstructing unemployment: developments in Britain in the interwar years', *Economic History Review*, 2nd series, vol. 44, no. 4, 1991.

Wilkinson, E., *The Town That Was Murdered*, 1939.

Williamson, P., *National Crisis and National Government: British Politics, Economy and Empire, 1926–32*, 1992.

Winter, J., 'Infant mortality, maternal moratity and public health in Britain in the 1930s', Journal of European Economic History, vol. 8, 1979.

Winter, J. (ed.), *The Working Class in Modern British History: Essays in Honour of Henry Pelling*, 1983.

United States

Badger, A., *The New Deal: the Depression Years, 1933–1940*, 1989.

Blumberg, B., *The New Deal and the Unemployed: the View from New York City*, 1979.

Brody, D., *Workers in Industrial America: Essays on the 20th Century Struggle*, 1980.

Chandler, L., *America's Greatest Depression*, 1970.

Eisenberg, P. and Lazarfeld, P., 'The psychological effects of unemployment', *Psychological Bulletin*, vol. 35, no. 6, June 1938.

Folsom, F., *America before Welfare*, 1991.

Ford, H., *Moving Forward*, 1931.

Fried, A., *Communism in America: a History in Documents*, 1997.

Gould, S., *The Mismeasure of Man: Revised and Updated*, 1996.

Hopkins, H., *Spending to Save*, 1937.

Ickes, H., *The Secret Diary of Harold L. Ickes*, 3 vols, vol. 1: *1933–5*, 1954.

IEA Health and Welfare Unit (ed.), *Charles Murray and the Underclass: the Developing Debate*, 1996.

Keyssar, A., *Out of Work: the First Century of Unemployment in Massachusetts*, 1986.

Leah, D., '"United we don't eat": the creation of the Unemployed Councils in 1930', *Labor History*, vol. 8, 1967.

Lopes, R., 'The economic depression and public health', *International Labour Review*, no. 29, 1934.

Lowitt, R. and Beasley, M., *One Third of a Nation: Lorena Hickok Reports on the Great Depression*, 1981.

Lubove, R., *The Struggle for Social Security 1900–35*, 1968.

Lynd, R. and Lynd, H., *Middletown in Transition: a Study in Cultural Conflicts*, 1937.

Matthews, K. and Benjamin, D., *US and UK Unemployment between the Wars: a Doleful Story*, 1992.

McElvaine, R.(ed.), *Down and Out in the Great Depression: Letters from the 'Forgotten Man'*, 1983.

McElvaine, R., *The Great Depression: America 1929–41*, 1984.

Nelson, D., *Unemployment Insurance: the American Experience 1915–35*, 1969.

New Deal Network: '*http://newdeal.feri.org*'

Piven, F. and Cloward, R., *Regulating the Poor: the Functions of Public Welfare*, 1974.

Piven, F. and Cloward, R., *Poor People's Movements: Why They Succeed, Why They Fail*, 1977.

Rosenzweig, R., 'Radicals and the jobless: the Musteites and the Unemployed Leagues 1932–6', *Labor History*, vol. 16, 1975.

Rosenzweig, R., 'Organising the unemployed: the early years of the Great Depression 1929–33', *Radical America*, no. 10, 1976.

Rosenzweig, R., '"Socialism in our time": the Socialist Party and the unemployed', *Labor History*, vol. 20, 1979.

Sternsher, B. (ed.), *Hitting Home: the Great Depression in Town and Country*, 1970.

Terkel, S., *Hard Times: an Oral History of the Great Depression*, 1970.

Trout, C., *Boston: The Great Depression and the New Deal*, 1977.

Verba, S. and Schlozman, K., 'Unemployment class consciousness and radical politics: what didn't happen in the 1930s', *Journal of Politics*, vol. 39, 1977.

Wolfskill, G., *The Revolt of the Conservatives: a History of the American Liberty League 1934–1940*, 1962.

Continental Europe

Alber, J., 'Government responses to the challenge of unemployment: the development of unemployment insurance in Western Europe', in Flora, P. and Heidenheimer, A. (eds), *The Development of Welfare States in Europe and America*, 1984.

Croucher, R., 'Communist unemployed organisations between the wars, ' *Archiv für Sozialgeschichte*, vol. 30, 1990.

Eichengreen, B. and Hatton, T. (eds), *Interwar Unemployment in International Perspective*, 1988.

Evans, R. and Geary, D. (eds), *The German Unemployed: Experiences and Consequences of Mass Unemployment from the Weimar Republic to the Third Reich*, 1987.

Fallada, H., *Little Man – What Now?*, 1933.

Fischer, C., *German Communists and the Rise of the Nazis*, 1991.

Fuss, H., 'Unemployment and employment among women', *International Labour Review*, vol. 31, no. 4, April 1935.

Grytten, O., 'The scale of Norwegian labour unemployment in international perspective', *Scandinavian Economic History Review*, vol. 42, no. 2, 1995.

Guérin, D., *The Brown Plague: Travels in Late Weimar and Early Nazi Germany*, 1994.

Instytut Gospodarstwa Spolecznego, *Pamietniki Bezrobotnych*, 1933.

Jahoda, M., Lazarfeld, P. and Zeisel, H., *Marienthal: the Sociography of an Unemployed Community*, 1972.

Kershaw, I., *Public Opinion and Political Dissent in the Third Reich: Bavaria 1933–1945*, 1983.

Landau, L., Panski, J. and Strzelecki, E., *Chômage des Paysans*, 1939.

Lopes, R., 'The economic depression and public health', *International Labour Review*, vol. 29, no. 6, June 1934.

McDermott, K. and Agnew, J., *The Communist International: a History of International Communism from Lenin to Stalin*, 1996.

Mitchell, B., *European Historical Statistics 1750–1970*, 1981.

Mommsen, W.J. (ed.), *The Emergence of the Welfare State in Britain and Germany 1850–1950*, 1981.

Noakes, J., 'Social outcasts in the Third Reich', in Bessel, R. (ed.), *Life in the Third Reich*, 1987.

Salais, R., Baverez, N. and Reynaud, B., *L'Invention du Chômage: Histoire et Transformations d'une Catégorie en France des Années 1890 aux Années 1980*, 1986.

Stachura, P.(ed.), *Unemployment and the Great Depression in Weimar Germany*, 1986.

Statistisches Jahrbuch für das Deutsche Reich.

Thibert, M., 'Economic depression and the employment of women', *International Labour Review*, vol. 27, nos 4 and 5, April and May 1933.

Tidsskrift fȲr Arbeiderbewegelsens Historie, no. 1, 1983.

Vanthemsche, G., 'Unemployment insurance in interwar Belgium', *International Review of Social History*, vol. 35, no. 3, 1990.

Woytinsky, W., *The Social Consequences of the Economic Depression*, 1936.

Zawadzki, B. and Lazarfeld, P., 'The psychological effects of unemployment', *Journal of Social Psychology*, vol. 6, 1935.

Zimmerman, E., 'The 1930s world economic crisis in 6 European countries: a first report on the causes of political instability and reaction to crisis', in Johnson, P. and Thompson, W. (eds), *Rythmns in Politics and Economics*, 1985.

Index